Shannon M. Hilliker
**Second Language Teaching and Learning through Virtual Exchange**

# Trends in Applied Linguistics

Edited by
Ulrike Jessner

**Volume 29**

# Second Language Teaching and Learning through Virtual Exchange

Edited by
Shannon M. Hilliker

**DE GRUYTER**
MOUTON

ISBN 978-3-11-135673-0
e-ISBN (PDF) 978-3-11-072736-4
e-ISBN (EPUB) 978-3-11-072746-3
ISSN 1868-6362

**Library of Congress Control Number: 2021947923**

**Bibliographic information published by the Deutsche Nationalbibliothek**
The Deutsche Nationalbibliothek lists this publication in the Deutsche Nationalbibliografie;
detailed bibliographic data are available on the Internet at http://dnb.dnb.de.

© 2023 Walter de Gruyter GmbH, Berlin/Boston
This volume is text- and page-identical with the hardback published in 2022.
Cover design: Martin Zech, Bremen, using a photo by Roswitha Schacht/morguefile.com
Typesetting: Integra Software Services Pvt. Ltd.
Printing and binding: CPI books GmbH, Leck

www.degruyter.com

This book is dedicated to those around the world that I have had the pleasure to interact with because of my involvement in virtual exchange and because they took a chance to work with me, work with my students, attend a presentation, or believed in this book enough to contribute. May we never stop educating and being educated in an international arena where we share language and culture with one another as freely as I have experienced with all of the educators and students I have had the pleasure to interact with.

# Preface

In the Fall of 2000 I took my first online class during my master's in TESOL (Teaching English to Speakers of Other Languages). The course was offered online which made sense considering the course was Using Media in the Language Classroom. More than the content made a lasting impression on me, the course resonated with me because of the format. I was able to engage with the material during the time of day when I was most productive (after midnight) and I took chances and shared ideas in discussions like no other time in my college career. As an example, I clearly remember recording myself singing for a lesson plan to use demonstrate use of audio with English Language Learners (ELLs). I don't sing. Ultimately that class that was designed and orchestrated by an amazing professor led me to pursue my doctorate.

During my doctorate in the early 2000s online learning started to become popular. I had the opportunity to teach my first class online in 2003, that same class I described above, and fell in love with instructing courses online. I have been teaching that way ever since either fully online or face-to-face classes with an online component. My dissertation research focused on the affordances of idea exchange for ESL (English as a Second Language) teachers and my study confirmed that for teachers learning about how to use technology in the classroom the online environment worked. There is continued confirmation that online learning, when designed and supported correctly, can provide unique learning opportunities for students in countless disciplines.

Around 2010 I was selected to be a faculty fellow for SUNY (State University of New York) COIL (Collaborative Online International Learning) where I was introduced to the idea of faculty and students working together across universities, schools, disciplines, borders, and topics to engage in a global experience tied to coursework. I formally learned the tenants of COIL and heard about previous COIL courses and experiences. In addition, I was paired up with a faculty member in Turkey and was supported by excellent instructional designers to plan a six-week exchange between ELLs in the United States with English as a Foreign Language (EFL) students in Turkey. Ultimately, the partnership fell through and I didn't get to deliver that project to my students. Nowadays, in my field, we call these projects virtual exchange. In this book the authors use different words such as tele-tandem and telecollaboration as synonyms for virtual exchange. All of these terms used to describe collaboration between those in different cultures are valid, storied, and researched so the authors in this book were free to use the label of their choosing. Although it has evolved over the time I have been involved, because of the research that is published much like the studies contained in this book, one thing remains clear to me- language and culture exchange is mutually beneficial for faculty and students involved even when it doesn't materialize as planned. The failed exchange between my students and Turkey and communication failures between exchanges that do take place are significant points of learning. Over the last several years I have been doing exchanges in all my courses. All of them have successes and failures that we can learn and grown from and indeed my research shows that everyone involved has grown over time because of our global connections.

Being in the field of TESOL it has always been clear to me that virtual exchange makes sense for both language and cultural exchange. It is good for teacher candidates to collaborate with other teacher candidates to hone their pedagogical skills and learn about education in different cultures and it is beneficial for teacher candidates to learn from ELLs both cultural issues as well as how to support their language acquisition. In addition, it is constructive for language learners to learn from one another and get authentic language practice. I have had the pleasure to consult on many exchange projects, give presentations, and travel to talk to faculty in several fields to tout the benefits of global connections for students. The 21$^{st}$ century demands that students can communicate and work in diverse situations. The excellent news is the students on both ends of the exchange benefit in different ways. Also, during a global pandemic and Covid-19 online learning including virtual exchanges have gone on with little or no interruption when some other aspects of education were forced to stop.

My students and I have participated in virtual exchanges and I started collecting data formally on each exchange and publishing the results starting in the Fall of 2018. I have led virtual exchanges that pair teacher candidates learning about English linguistics and grammar with ELLs around the world. The authentic language produced allows teacher candidates to analyse authentic language based on course topics and the language learners receive native or near native speaker conversation partners. I have paired teacher candidates in their practicum work with other teacher candidates in Poland and Colombia to discuss the pedagogical practices within the four language modalities (reading, writing, listening, and speaking). I have devised exchanges where teachers candidates within the United States at different universities look at photos of technology use in the classroom at different time periods to discuss the evolution of teaching practices, TESOL teacher candidates paired with students working towards taking the TOEFL (Test of English as a Foreign Language) to improve their speaking based around culture community topics and formal essay writing, and teacher candidates paired with other teacher candidates to discuss the United Nation's Sustainable Development Goals. From these exchanges not only have countless teacher candidates and language learners had the invaluable experience of working with partners outside of their own classrooms, I have had the privilege to publish the fruits of that work on topics such as the use of video in teacher reflection (Lenkaitis, Hilliker, and Roumeliotis, 2020; Loranc-Paszylk, Hilliker,and Lenkaitis in press), the expansion of teacher candidates' linguistic knowledge as a result of a virtual exchange (Hilliker, Lenkaitis, and Ramirez 2020) including pragmatic awareness (Hilliker, Lenkaitis, and Bouhafa 2020), how virtual exchange can give teacher candidates more clinical experiences such as an alternative to study abroad (Hilliker 2020; Hilliker, Loranc-Paszylk,and Lenkaiti 2020), and the increase of global awareness as a result of virtual exchange (Lenkaitis, Loranc-Paszylk, and Hilliker 2019).

# Contents

Preface —— VII

Introduction —— 1

## Language and virtual exchange

Paul Wicking
**Chapter 1**
**Learning-oriented assessment in an international virtual exchange —— 9**

Eucharia Donnery
**Chapter 2**
**From demotivation to Intercultural Communicative Competence (ICC): Japanese university learner journeys in the International Virtual ExchangeProject (IVEProject) —— 35**

Alberto Andujar, Paloma Mármol Trapote
**Chapter 3**
**Annotating appraisal in a mobile telecollaboration project: A linguistic analysis of students' engagement —— 49**

Carolin Fuchs, Bruce Tung, Bill Snyder
**Chapter 4**
**Learner appropriation of genre in a US-China virtual exchange —— 73**

Kaishan Kong
**Chapter 5**
**"Zoom" in and speak out: Virtual exchange in language learning —— 97**

## Culture and virtual exchange

Anna Nicolaou, Ana Sevilla-Pavón
**Chapter 6**
**Developing intercultural communicative competence in ESP contexts through virtual exchange: An ecological perspective —— 117**

Martin Parsons, Mikel Garant, Elizaveta Shikhova
Chapter 7
Video exchange telecollaboration: Towards developing interculturality in EFL environments —— 145

Eduardo Viana da Silva, Ana Cristina Biondo Salomão
Chapter 8
Taking action in a virtual exchange with Brazilian and U.S. students —— 161

Clara Bauler, Devin Thornburg, Óscar Ceballos, Carlos Pineda, Esther Kogan, Pirjo Sorri
Chapter 9
Tackling problems, finding solutions: Creativity and collaboration in cross-cultural virtual exchange during a pandemic —— 189

## Teacher education and virtual exchange

Chesla Ann Lenkaitis
Chapter 10
Integrating the United Nations' Sustainable Development Goals into a teacher preparation program: Developing content for virtual exchanges —— 209

Shannon M. Hilliker, Devindi Samarakkody
Chapter 11
Enhancing ELLs' understanding through the use of examples, questions, and native language connections during virtual exchange —— 225

Alexandra Laletina, Anna Zhiganova, Elena Gritsenko
Chapter 12
Developing linguistically responsive pedagogy among K-12 mainstream teacher candidates through virtual exchange —— 245

Blanka Babická, Barbara Loranc-Paszylk, Josef Nevařil
**Chapter 13**
**Virtual exchange to enhance English language teacher trainees'
professional development – insights from a Czech-Polish project —— 263**

**Conclusion —— 281**

**Index —— 285**

# Introduction

I have been lucky to work with several faculty around the world so our students can exchange and share ideas outside of those they are exposed to in their own cultures. This book contains chapters from several of my colleagues who I have done virtual exchange within the past, colleagues I have met because of our mutual interest in virtual exchange, colleagues of colleagues, and scholars that I have now connected with because of this book. I can tell that every single author in this book has organized a virtual exchange. It takes a lot of time and organization to collaborate with others in a different language and/or culture. When contributing to this book the authors showed that same time management and organization it takes to organize a solid virtual exchange as they worked tirelessly to contribute their research and knowledge in this volume. I am especially excited about the research presented in each chapter not just because of the quality of the research presented, but that all authors were generous in sharing the details of the activities within their exchanges so that they may be adapted into other contexts. They have all contributed to furthering my knowledge in the field with each contribution that focuses on culture and language learning through virtual exchange.

To this end this book is organized into three sections 1) research on exchanges focused on language, 2) research on exchanges focused on culture, and 3) research on exchanges focused on language teacher education. I will conclude by introducing each chapter in the book-

# Language and virtual exchange

Chapter 1 is titled Learning Oriented Assessment in an International Virtual Exchange. In this chapter Wicking presents a case study of a virtual exchange between foreign language learning university students in New York and students in central Japan. He studies learning oriented assessments that can be used to measure student second language acquisition goals that go beyond a participation grade. Included in his study are data that uncovered how different second language learning goals were (or were not) supported by the exchange. The title for Chapter 2 is From Demotivation to Intercultural Communicative Competence (ICC): Japanese University Learner Journeys in the International Virtual Exchange Project (IVEProject). In Donnery's chapter she discusses a long term three semester collaboration between Japanese and Colombian university students. The focus of this chapter is on three Japanese non-English major computer science students. She explains their accomplishments both linguistically and culturally during their exchange, particularly with respect to their gains in intercultural communicative competence as evidenced in their writings. Chapter 3 by Andujar and Trapote investigates a telecollaboration project between a Spanish and a North American university using WhatsApp. They specifically explore engagement and attitude in the discourse of the students' messages to one another. They outline the intercultural exchange of participants when discussing their own culture, the L2 culture, and the topic under discussion. Their chapter is called Annotating Appraisal in a Mobile Telecollaboration Project: A Linguistic Analysis of Students' Engagement. Fuchs, Tung, and Snyder contribute Chapter 4 by exploring Chinese EFL learners' appropriation of written academic genres (statements of purpose and business letters) in a virtual exchange with student teachers in the US. Genre writing tasks were designed by US student teachers and mediated by the EFL teacher. Their case study explores to what extent learners master genre structures based on the pedagogical support provided by the student teachers. This chapter is called Learner Appropriation of Genre in a US-China Virtual Exchange. The final chapter in this section, Chapter 5, is titled "Zoom" in and Speak Out: Virtual Exchange in Language Learning. In this chapter Kong explores the benefits of virtual exchange in a beginning-level Chinese class. In particular, the author examines two Chinese language learners' language development and learner autonomy after virtual exchange meetings with native speakers for 10 weeks. The two participants produced a larger number of words and enhanced lexical richness in their video presentations. The positive virtual exchange experience helped them activate their agency to take charge of their learning by asking questions to fulfill their learning needs and by taking risks to use the target language.

## Culture and virtual exchange

In Chapter 6 Nicolaou and Sevilla-Pavón focus on a content-based English for Specific Purposes (ESP) virtual exchange where the students are studying similar Business English courses. This study discusses findings from pre- and post-exchange questionnaires and from focus groups interviews and reflection papers. The authors indicate intercultural communicative competence growth and the acquisition of discipline-specific knowledge in their participants. They call their chapter Developing Intercultural Communicative Competence in ESP Contexts Through Virtual Exchange: An ecological perspective. Chapter 7, Video-Exchange

Telecollaboration: Towards Developing Interculturality in EFL Environments, by Parsons, Garant, and Shikhova is based upon an ongoing collaborative, transnational video podcasting project between students in higher education in Japan, China, and Russia. The authors describe the components of their project highlighting the importance of the instructor guided activities that ultimately supported their students' greater understanding of one another. Pre- and post-project questionnaires were administered to assess students' attitudes towards the other countries and results from the surveys indicate improved attitudes towards the other countries in the project and differing digital skill bases in the three cohorts of students. Viana da Silva and Salomão's Chapter 8 focuses on a tele-tandem project between university students from Brazil and the United States. The participants engaged with the topics of the Amazon Forest and Indigenous populations. The authors point to the importance of forming globally competent citizens and highlight the pedagogical applications of the "take action" component of the Global Competence Matrix. The title of this chapter is Taking Action in a Virtual Exchange with Brazilian and U.S. Students. In the last chapter in this section, Chapter 9, Bauler, Thornburg, Ceballos, and Piñeda use action research to examine their virtual exchange between multilingual high school students from Sevilla, Spain and freshman undergraduate students from New York, USA, who engaged in virtual cross-cultural dialogue through the English language medium. The chapter titled Problems, Finding Solutions: Creativity and Collaboration in Cross-Cultural Virtual Exchange during a Pandemic focuses on the conversations was on multilingualism, empowering both groups of students to examine linguistic diversity as a tool to promote multiculturalism, tolerance, and dialogue. They not only highlight the tasks and reactions from the students, but also lessons they learned especially considering Covid-19. In addition, they provided pointed recommendations for practitioners.

## Teacher education and virtual exchange

Lenkaitis' Chapter 10 focuses on a six-week exchange where four second language (L2) teacher candidates met weekly with participants from Poland to discuss the Sustainable Development Goals (SDGs) that were the most important to them. Not only did the teacher candidates learn more about global issues, but the exchange also impacted their pedagogies which is particularly important for L2 classrooms. She titled her work Integrating the United Nations' Sustainable Development Goals into a Teacher Preparation Program: Developing Content for Virtual Exchanges. Hilliker and Samarakkody's submission for

Chapter 11 is called Enhancing ELLs' Understanding Through the Use of Examples, Questions, and Native Language Connections During Virtual Exchange. This study focuses on a virtual exchange that connected ELLs in a Colombian university and TESOL teacher candidates and undergraduates majoring in linguistics in a university in the US. These partners used questions, examples, and students' native language in this collaboration, putting together two streams of knowledge in discussing how to enhance communicative business English skills. It thereby benefited ELLs in understanding what makes a good business pitch and the participants in the USA gaining the experience of assisting ELLs. The results of this virtual synchronous partnership discuss how native/near native speakers of English and EFL learners in Colombia co-constructed their knowledge. The authors of Chapter 12, Developing Linguistically Responsive Pedagogy Among K-12 Mainstream Teacher Candidates Through Virtual Exchange, Laletina, Zhiganova, and Gritsenko analyse a virtual exchange project between mainstream teacher candidates in rural northeastern US and Russian learners of English. Their findings suggest that virtual exchange positively contributes to mainstream teacher candidates' sensitivity to the English language and American culture and boosts their confidence interacting with multilingual students. An important implication of the study is that there is a need for more linguistics-related training in mainstream teacher education. Finally, in Chapter 13, Babická, Loranc-Paszylk, and Nevařil provide Virtual Exchange to Enhance English Language Teacher Trainees' Professional Development – Insights from a Czech-Polish Project. They examine affordances of telecollaboration between two graduate-level master's programmes offering qualifications for teaching English as a foreign language in the Czech Republic and Poland. In the chapter they discuss teacher trainees' perceived benefits and challenges of intercultural telecollaborative exchanges, its affordances in developing their professional expertise in both collaboration and peer assessment.

Takes together the chapters in this book provide solid research in support of using virtual exchange in language teaching and learning. Each chapter contributes to the growing body of knowledge on virtual exchange and there are concrete ideas in this book that can be translated to different contexts. By sharing experiences and the results of the research in this book it is my hope that virtual exchange can continue to expand, and language learners and teachers of language learners can continue to gain valuable insight from their peers around the globe. Additionally, that faculty members at institution of higher education continue to collaborate with one another and strive to implement these exchanges to support their curricula and continue to grow as educators because of their international connections.

# References

Hilliker, Shannon. M. 2020. Virtual exchange as a study abroad alternative to foster language and culture exchange in TESOL teacher education. *The Electronic Journal for English as a Second Language. 23* (4). 1–13. Retrieved from http://www.tesl-ej.org/wordpress/issues/volume23/ej92/ej92a7/

Hilliker, Shannon. M., Barbara Loranc-Paszylk & Chesla Ann Lenkaitis. 2020. Transforming language teacher education: Utilizing virtual exchange as an alternative to study abroad. In Laura Baecher (ed.), *Study Abroad in Teacher Education: Transformative Learning at the Global Scale*. Routledge.

Hilliker, Shannon Marie, Chesla Ann Lenkaitis & Yahya Bouhafa. 2020. The role of intercultural virtual exchanges in developing pragmatic awareness. In C-C. Lin & C. Zaccarini (Eds.). *Internationalization in Action: Leveraging Diversity and Inclusion in Globalized Classrooms*. Bern, Switzerland: Peter Lang.

Hilliker, Shannon M., Chesla Ann Lenkaitis & Angie Ramirez. in press. Expanding teacher candidate linguistic knowledge: Analyzing recorded virtual exchange sessions. *EUROCALL Review*.

Lenkaitis, Chesla Ann, Shannon M. Hilliker & Kayla Roumeliotis. 2020. Teacher candidate reflection and development through virtual exchange. *IAFOR Journal of Education. 8* (2). 127–141. doi: 10.22492/ije.8.2.07

Lenkaitis, Chesla Ann, Barbara Loranc-Paszylk & Shannon M. Hilliker. 2019. Global awareness and global identity development among foreign language learners: The impact of virtual exchanges. *MEXTESOL Journal 43*(4). 1–11. Retrieved from https://mextesol.net/journal/index.php?page=journal&id_article=14468

Loranc-Paszylk, Barbara, Shannon M. Hilliker & Chesla Ann Lenkaitis, C. A. in press. Virtual exchange in teacher education: Facilitating reflection on teacher practice through the use of video. *TESOL*.

# Language and virtual exchange

Paul Wicking
# Chapter 1
# Learning-oriented assessment in an international virtual exchange

Within the relatively short history of international virtual exchange (IVE), assessment has long proved a challenge. The inherent messy nature of bringing together classes from diverse cultural contexts and often with differing course goals has made traditional assessment approaches problematic. Further complications arise with mismatching program schedules (Bueno-Alastuey and Kleban 2016), the huge volume of data that can be assessed (Andresen 2009), institutional constraints which limit teachers' freedom to choose assessment methods (Nissen 2016), and the practical demands of overseeing the exchange which may leave little time available for comprehensive assessment. Moreover, if the exchange involves a genuinely collaborative task, distinguishing one learner's work from another for assessment purposes can further exacerbate the problem. Çiftçi and Savaş (2018) have therefore concluded that assessment is one of the key challenges facing language and intercultural learning in virtual exchange. After outlining the various challenges that assessment poses to IVE programs, O'Dowd (2010) noted that because many teachers are unsure how telecollaborative tasks should be assessed, the common default position when it comes to assessment is often a participation grade. Yet even though practical realities have often made this the case, a more satisfactory approach is warranted, as merely taking part in a virtual exchange cannot be equated with having learned something.

International virtual exchange, also known as telecollaboration (O'Dowd 2018) and online intercultural exchange (OIE) (Lewis and O'Dowd 2016), is a pedagogical practice that engages geographically and culturally distant learners in collaborative work. The desired learning outcomes of IVE can be many and varied. They are largely contingent upon the course goals of each class, but in addition to second language acquisition, they may also include the development of digital literacy, cross-cultural understanding, creativity, and collaboration skills. This is one of the strengths of telecollaboration, as it is able to actively promote the development of multiple skills needed to succeed in the

---

**Acknowledgements:** This paper uses data gathered as part of a project supported by a grant-in-aid from the Japan Society for the Promotion of Science (KAKENHI), no. 18K00802.

---

**Paul Wicking,** Meijo University, Faculty of Foreign Studies, e-mail: wicking@meijo-u.ac.jp

modern interconnected world – skills identified by Guth and Helm (2010) as foreign language skills, intercultural communicative competence, and new online literacies. Ideally, the methods of assessing such outcomes would support and propel learners toward greater achievement; in other words, assessment would be learning oriented. Assessment exerts a strong influence over classrooms by focusing learner effort, guiding the paths of learning, measuring educational attainment, and increasing intrinsic and extrinsic motivation. If assessment methods are poorly aligned with desired outcomes, the risk is that learners would be distracted, demotivated, and discouraged in their learning paths.

Improved assessment practice can have a dramatic and positive effect on the amount of learning that takes place (Black and Wiliam 1998; Pereira, Flores, and Niklasson 2016). The last two decades have seen a surge in research concerning effective assessment theory building and practice, which can provide a framework for IVE practitioners when using assessment tasks to support second language acquisition. The broad trend of this research has been to take the focus away from the summative purposes of assessment (i.e. quantifying and measuring learners' level of achievement) and instead emphasize the formative purposes (i.e. supporting learners to progress to a higher level of knowledge and ability). Following this trend, the present study is an investigation of assessment *for* second language acquisition, rather than assessment *of* second language acquisition. This chapter firstly presents the theoretical background of learning-oriented assessment (LOA), and secondly explores data collected from a case study of a program guided by LOA principles.

# 1 Literature review

## 1.1 Theoretical background of learning-oriented assessment

The term *learning-oriented assessment* refers to a way of conceptualizing and practicing assessment which prioritizes learning above all other considerations (Carless 2015; Jones and Saville 2016; Turner and Purpura 2016). It rejects the notion that summative and formative assessments are in opposition to each other but sees them working together to aid learning. LOA seeks to make learning the highest priority in the classroom, so that all other activities including assessment serve the purpose of learning. As such, it draws from a wide pool of formative assessment frameworks, such as authentic assessment (Frey et al. 2012), dynamic assessment (Poehner 2007), assessment for learning (Assessment Reform Group 2002), and teacher-based assessment (Davison and Leung 2009).

Within the field of SLA, there is no widely accepted model of LOA. Although Jones and Saville (2016) proposed a model of LOA that considers evidence of learning at the micro and macro level, their model makes little allowance for the highly situated and contextualized nature of learning environments. Turner and Purpura (2016: 260) noted, "Due to the variability in and unpredictability of context and the diverse characteristics of classroom agents in classrooms, it appears unrealistic to propose a model of LOA". Any educator who attempts to develop assessment methods that are effective in promoting learner growth will have to pay careful attention to the particular cultural systems of relations and social structures of the context within which that assessment takes place (Elwood and Murphy 2015). However, while sociocultural particularities preclude the creation of a one-size-fits-all model of LOA, there do exist some generally agreed-upon principles, as outlined below. These principles informed the methods of assessment that were implemented in the case study which follows.

## 1.2 Principles of learning-oriented assessment

### 1.2.1 Creating authentic and cognitively complex tasks

Tasks used in IVE must be well-constructed, as participation in a virtual exchange by itself is not a sufficient condition for effective and motivated language learning (Hauck and Youngs 2008). As authentic assessment is a feature of LOA, assessment tasks should be aligned as closely as possible with the real world, and so reflect what learners will be doing once they leave the classroom (Lynch 2003). In the post-COVID-19 world with reduced opportunities for travel, this would likely entail virtual meetings, collaboration on online documents, video presentations, text chat, and other activities that are a staple of international virtual exchanges.

In addition, authentic assessment tasks are also performance-based, cognitively complex, and require collaboration among students or with the teacher (Frey et al. 2012). When undertaking assessment which is performance-based (or task-based), information is elicited that is both product-based and process-based. In other words, it examines whether the outcome of the task was achieved, and whether the students were actively engaged when they performed the task (Ellis 2018). Cognitive complexity comes from having learners participate in the manipulation of information and ideas as they co-construct knowledge, as opposed to just memorizing and reciting facts. The collaborative requirement is based on the premise that cognitive development takes place when a learner engages with others, thus making social interaction a necessary condition for learning. In an IVE program, this interaction is online.

Carless (2009) stated that LOA tasks: (a) are aligned with curriculum objectives; (b) engage students with work over time (rather than one-shot final exams); (c) are related to real-world tasks; and (d) are more cooperative than competitive. The first specification poses a challenge for IVE programs, as it may be that the partner institutions have differing curriculum objectives. However, even though designing tasks that align with the goals of both institutions could be problematic, with careful planning it is possible (Bueno-Alastuey and Kleban 2016).

When the goal is second language acquisition, task design in an IVE can draw inspiration from task-based language learning and teaching. Ellis (2003) suggested that there are six criterial features of which tasks comprise: tasks have a plan for learner activity; they focus primarily on meaning; they engage with real-world language use; they have a focus on one or all of the four language skills; they require learners to use cognitive skills in order to accomplish them; and they have a clearly defined learning outcome. Thomas and Reinders (2012) have shown that tasks can be an effective tool when combined with computer-mediated communication technologies. The principles of task-based learning and teaching provide a solid framework to guide the creation and implementation of assessment tasks in IVE which promote second language acquisition.

### 1.2.2 Clarifying goals and criteria for success

Clarifying and sharing with students the goals of the task and the criteria for success is a key principle for assessment that promotes learning (Assessment Reform Group 2002; Black and Wiliam 2009). For learners to work towards a learning goal, they must have a clear understanding of what that goal is. In the field of SLA, the Common European Framework of Reference (CEFR) descriptors, along with their Can-Do statements, have been established as the key reference for setting goals and directing learner efforts. Apart from language learning, however, the goals of an IVE can range across a whole spectrum of competencies, including intrapersonal communication, interpersonal communication, digital literacy, creative thinking, critical thinking, and other domains of $21^{st}$ century skills. The particular goals should be made explicit at the start of the exchange.

Sadler and Dooly (2016) found that a very clear set of expectations was crucial for a successful online exchange. They provided students with a telecollaborative activities contract, which detailed attitudes and behaviours the students were expected to exhibit during the exchange. This also provided the basis for peer and instructor evaluation. Due to the nature of IVE, it is very likely that partner classrooms will have a different set of desired linguistic and/or cultural outcomes, but having clearly stated objectives which are made explicit to learners will go a long way towards having a successful exchange (Bueno-Alastuey and Kleban 2016). When learners are aware of the desired outcomes of an IVE, they are able to focus their effort and attention on those areas. Moreover, research has suggested that more intense collaboration is generated when task instructions include clearly communicated goals, as opposed to instructions that have detailed procedural steps without goal clarity (Muller-Hartmann and Kurek 2016).

One practical way this can be achieved is through the creation and use of rubrics. Jonsson and Panadero (2017) argued that rubrics facilitate student learning in several ways. For instance, rubrics support learners in understanding desired outcomes and assessment criteria, which serve not only to evaluate work that has been completed but also to feed-forward by focusing effort on future work. Rubrics also facilitate self-regulated learning by aiding learners in monitoring and evaluating their own work and in planning and performing the task. Their review of research into rubrics recommended that rubrics not include any numerical scores, but instead focus on an analytical assessment of strengths and weaknesses.

### 1.2.3 Activating students as instructional resources for one another

Another key strategy for LOA is activating students as instructional resources for one another (Black and Wiliam 2009). This principle underlies many IVE programs today, such as e-tandem (O'Rourke 2007). Students have expert knowledge of the language and culture in which they live, and so can provide insights into vocabulary, pragmatics, and language form, as well as provide a model of pronunciation and natural expressions. However, even though students have said they appreciate individualized feedback from their cross-cultural partner, they do not actively provide such feedback if the teacher does not give them explicit directions to do so (Ware and O'Dowd 2008). It is therefore beholden on the teacher to train students in methods of giving feedback and integrating the provision of feedback into task requirements.

In addition to feedback from a cross-cultural peer in an IVE, it is also possible that peers within the same classroom can support, encourage and instruct one another in the target language through peer feedback (Villamil and de Guerrero 2006). Students may need assistance and instruction in a whole range of different areas, including language use, making sense of feedback, technical and software-related issues, interpreting the meaning of messages, and so on. While a teacher will have great difficulty in responding to every individual need in a large class, students are often able to have those needs met by a classmate.

### 1.2.4 Developing students' abilities to evaluate their own learning

Assessment that promotes learning will seek to develop students as self-assessors and effective lifelong learners (Sambell, McDowell, and Montgomery 2013). When students are skilled at self-assessment, their dependence on the teacher decreases, as they can identify their own strengths and weaknesses and then focus their efforts on areas that need improvement. Empowering students to take ownership of their own learning, to make their own educational decisions and to set their own course will enable them to continue life-long learning that extends well beyond their time in the classroom.

Many educational scholars agree that self-assessment is not just good practice, but it plays an essential role in the learning process (Little and Erickson 2015). Indeed, students are continually monitoring and evaluating their own performances, whether the teacher acknowledges it or not (Nicol and Macfarlane-Dick 2006). As Black and Wiliam stated, "The issue is therefore not whether to initiate self-assessment – self-assessment is inherent in any classroom activity – but to make it more overt as a step to improvement" (2012: 215). When students engage in formal practices of self-evaluation, their insights are often profound and multifaceted. Huang's (2016) study into self-assessment on an English speaking performance task suggested that common teacher feedback shortcomings are often overcome through self-assessment; shortcomings such as a misalignment of perceptions between teacher and learners, a misunderstanding of feedback intent, and problems with the comprehensibility of feedback content. Moreover, the study found that learners' self-feedback reached a level of breadth and depth that would be very difficult to match by a typical teacher. This is because learners have detailed knowledge of their own learning history and level of effort, in addition to time that can be spent in scrutinizing their own performance outcomes.

The importance of providing an opportunity for analysis, reflection, and self-evaluation in virtual exchanges has been widely acknowledged (Lewis et al. 2016; Martí and Fernández 2016; Muller-Hartmann and Kurek 2016). This can be achieved through self-evaluation sheets, group discussions, short activity reports, or learner journals. Students can be encouraged to keep a log of language features which they have noticed and vocabulary they hope to remember. In this way, students are engaging in deeper levels of reflection and not just giving themselves a score, as self-assessment that is merely self-rating is unlikely to yield pedagogically informative results (Little and Erickson 2015).

In addition, learners should be encouraged to examine the awkward and stressful aspects of the exchange, reflecting upon the causes and considering how they may be better handled in the future. When evaluating their own performance in an interaction, any contradictions and tensions that arose should be taken as opportunities for growth and intercultural learning (Priego and Liaw 2017). In this way, sources of cultural friction can be appreciated, rather than considered as something to be cleansed or avoided (Belz 2002), so that their function as transformative agents can be valued and appreciated (Helm 2016).

### 1.2.5 Providing feedback that enhances ongoing learning

Of central importance to a learning-oriented approach to assessment is the act of giving feedback (López-Pastor and Sicilia-Camacho 2017), as research suggests that more effective methods of giving feedback will lead to more effective learning (Ferris 2010). This feedback should be both from formal sources, such as the teacher, and informal sources, such as from pair work and collaborative group work (Sambell, McDowell, and Montgomery 2013). Furthermore, the learner should be given the opportunity to employ that feedback in order to progress to a higher level of learning. This is a key component of LOA practice. In fact, Turner and Purpura (2016) argued that if there is no evidence that feedback has resulted in some kind of L2 system change, then that assessment cannot be considered as learning oriented.

IVE has generally been rich in informal feedback, as students produce linguistic messages in interaction with others, and then observe how those messages are received and interpreted. This feedback then gives some indication of how successful the exchange was. Formal feedback, however, poses a greater challenge. Moreover, finding evidence that this feedback led to L2 system change is highly problematic. One way this could be done, as suggested by Ware and O'Dowd (2008), is through using portfolios and learner diaries as ways for students to demonstrate linguistic and cultural learning gains. These provide an opportunity for students to reflect upon the feedback they have received and record new linguistic structures and lexical items that have been incorporated into their L2 repertoire.

Whether feedback leads to learner growth is also influenced by whether students have a fixed mindset or a growth mindset (Forsythe and Johnson 2017). Students with a fixed mindset are more likely to adopt defensive behaviours when given feedback, in order to protect their self-esteem. Conversely, students with a growth mindset are more likely to appreciate critical feedback and view it as a positive aspect of their learning. Those with a fixed mindset can be helped to make productive use of feedback through the development of feedback literacy. Engaging students in meta-dialogues concerning the processes and strategies of assessment, having students discuss feedback together, and requiring students to demonstrate how they have used previous comments in subsequent work are all effective ways to develop feedback literacy (Carless and Boud 2018).

## 2 Case study context and program design

A case study was conducted in order to explore how the above principles of LOA might support second language acquisition in an IVE. The first two principles of LOA concern task creation and goal clarification, which occur in the task design stage. The following three principles are concerned with peer and self-assessment that lead to further learning, and so happen at the task evaluation stage. The present case study seeks to explore this evaluation stage (Figure 1.1).

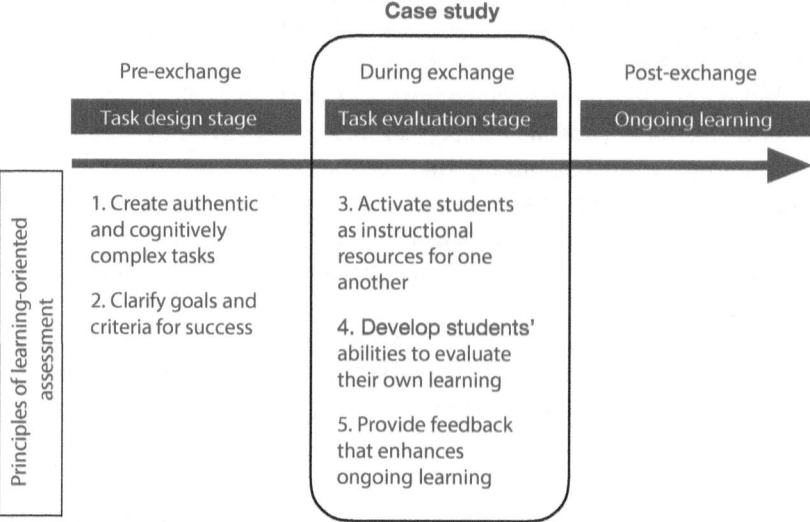

**Figure 1.1:** Focus of the case study.

Case studies focus upon a "bounded instance" (Nunan and Bailey 2009: 161) which, in this study, was an eight-week exchange program between three institutions of higher education: one in New York and two in central Japan. Although the results of case studies cannot be reliably generalized to wider populations, a sufficiently thick description of setting, participants and phenomena will allow for transferability; that is, the ability of readers to determine how applicable and congruent the findings are to their own context (Brown 2014; Duff 2008.)

The participants in New York were third- and fourth-year college students majoring in business and taking an advanced Japanese language course, while the participants in Japan were first- and second-year students majoring in English. Due to the small class sizes of the schools in Japan, it was decided to combine two classes so that there would be enough numbers for each student in New York to have one partner. In total, there were 44 participants: 22 from New York and 22 from central Japan. While foreign language acquisition was the primary goal, the broader aim of the program was to develop students' transversal competencies in domains such as critical and innovative thinking, interpersonal skills, global citizenship, and information and communication technology skills (Care and Luo 2016).

As academic semesters in the US have different starting and finishing dates to Japan, there was an overlap of eight weeks during which the IVE program was able to run. Three tasks, in order of increasing complexity, were completed during this time (Figure 1.2). Both the US and Japanese students were completing a course in which the IVE was only one component (15% of the total course grade in the US and 10% in Japan), and so time spent on the IVE was limited to approximately 30 minutes a week. The Japanese students were enrolled in a standardized course as part of a comprehensive university curriculum, which meant that the IVE was an add-on, unlike other courses where virtual exchange is not only integral to course design but is often the hub (Nissen 2016).

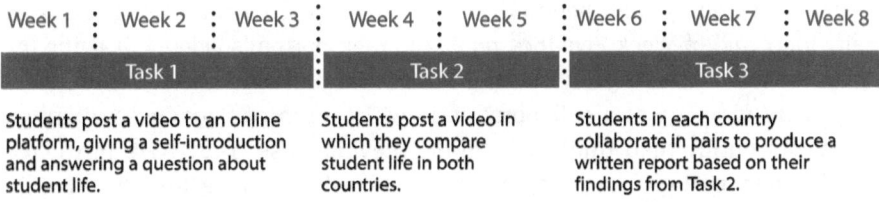

**Figure 1.2:** IVE program schedule.

Contextual features of the exchange informed the design of different aspects of the program, such as the choice between synchronous and asynchronous tools (Çiftçi and Savaş 2018). In order to provide an opportunity for more linguistically complex statements, it was decided to combine the asynchronous tools of video upload (via the Flipgrid™ platform) and online word processing (via Google Docs) to facilitate the exchange. There were three main task types, as categorized by O'Dowd and Ware (2009): information exchange, comparison, and collaboration. There was a common theme that ran through all three tasks (student life), and these tasks were carefully sequenced so that each one built upon the previous interaction (Ware and O'Dowd 2008).

## 2.1 Description of the tasks

Task 1 was an information exchange that required students to upload a video to a shared website, introducing themselves and answering the question, "How does a typical university student at your school spend his/her week?". Konishi (2017) advocated using both languages in a language exchange situation with Japanese students, as it decreases anxiety. Students were instructed to speak their country's language first, and then repeat everything in the target language (i.e. students in Japan would speak Japanese first, and then speak in English), and all 44 students were able to view all the videos. In the first and second week, videos were uploaded. In the third week, each student was assigned one overseas partner, to whom they posted a video reply in response to the first video. They remained with the same partner for all three tasks.

Task 2 was another video production, requiring students to watch a selection of videos from Task 1 and draw some conclusions, making a comparison between students' schedules in Japan and the U.S. In this video, too, they spoke first in their home language and then in the target language. In Week Four they posted their video, and in Week Five they replied to their partner's video, critiquing the comments and answering any questions from their partner.

Finally, Task 3 was a collaboration in which each pair produced a written report, presenting their findings from the previous task. They were instructed to make the report one A4 page, to include at least one image, and to write it in both Japanese and English. Each student was to write in their target language, with help from comments and suggestions given by their partner. Language learning gains can be greatly improved when tasks are designed to give importance to linguistic accuracy, and when students take on the role of language expert or tutor (Lewis and O'Dowd 2016). Students were therefore told they would be graded on the quality of their writing, and to give as much support as they could to their partner, pointing out language errors without explicitly correcting them. The final report was sent as a PDF to each teacher.

## 2.2 Assessment

An assessment scheme was created, founded upon the five LOA principles mentioned above: creating authentic and cognitively complex tasks, clarifying goals and criteria for success, activating students as instructional resources for one another, developing students' abilities to evaluate their own learning, and providing feedback that enhances ongoing learning. Students completed an online peer and self-assessment form at the end of each of the three tasks. As the forms were online, students could use their smartphone in class to complete the assessment, and the teacher was instantly provided with a spreadsheet of collated responses. These assessment forms contributed to students' grades, as peer assessment can be as equally valid and reliable as teacher assessment (Topping 2009). It was decided not to build anonymity into the peer assessment as, when training is provided, revealing the identity of the peer assessor can lead to greater appreciation of the feedback (Li 2017).

The Task 1 assessment form directed students' attention to various aspects of language and culture that were being covered during the course, such as facial expressions, pronunciation, vocabulary, grammar, ideas and so on. There were two questions that required a score of one to five, followed by a series of free-response questions that prompted students to evaluate their partner's work and to reflect upon their own performance (Figure 1.3).

---

Did you understand your partner's main point?
*(No, not at all.)*   1   2   3   4   5   *(Yes, completely.)*

Did your partner communicate his/her ideas clearly?
*(No, not at all.)*   1   2   3   4   5   *(Yes, completely.)*

What did your partner do well?

How can your partner improve next time?

What did you do well?

How can you improve next time?

Think about your personal weekly schedule. Is it typical of other students in your country? Why or why not?

---

**Figure 1.3:** Peer and self-assessment form, Task 1.

The form for Task 2 directed students to make a categorical response of "yes" or "no" to a question about whether their partner said their opinion and whether they had given a reason for it. There were also three questions asking about their partner's pronunciation, use of natural expressions, and intercultural understanding, attached to a scoring system ranging from one to five points (Figure 1.4).

> Did your partner say his/her opinion?
> ☐ yes   ☐ no
>
> Did your partner give a reason or an example for his/her opinion?
> ☐ yes   ☐ no
>
> Did your partner speak clearly with good pronunciation?
> (No, not at all.)   1   2   3   4   5   (Yes, very much.)
>
> Did your partner use natural expressions?
> (No, not at all.)   1   2   3   4   5   (Yes, very much.)
>
> Did your partner show an understanding of student schedules in your country?
> (No, not at all.)   1   2   3   4   5   (Yes, very much.)
>
> What did your partner do well?
>
> How can your partner improve next time?
>
> What did you do well?
>
> How can you improve next time?

**Figure 1.4:** Peer and self-assessment form, Task 2.

Task 3 was the final task of the project. The assessment form had two parts. Part I had students read a report written by another pair and assess it. The assessment consisted of four items with a score of one to five for each item. As this was the final task, it was more summative in focus. Part II was an exercise in self-assessment, with students reporting how they communicated with their partner, and reflecting upon how successful their collaboration had been (Figure 1.5).

After completion, the teacher collected the online peer feedback and gave it to each student, printed on paper, together with teacher feedback. This teacher feedback was given via a descriptive rubric but without a numerical score, with each domain of assessment evaluated at a level ranging from "excellent" to "failure". The teacher also provided additional feedback on the sheet through written comments that focused on particular linguistic areas which could be improved.

A major challenge in designing the assessment scheme was providing an opportunity for students to use their feedback to *feed-forward* to subsequent work.

> Whose report did you read?
>
> Did the report accurately describe student life in both NewYork and Japan?
> (No, not at all.)   1   2   3   4   5   (Yes, very much.)
>
> Did the report contain interesting or unusual insights?
> (No, not at all.)   1   2   3   4   5   (Yes, very much.)
>
> Was the language clear and easy to understand?
> (No, not at all.)   1   2   3   4   5   (Yes, very much.)
>
> Was the report nicely designed and presented?
> (No, not at all.)   1   2   3   4   5   (Yes, very much.)
>
> How did you communicate with your partner? (Check all that apply.)
> ☐ comments in Google Docs   ☐ email   ☐ Line   ☐ Skype   ☐ other
>
> How much time do you think you spent communicating with your partner for Task 3?
> ☐ less than 1 hour   ☐ 1~2 hours   ☐ 2~3 hours   ☐ more than 3 hours
>
> Did you and your partner work well together?
> (No, not at all.)   1   2   3   4   5   (Yes, very much.)
>
> Why?

**Figure 1.5:** Peer and self-assessment form, Task 3.

Unless students have an opportunity to learn from their feedback and make improvements in later tasks, that feedback has limited value. However, the practical reality was that there was just not enough time to repeat tasks within the IVE program. This challenge was overcome by having students repeat similar tasks to the IVE as part of their regular course work. As the IVE was an add-on component to a standardized course there were, in effect, two instructional strands running alongside each other: the regular course strand and the IVE strand (Figure 1.6). By having students rehearse and repeat video tasks in class as part of their regular course work, the feedback from these tasks could be used as a proxy for feedback from IVE tasks.

In practice, for the first five weeks students produced weekly videos for their classmates which were not shown to the partner school. Video replies were made by classmates and the teacher, with teacher comments addressing

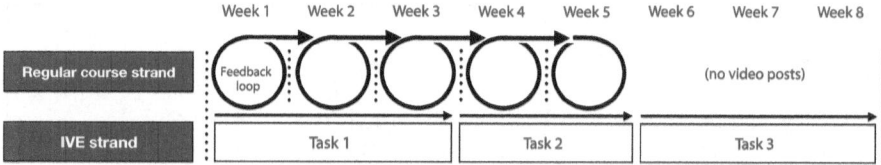

**Figure 1.6:** The two instructional strands.

linguistic areas such as pronunciation, expression and vocabulary. This feedback was a resource for students to draw upon when making their videos for the virtual exchange in Task 1 and Task 2.

# 3 Data collection and analysis

Past research into virtual exchanges has revealed much variation in responses between participants, and so reveals the importance of multiple methods of data collection and analysis in order to approach the object of study from multiple perspectives (Avgousti 2018). In this study, there were three sources of data which were merged into a dataset: (1) peer evaluation forms; (2) written self-reflections ; and (3) semi-structured interviews with students.

Written data were provided through peer evaluation forms and self-reflections. In total, 354 responses were collected from 44 students who took part in the exchange. These underwent a qualitative content analysis (Schreier 2012). First, the main categories were decided upon – in this case, they were the five domains of transversal competencies, plus "other". Second, as this study is primarily interested in the linguistic component of interpersonal communication, subcategories in that domain were created in a data-driven way from the responses. The subcategories were: vocabulary and expressions, grammar, pronunciation, clear and understandable ideas, and facial expression.

Oral data were provided through interviews with 19 students who were randomly selected: ten from Japan and nine from the US. Interviews were conducted in the final weeks of the course after the IVE had been completed, face-to-face with a researcher who was not the classroom teacher. The interviews were semi-structured and avoided leading questions, instead utilizing more general questions such as, "What did you think about this?" and "Tell me about that," in order to encourage participants to give their own voice to their lived experience. The interview data were fully transcribed and then coded by two researchers in N-Vivo for Mac (version 12). The data were coded according to eight themes: the five domains of transversal competencies, plus self-assessment, peer feedback, and teacher feedback. An initial coding comparison query revealed a modest amount of difference, which was negotiated by the researchers. A second round of coding and subsequent coding comparison resulted in a Kappa coefficient of 0.80, suggesting high inter-rater reliability. During the coding process, analytic memoing (Miles, Huberman, and Saldaña 2020) was employed, in which notes were written as declarative statements of emergent truth. Subsequent triangulation of data sources then caused these statements to be confirmed, revised or annulled.

## 4 Results and discussion

When engaging in peer assessment, students were instructed to provide their partner with feedback according to a general question, "What did your partner do well?", and then to provide some feed-forward by addressing, "How can your partner improve next time?". Those same two questions were then posed to themselves, encouraging students to reflect upon their own performance. In terms of volume, the most amount of feedback focused on interpersonal skills, of which performance in the foreign language is a component (Table 1.1).

**Table 1.1:** Number of comments in the main categories.

|  | Critical and innovative thinking | Inter-personal skills | Intra-personal skills | Global citizenship | ICT skills | Other | Total |
|---|---|---|---|---|---|---|---|
| Total comments | 36 | 250 | 16 | 12 | 16 | 24 | 354 |

Although the educators in this course had aims which hoped to develop a range of transversal competencies, the primary focus was on interpersonal skills, and foreign language skills in particular. The number of student comments in this domain indicates this focus was shared by students. There were 250 comments addressing interpersonal skills, broadly defined as all those linguistic and para-linguistic skill areas listed in Table 1.2.

Table 1.2: Number of comments addressing linguistic and interpersonal skills and other competencies.

| | Linguistic and interpersonal skills | | | | | | Other transversal competencies | Total |
|---|---|---|---|---|---|---|---|---|
| | Vocabulary and expressions | Grammar | Pronunciation | Clear and understandable ideas | Facial expression | Other interpersonal skills | | |
| **Peer assessment** | | | | | | | | |
| What did your partner do well? | 8 | 8 | 44 | 4 | 2 | 8 | 19 | 93 |
| How can your partner improve next time? | 8 | 21 | 20 | 3 | 5 | 3 | 24 | 84 |
| **Self-assessment** | | | | | | | | |
| What did you do well? | 2 | 3 | 18 | 8 | 6 | 3 | 45 | 85 |
| How can you improve next time? | 13 | 13 | 37 | 4 | 5 | 4 | 16 | 92 |
| Total | 31 | 45 | 119 | 19 | 18 | 18 | 104 | 354 |

## 4.1 Activating students as instructional resources for one another

When asked to comment freely on aspects of their partner's and their own performance, students overwhelmingly chose to comment on pronunciation. Issues of grammar and vocabulary were commented on much less, indicating that students' attention was mainly oriented towards clarity of speech.

When giving positive feedback, students mainly mentioned pronunciation as being something that their partner did well. Some representative comments are: "She spoke clearly and her pronunciation was good," from a US student, and "He's Japanese was very fluently," from a Japanese student. However, while they praised their partner for clear pronunciation, students viewed their own pronunciation as something which they needed to improve, more so than any other area.

When asked to identify weak areas that could be improved in the future, students advised their partner to focus on grammar (21 comments) more than any other linguistic skill. Some of these comments were of a general nature, such as, "Improving on grammar towards the end of the video." However, many comments were clear and explicit, from both the U.S. students and Japanese students. One US student wrote, "A verb from the last question was missing: why *don't* you have . . .", while another wrote, "Don't forget to include articles in your sentences, and make your words plural if you are describing more than one thing." A student from Japan commented, "Her Japanese is very good. If she had better practice to *joshi* (particles), l think she will be more better", and another advised to improve "conjunction such as ~*nanode, ~dakara*". The number and clarity of the comments suggest that students were successfully activated as instructional resources for each other (Black and Wiliam, 2009), with most students feeling comfortable in their role as teacher of their native language. It is also interesting that students saw themselves and their partners in the role of teacher, despite the fact that during this program they were never actually instructed to 'teach' their partner anything. Kano commented in her interview, "It was like there was a whole bunch of teachers. We were able to teach them new things and they were able to teach us new things." When interviewed, students reported specifically learning grammar, vocabulary, verbs, adjectives, and writing sentences from their partners. Andresen (2009) noted that the primary difficulty with assessing online forums is the vast amount of data that can be assessed. The results here suggest that students can effectively engage in assessment of each other, thus reducing some of the workload for the teacher.

## 4.2 Developing students' abilities to evaluate their own learning

When evaluating what they themselves did well, less than half the written reflections (40 comments) addressed interpersonal and linguistic areas, instead focusing on other competencies (45 comments). Comments were quite diverse, such as, "I met the criteria of the assignment, the time length, and by the due date"; "I spend quite a good amount of time to shoot the video and editing it to make it interesting"; and "I'm not afraid of making mistakes and I spoke with joy and fun." Students were more likely to evaluate themselves well in intrapersonal areas such as attitude and effort, rather than linguistic competence.

Students more often saw their own performance weaknesses as not related to lexis or sentence construction, but in the area of pronunciation. Written comments on the self-reflection forms were made such as, "I would like to improve on pronouncing the words correctly. I also think I should still practice more so that I could speak a little quicker and clearer"; "I have to learn English pronounce again and again"; and "(Next time I should) give a smoother delivery while speaking Japanese by having less pauses to think." When evaluating their own performance, comments suggest some students were closely watching the performance of others and making judgments based on a comparison with their peers. One student wrote, "I think I am going a little faster than others and I should slow down."

This finding is supported by the interview data. The participants Tom, Ruth and Rina all said they watched their classmates' videos and evaluated their own performance in light of those. Rina (Japan) said:

> The video that I made, I compared to videos made by other students in my class, and compared to them, how was I able to do it? Did I prepare properly?, and stuff like that. Also, what was my level of English like, compared to other people?

Having students engage in self-evaluation caused them to watch the performance of classmates closely, to notice where their strengths and weaknesses lie in comparison with their peers. This reflection provided a foundation for the development of learner autonomy, as also argued by Dam and Legenhausen (2011). Hannah (U.S.) said,

> (Self-evaluation) helps me to see, oh, this is what my work looks like. This is what I wanted, this is how I want to improve, this is what I want to do better. And by seeing that, that's something that I want, rather than [my teacher] telling me, 'Oh, you need to work on this.' It makes me see, oh, that I want to continue learning.

In addition to comparing themselves with peers, just the act of watching their own video brought to light L2 weaknesses which had hitherto been hidden. Dave (U.S.) said:

> I never really recorded myself speaking for a speech, essentially. All my speeches I've done in the past all are in person. I didn't have to send it or record it. So this time got me really uncomfortable to record myself. And I'm not going to lie, the two-minute videos that we had to do– I spent, like, an hour and a half just re-recording them over and over again. So yeah, that's definitely something that kind of opened my eyes to how uncomfortable I am with this kind of stuff. Because I just started thinking that I'm getting better at public speaking, and then now that the video hit me, I was like, damn! I could really– I'm missing in this section. That kind of thing.

Students were continually casting an evaluative eye over their own performances as well as that of their classmates and overseas partners. This provided a foundation for self-regulated learning (Nicol and Macfarlane-Dick, 2006), as well as an opportunity for them to develop their own evaluative expertise, which is an essential component of an instructional system that aims to promote learning (Sadler, 1989).

## 4.3 Providing feedback that enhances ongoing learning

The design of the program allowed students to get quick and timely feedback from their partner, which was appreciated by Melanie (U.S.), who said in her interview: "We were able to communicate with them and get really soon feedback from them, the video the following week or something like that." While the reception of such timely feedback was conducive to learning, the giving of feedback also was beneficial. Doing peer assessment helped Melanie with meta-linguistic awareness. She said, "I think it helps me view English from an outside perspective of not being a native speaker and having also to learn the grammar structure of English as well."

Engaging in peer assessment oriented students to focus on learning, and not just take the whole exchange lightly or of limited educational value. Dave (U.S.) said,

> It's always nice to get feedback on yourself. But doing this assessment definitely reminds me that this is an assignment. This is not just me talking to and making a friend. This is assigned to me – a person that's assigned to me to work on something together.

An assessment cannot be described as learning oriented unless it actually leads to L2 development (Turner and Purpura, 2016). While this is difficult to demonstrate, participants did report that they tried to incorporate comments from peer feedback in subsequent tasks. When interviewed, Tom (U.S.) said, "[My teacher] kind of showed us our feedback and I tried to take that to mind when I was doing my second video." Saki (Japan) also used comments from Dave to feed-forward into her second video. In her self-evaluation, she wrote that she prepared well the second time, and when interviewed, she said the reason for that was Dave advised her to practice more.

Students received feedback from both formal (teacher) and informal (peer) sources, as recommended by Sambell, McDowell, and Montgomery (2013). A major theme in the interview data was how teacher feedback was received differently to peer feedback. Teacher assessment was considered useful for the form and mechanics of language, whereas peer assessment functioned to motivate and improve practical communication skill. Dee (U.S.) said,

> I feel like with [my teacher], correction kind of feels like a reprimand. With my partner, it just feels kind of like, hey, you should do this. Kind of like a little easier and chilled back. . . It just feels like a little more relaxed, kind of like a friendly setting. . . Like, I'm going through the same things as you are. Here's just what I suggest. Take it or leave it.

Saki (Japan) also commented on the rapport between a fellow-learner that effected feedback. She said, "Receiving comments from Dave was more 'real'. He's studying Japanese and I'm studying English and we're the same age and understand what each other is going through." However, both teacher and peer feedback were equally valued. Masa (Japan) said, "Teacher assessment is quite different . . . It's good to hear some different perspectives, not just one person, to have a few different people give me advice." Hazuki (Japan) said,

> My partner can tell me whether she could understand what I was saying or not. She's the only one who can tell me that. If she didn't really understand what I was talking about, she can let me know, "Is this what you were trying to say?". She can tell me how she feels about my video, and that is really good for me to hear. The teacher tells me about the mistakes in my sentences, and tells me that I should use these words instead, and gives me advice about stuff like that. But I really want to hear the impressions from a person to whom I'm just speaking normally.

While an LOA approach to assessment had many perceived benefits for language learning, the biggest challenge presented by the data is that of making peer feedback more comprehensible. Some of the comments on the peer assessment forms were difficult to understand, while other comments were of such a general nature that they could not effectively feed forward into any useful L2 development. A small number of students interviewed mentioned that some feedback was puzzling and sometimes contradictory. It has been suggested that training can help improve the relevance of peer comments by promoting the citation of particular skills (Saito, 2008). A challenge for the future, therefore, is to train students in making their peer feedback more targeted and explicit so that it can productively contribute to their partner's language development. Having students discuss their feedback together in class may also deepen their understanding and improve their feedback literacy (Carless and Boud, 2018).

The main limitation of the present study is that it relies on students' self-reporting of language learning gains. While it can be argued that students have a very intimate and unique insight into their own learning progress, it is also probable that individual personality and mindset would colour some of their self-evaluations. Future research would do well to gather evidence from learners' language output as a more objective measure of the degree of second language acquisition within a program founded on LOA principles.

# 5 Conclusion

The case study described in this chapter is an exploration of how a virtual exchange program could be developed using theoretical principles of assessment practice to support language learning. The data indicate that LOA as operationalized in this virtual exchange program supported SLA in cognitive and affective dimensions. Students noticed their own errors in language production by engaging in self-evaluation, they received explicit feedback and correction from their overseas partner and the teacher, and then were provided with an opportunity to use that feedback to improve their language output in subsequent tasks. In addition, the design of the assessment methods worked to build intrinsic motivation through authentic interaction with intercultural peers, and extrinsic motivation through comprehensive assessment which contributed towards their final grade for the course. The highly situated nature of case studies means that one must be cautious about generalization to other contexts. However, it is hoped that some of the ideas presented here would be helpful to educators seeking to move beyond a participation score for virtual exchange programs and instead utilize the power of assessment to propel learners to greater language attainment.

# References

Andresen, Martin. 2009. Asynchronous discussion forums: Success factors, outcomes, assessments, and limitations. *Journal of Educational Technology & Society*. 12 (1). 249–257. http://www.jstor.org/stable/jeductechsoci.12.1.249

Assessment Reform Group. 2002. Assessment for Learning: 10 principles. https://www.aaia.org.uk/storage/medialibrary/o_1d8j89n3u1n0u17u91fdd1m4418fh8.pdf

Avgousti, Maria. 2018. Intercultural communicative competence and online exchanges: A systematic review. *Computer Assisted Language Learning*. 31 (8). 819–853. https://doi.org/10.1080/09588221.2018.1455713

Belz, Julie. 2002. Social dimensions of telecollaborative foreign language study. *Language Learning & Technology*. 6 (1). 60–81.

Black, Paul & Dylan Wiliam. 1998. Assessment and classroom learning. *Assessment in Education: Principles, Policy & Practice*. 5 (1). 7–74. https://doi.org/10.1080/0969595980050102

Black, Paul & Dylan Wiliam. 2009. Developing the theory of formative assessment. *Educational Assessment, Evaluation and Accountability*. 21 (1). 5–31. https://doi.org/10.1007/s11092-008-9068-5

Black, Paul & Dylan Wiliam. 2012. Developing a theory of formative assessment. In John Gardner (ed.), *Assessment and Learning* (2nd ed.), 206–229. London: Sage.

Brown, James D. 2014. *Mixed Methods Research for TESOL*. Edinburgh: Edinburgh University Press.

Bueno-Alastuey, M. Camino & Marcin Kleban. 2016. Matching linguistic and pedagogical objectives in a telecollaboration project: A case study. *Computer Assisted Language Learning*. 29 (1). 148–166. https://doi.org/10.1080/09588221.2014.904360

Care, Esther & Rebekah Luo. 2016. Assessment of transversal competencies: Policy and practice in the Asia-Pacific Region. UNESCO Bangkok. http://unesdoc.unesco.org/images/0024/002465/246590E.pdf

Carless, David. 2009. Learning-oriented assessment: Principles, practice and a project. In Luanna Meyer, Susan Davidson, Helen Anderson, Richard Fletcher, Patricia Johnston & Malcolm Rees (eds.), *Tertiary Assessment and Higher Education Student Outcomes: Policy, Practice and Research*, 79–90. Wellington, New Zealand: Ako Aotearoa.

Carless, David. 2015. Exploring learning-oriented assessment processes. *Higher Education*. 69 (6). 963–976. https://doi.org/10.1007/s10734-014-9816-z

Carless, David & David Boud. 2018. The development of student feedback literacy: Enabling uptake of feedback. *Assessment & Evaluation in Higher Education*. 43 (8). 1315–1325. https://doi.org/10.1080/02602938.2018.1463354

Çiftçi, Emrullah Yasin & Perihan Savaş. 2018. The role of telecollaboration in language and intercultural learning: A synthesis of studies published between 2010 and 2015. *ReCALL*. 30 (3). 278–298. https://doi.org/10.1017/S0958344017000313

Dam, Leni & Lienhard Legenhausen. 2011. Explicit reflection, evaluation, and assessment in the autonomy classroom. *Innovation in Language Learning and Teaching*. 5 (2). 177–189. https://doi.org/10.1080/17501229.2011.577533

Davison, Chris & Constant Leung. 2009. Current issues in English language teacher-based assessment. *TESOL Quarterly*. 43 (3). 393–415. https://doi.org/10.1002/j.1545-7249.2009.tb00242.x

Duff, Patricia. 2008. *Case Study Research in Applied Linguistics*. New York: Lawrence Erlbaum Associates.

Ellis, Rod. 2003. *Task-Based Language Learning and Teaching*. Oxford: Oxford University Press.

Ellis, Rod. 2018. *Reflections on Task-Based Language Teaching*. Bristol, UK: Multilingual Matters.

Elwood, Jannette & Patricia Murphy. 2015. Assessment systems as cultural scripts: A sociocultural theoretical lens on assessment practice and products. *Assessment in Education: Principles, Policy & Practice*. 22 (2). 182–192. https://doi.org/10.1080/0969594X.2015.1021568

Ferris, Dana R. 2010. Second language writing research and written corrective feedbackin SLA: Intersections and practical applications. *Studies in Second Language Acquisition*. 32 (2). 181–201. https://doi.org/10.1017/S0272263109990490

Forsythe, Alex & Sophie Johnson. 2017. Thanks, but no-thanks for the feedback. *Assessment & Evaluation in Higher Education*. 42 (6). 850–859. https://doi.org/10.1080/02602938.2016.1202190

Frey, Bruce B., Vicki L. Schmitt & Justin P. Allen. 2012. Defining authentic classroom assessment. *Practical Research, Assessment, and Evaluation*. 17 (2). https://doi.org/10.7275/SXBS-0829

Guth, Sarah & Francesca Helm (eds.). 2010. *Telecollaboration 2.0*. Bern: Peter Lang International Academic Publishers.

Hauck, Mirjam & Bonnie L. Youngs. 2008. Telecollaboration in multimodal environments: The impact on task design and learner interaction. *Computer Assisted Language Learning*. 21 (2). 87–124. https://doi.org/10.1080/09588220801943510

Helm, Francesca. 2016. Facilitated dialogue in online intercultural exchange. In Robert O'Dowd & Tim Lewis (eds.), *Online Intercultural Exchange: Policy, Pedagogy, Practice*, 150–172. New York: Routledge.

Huang, Shu-Chen. 2016. Understanding learners' self-assessment and self-feedback on their foreign language speaking performance. *Assessment & Evaluation in Higher Education*. 41 (6). 803–820. https://doi.org/10.1080/02602938.2015.1042426

Jones, Neil & Nick Saville. 2016. *Learning Oriented Assessment: A Systemic Approach*. Studies in Language Testing 45. Cambridge: Cambridge University Press.

Jonsson, Anders & Ernest Panadero. 2017. The use and design of rubrics to support assessment for learning. In David Carless, Susan M. Bridges, Cecilia Ka Yuk Chan & Rick Glofcheski (eds.), *Scaling up Assessment for Learning in Higher Education*, 99–111. Singapore: Springer.

Konishi, Masae. 2017. Effects of international online video talk in a language exchange situation on Japanese EFL college students taking a teacher training program. *Language Education & Technology*. 54. 113–133.

Lewis, Tim, & Robert O'Dowd. 2016. Online intercultural exchange and foreign language learning: A systematic review. In Robert O'Dowd & Tim Lewis (eds.), *Online Intercultural Exchange: Policy, Pedagogy, Practice*. 21–68. New York: Routledge.

Lewis, Tim, Breffni O'Rourke & Melinda Dooly. 2016. Innovation in language learning and teaching – Online Intercultural Exchange. *Innovation in Language Learning and Teaching*. 10 (1). 1–5. https://doi.org/10.1080/17501229.2015.1133541

Li, Lan. 2017. The role of anonymity in peer assessment. *Assessment & Evaluation in Higher Education*. 42 (4). 645–656. https://doi.org/10.1080/02602938.2016.1174766

Little, David & Gudrun Erickson. 2015. Learner identity, learner agency, and the assessment of language proficiency: Some reflections prompted by the Common European Framework of Reference for Languages. *Annual Review of Applied Linguistics*. 35. 120–139. https://doi.org/10.1017/S0267190514000300

López-Pastor, Victor & Alvaro Sicilia-Camacho. 2017. Formative and shared assessment in higher education: Lessons learned and challenges for the future. *Assessment & Evaluation in Higher Education*. 42 (1). 77–97. https://doi.org/10.1080/02602938.2015.1083535

Lynch, Richard. 2003. Authentic, performance-based assessment in ESL/EFL reading instruction. *The Asian EFL Journal5* (4). http://www.asian-efl-journal.com/dec_03_rl.pdf (accessed 12 July 2019)

Martí, Natalia Morollon & Susana S. Fernández. 2016. Telecollaboration and sociopragmatic awareness in the foreign language classroom. *Innovation in Language Learning and Teaching*. 10 (1). 34–48. https://doi.org/10.1080/17501229.2016.1138577

Miles, Matthew B., Michael A. Huberman & Johnny Saldaña. 2020. *Qualitative Data Analysis: A Methods Sourcebook* (4th ed.). Los Angeles: Sage.

Muller-Hartmann, Andreas & Malgorzata Kurek. 2016. Virtual group formation and the process of task design in online intercultural exchanges. In Robert O'Dowd & Tim Lewis (eds.), *Online Intercultural Exchange: Policy, Pedagogy, Practice*. 131–149. New York: Routledge.

Nicol, David J. & Debra Macfarlane-Dick. 2006. Formative assessment and self-regulated learning: A model and seven principles of good feedback practice. *Studies in Higher Education*. 31(2). 199–218. https://doi.org/10.1080/03075070600572090

Nissen, Elke. 2016. Combining classroom-based learning and online intercultural exchange in blended learning courses. In Robert O'Dowd & Tim Lewis (eds.), *Online Intercultural Exchange: Policy, Pedagogy, Practice*. 173–191. New York: Routledge.

Nunan, David & Kathleen M. Bailey. 2009. *Exploring second language classroom research*. Boston, MA: Heinle.

O'Dowd, Robert & Paige Waire. 2009. Critical issues in telecollaborative task design. *Computer Assisted Language Learning*. 22 (2). 173–188. https://doi.org/10.1080/09588220902778369

O'Dowd, Robert. 2018. From telecollaboration to virtual exchange and the role of UNICollaboration: An overview of where we stand today. *Journal of Virtual Exchange*. 1 (1). 1–23.

O'Rourke, Breffni. 2007. Models of telecollaboration (1): E(tandem). In Robert O'Dowd (ed.), *Online Intercultural Exchange: An Introduction for Foreign Language Teachers*. 41–62. Bristol, UK: Multilingual Matters.

Pereira, Diana, Maria A. Flores & Laila Niklasson. 2016. Assessment revisited: A review of research in Assessment and Evaluation in Higher Education. *Assessment and Evaluation in Higher Education*. 41 (7). 1008–1032. https://doi.org/10.1080/02602938.2015.1055233

Poehner, Matthew E. 2007. Beyond the Test: L2 Dynamic Assessment and the Transcendence of Mediated Learning. *The Modern Language Journal*. 91 (3). 323–340. https://doi.org/10.1111/j.1540-4781.2007.00583.x

Priego, Sabrina & Meei-Ling Liaw. 2017. Understanding different levels of group functionality: Activity systems analysis of an intercultural telecollaborative multilingual digital storytelling project. *Computer Assisted Language Learning*. 30 (5). 368–389. https://doi.org/10.1080/09588221.2017.1306567

Sadler, D. Royce. 1989. Formative assessment and the design of instructional systems. *Instructional Science*. 18 (2). 119–144. https://doi.org/10.1007/BF00117714

Sadler, Randall & Melinda Dooly. 2016. Twelve years of telecollaboration: What we have learnt. *ELT Journal*. 70 (4). 401–413. https://doi.org/10.1093/elt/ccw041

Saito, Hidetoshi. 2008. EFL classroom peer assessment: Training effects on rating and commenting. *Language Testing*. 25 (4). 553–581. https://doi.org/10.1177/0265532208094276

Sambell, Kay, Liz McDowell & Catherine Montgomery. 2013. *Assessment for Learning in Higher Education*. New York: Routledge.

Schreier, Margrit. 2012. *Qualitative Content Analysis in Practice*. Los Angeles: Sage.

Thomas, Michael & Hayo Reinders (eds.). (2012). *Task-Based Language Learning and Teaching with Technology*. New York: Bloomsbury Academic.

Topping, Keith J. 2009. Peer assessment. *Theory into Practice*. 48 (1). 20–27. https://doi.org/10.1080/00405840802577569

Turner, Carolyn E. & James E. Purpura. 2016. Learning-oriented assessment in second and foreign language classrooms. In Dina Tsagari & Jayanti Banerjee (eds.), *Handbook of Second Language Assessment*, 255–272. Berlin: De Gruyter Mouton.

Villamil, Olga S. & Maria C. M. de Guerrero. 2006. Sociocultural theory: A framework for understanding the social-cognitive dimensions of peer feedback. In Ken Hyland & Fiona Hyland (eds.), *Feedback in Second Language Writing*, 23–41. Cambridge: Cambridge University Press.

Ware, Paige & Robert O'Dowd. 2008. Peer feedback on language form in telecollaboration. *Language Learning & Technology*. 12 (1). 43–63.

Eucharia Donnery
# Chapter 2
# From demotivation to Intercultural Communicative Competence (ICC): Japanese university learner journeys in the International Virtual ExchangeProject (IVEProject)

For many Japanese students, the exam-focus of compulsory English classes at the junior and senior high levels often creates the impression that English is for passive testing purposes, rather than active communication, a perception that extends into the compulsory English university system (Nagatomo 2012). Within the context of English education in Japan, on completion of the six-year cycle of junior and senior high schools, the average Japanese university student tends to have good test-taking skills, excelling in the grammar and grammar-translation sections in particular. Unsurprisingly, the repetitive nature of this type of learning has left many Japanese students demotivated and jaded towards English, which has been taught as if it were complicated mathematical formulae for, what Ushioda (2013) terms *exam hell*. When language is taught in this way in which there is merely a correct or incorrect answer, leaving little room for creativity and/or ambiguity, students react in different ways: from polite passive-aggressive disinterest as individuals to open hostility as a class. Japan, as a predominantly monolingual and homogenous culture, is by no means unique in its production of citizens who are disinterested in other languages, such as Irish language learners in Ireland (Darmody & Daly 2015). Indeed, Nagatomo (ibid.) cites the results of Nagasawa's 2004 survey of English teaching practices at Japanese university level, which found 95% of classes were conducted in Japanese rather than English. This means that, for the majority of Japanese university students, there is little or no incentive – or even opportunity – to engage with authentic English within the set curriculum.

Although Ryan points out that "the literature on language learning in Japan presents a fascinating, though often depressing picture" (2009: 124), from a practical perspective, there can be tremendous opportunities for motivational change to occur within the Japanese university EFL context. Independent projects such as

---
**Eucharia Donnery,** Soka University, Japan, e-mail: eucharia@soka.ac.jp

Virtual Exchange (VE), which O'Dowd and O'Rourke describe as "the bringing together of learners from different cultural contexts for extended periods of online intercultural collaboration and interaction" (2019: 1) within the context of Second Language Acquisition (SLA), can allow university students to asynchronously experience and engage with authentic and meaningful communication. These kinds of VE projects can, in turn, foster ownership of English, self-confidence, and simultaneously develop Byram's *savoirs* of Intercultural Communicative Competence (ICC): attitudes, knowledge, skills of interpretation and relating, skills of discovery, and critical cultural awareness (1997: 34). Therefore, the aim of the present study is to explore changes in the development of intercultural communicative competence (ICC) particularly within the context of motivation and critical thinking through an international virtual exchange project, in which all participants communicated through the second language (L2) of English.

# 1 Literature review

## 1.1 Intercultural Communicative Competence (ICC)

In research starting as far back as 1997, Byram identified the aims of Intercultural Communicative Competence (ICC) as positive effects in what he called the areas of the "five savoirs": Attitudes, Knowledge, Interpreting/Relating Skills, Discovery/Interaction Skills, and Critical Cultural Awareness.

In 2001, Byram, Nichols and Stevens refined this model further to incorporate the world of the language learner and their place in it in terms of intercultural communicative competence (ICC), described as 'curiosity and openness, readiness to suspend disbelief about other cultures and belief about one's own', the most important ICC component (5). However, the following year, Byram, Gribova, and Starkey conceived this move towards ICC as the 'ability to ensure a shared understanding by people of different social identities' and the 'ability to interact with people as complex human beings with multiple identities and their own individuality' (2002: 10).

## 1.2 Process drama

Process drama (PD) within L1 can be summarized as a genre in which "the participants, together with the teacher, constitute the theatrical ensemble and engage in drama to make the meaningfor themselves" (Bowell & Heap 2001: 7). In PD, all classroom endeavours are viewed as part of a process rather than a final end product, as in a theatre-based approach. According to Bowell and Heap, there are six principles in the paradigm of the planning process: theme or learning area, context, roles, frame, sign and strategies (10). Within the process of preparation, there is a shape and a sense of where the process drama may go.

In the field of PD in Second Language Acquisition (SLA), Kao and O'Neill favored a more learner- and learning-centered interactive three-step approach; that of preparation (visual or textual cues, discussion, tableau + interview), dramatic scenes (role-plays), and reflection (writing-in-role) (1998: 18). This act of reflection was in keeping with the thoughts of the 20$^{th}$ century global disseminator of drama-in-education (DiE) in L1 Dorothy Heathcote, who stated that, with respect to the creation of meaningful experience, "without the power of reflection we have very little. It is reflection that permits the storing of knowledge, the recalling of power of feeling, and memory of past feelings" (1984: 97). This act of self-reflection occurs simultaneously through that of the character-in-role and the actor-self. Therefore, the aims of Kao and O'Neill's Open Communication Model are perhaps less complex than those of Byram's to verify: fluency, authenticity, confidence, challenge, and new classroom relations (1998: 16). From DiE, PD in SLA has developed into a highly structured pedagogy that promotes content and language integrated learning (CLIL).

## 1.3 Telecollaboration

Thorne's (2003) groundbreaking study documents English and French natives and language learners in mentor-learner relationship modes. However, in his study, there emerged the digital divide of what he termed *cultures-of-use*. In the interim, there has been accelerated development in democratization of the Internet, partly due to Moore's 1965 Law. The democratization of the Internet has taken place through the rapid advancement and accessibility of mobile devices, and Theis and Wong point to "the architecture of memory access" as being "ripe for innovation" (2017: 47). As Kern identifies, "with regard to language learning, the Internet . . . affords unprecedented opportunities for direct and inexpensive communication across huge distances" (2014: 340).

O'Dowd identifies the "important issue is that the practitioners and promoters of . . . virtual exchange work closer together to promote the overall goal of increasing the number of students who benefit from online intercultural exchange as part of their university education" (2018: 20). However, as Thorne argues, the use of technology in education is not a one-way street, "the implication for cultures-in-use is to expand our thinking to include the ontological possibility that it is not only humans that act on, with, and through technologies, but that technologies may also be acting on, with, and through us" (2018: 189).

## 1.4 International Virtual Exchange Project (IVEProject)

When the International Virtual Exchange Project (IVEProject) was established in 2005 by Eric Hagley, with the explicit goal to connect university students through English (2020b), online activities tended still towards the digital divide of the educational 'haves' versus the 'have nots.' Thanks to the aforementioned technological leap and the diminishment of the digital divide, the IVEProject introduced the first large-scale project with students not just from Japan and Colombia but also from China, Thailand, and Vietnam in 2015.

Hagley also makes the valid point in favor of this technological democratization when he argues that "without opportunities to interact on the international stage, EFL often became an academic activity with few chances to use English in real-world communicative events, nor were there chances to interact with a foreign culture. 'Real' communication between people who needed to use English to communicate was difficult to find in such environments. The Internet changed that" (2020a: 75). Since then, there have been almost 100 institutions from twenty countries taking part in the project with 20,000 students and 300 teachers from 15 countries (Hagley 2020b).

# 2 Method

## 2.1 Participants

Students of the Department of Applied Computer Sciences (CA) at a small mid-rank engineering institute in Japan take a compulsory-elective seminar course to a maximum of ten students called Team Project Learning (TPL), offered in the second and third years. All students must pass TPL in order to advance to fourth year; however, it is elective in that students can choose to study with the faculty member with the research area that corresponds best to their own research interest. The research areas that this TPL offered were those of PD in SLA, Intercultural Communicative Competence (ICC), and Computer Assisted Language Learning (CALL). This means that the non-English computer science majors came voluntarily into the seminar group in Spring 2018 for a three-hour session per week to explore these above research areas and foster groupwork using Deming's Plan-Do-Check-Act (PDCA) cycle, an educational model which Moen and Norman argue, has "roots in the scientific method and the philosophy of science for more than 400 years" (2009: 9). Because of length and time constraints, the analysis here focuses on three out of eight TPL students in the period from Fall 2018 to Fall 2019. This purposeful sampling is in order to facilitate the selection of what Patton calls "information-rich cases for study in depth" (1990: 16), therefore I chose to focus on the journeys of three particular students; one because of high levels of extroversion, one because of extreme introversion and the third because s/he had been a long-standing student in my classes from high school days, a program in which I teach five to ten times annually.

## 2.2 Task

In Fall 2018, the TPL students took part in a basic writing-in-role activity within the framework of PD projects, which became the start of the writing journey. In Spring and Fall 2019, the same students participated in the International Virtual Exchange Project (IVEProject). Building on the initial process drama project that incorporated WIR in the preceding semester, the students carried out two separate eight week-long, multi-stage, group blog-based[1] communication activities through the IVEProject over the two semesters. The students communicated in English throughout the IVEProject, where they were partnered with students of similar linguistic abilities, mostly from Servicio Nacional de Aprendizaje (SENA), the National Apprenticeship Service in Colombia.

From May 6th until June 10th during Spring 2019, the students wrote blogs under the following two-week topics:
1) Introductions
2) Food culture
3) Events in our lives
4) Final topic: What I learned

Within the two-week format, students read and commented on the writings from Colombia, while the Columbian students did likewise. Before writing the blogs, the eight Japanese students had discussions based on their understandings of what might be interesting for the Colombian students to read. This idea of having authentic communication *through* English with people of who also

---

[1] Further explanations of the IVEProject tasks are available in the FAQs: https://iveproject.org/.

were L2 English learners was an important one for the Japanese students, as it lowered language anxiety, allowing them to write freely. Before publication, students asked me to check their work individually, and then, as a group, we discussed some common issues, such as sentence length, punctuation and comprehensibility.

From October 14$^{th}$ until December 8$^{th}$, 2019, the students wrote blogs under the following topics:
1) Introductions and Daily Life
2) Communities and Relationships
3) Countries and Culture
4) Reflecting for a Better Future

In the same pattern as Spring 2019, the IVEProject progressed in two-week cycles of blogging and commenting. In this semester, there were discussions on written expression, style and the advantages and disadvantages of online software as a tool for self-checking written production.

## 3 Results and discussion

### 3.1 2018: Writing-in-role (WIR)

As discussed earlier, the WIR concluded each session of the weekly PD project and, as this was the first time for many to write creatively, there was no grammar requirement. Instead, the students were asked to write ten basic yet comprehensible sentences about their character from each drama. The PD drama chosen below and reproduced verbatim was thematically based on the civil disobedience that took place in Shibuya, Tokyo during October 31, 2018 that caused national outrage. The traditional Celtic Irish festival of Halloween as the night before the month of All Souls' had been filtered through the lens of the nineteenth-century Irish emigrants to the US, then subsequently reconstructed as a Japanese event which promoted unruly behavior amongst small, but significant, numbers of the 300,000 revelers. From a video-clip showing the overturning of a truck, the students led a discussion on the constitution of anti-social behavior in the context of intercultural experiences, especially behaviors that they would rather not be shown internationally. This, in turn, led to a discussion on personal safety which is lauded in Japan, in that many citizens are scrupulously honest and will try to reunite forgotten and/or misplaced items with the owners. However, Japan is not crime-free, and most students had had some experience of thievery, whether physically or online. This kind of self-reflective aspect of the PD projects had an enormous impact on the students, giving them much-needed confidence in their own English language abilities, whilst simultaneously allowing them to don the persona of their character from the particular drama.

|     | Aki[2]                                       | Taro                                  | Yuma                            |
| --- | -------------------------------------------- | ------------------------------------- | ------------------------------- |
| 1.  | I like to travel.                            | I'm kind.                             | My name is Yuma.                |
| 2.  | I went to Cebu.                              | I teach Japanese girl at "suri".[3]   | I'm 18 years old.               |
| 3.  | Cebu Island had a lot of culture shock.      | I wear bag in front of body.          | I had a phone stolen in Tokyo.  |
| 4.  | I was told the local people to be safe.      | I help Japanese people in America.    | I like watching baseball.       |
| 5.  | I did it.                                    | I'm like a hero.                      | My favorite food is sushi.      |
| 6.  | I was made a fool by my friend.              | My job is act of mercy.               | My hobby is playing video games.|
| 7.  | I also taught that friend about pickpockets. | I'm kind because my family is kind.   | I want to money.                |
| 8.  | Pickpockets is not good.                     | I can good at teaching.               | I want to go to Hawaii.         |
| 9.  | I want you to disappear from all over the world. | I was uncomfortable to help people. | I have two dogs.              |
| 10. | Japan is a peaceful country.                 | I love all human beings.              | My birthday is on Christmas Day.|

While the sentences may not be grammatically perfect, they are comprehensible and clear. These sentences show how this act of self-reflection, while perhaps lacking in "content which is cognitively and emotionally demanding" (Byram & Wagner 2018: 13), does demonstrate emerging sensibilities within these two realms.

---

2 All pseudonyms.
3 Pickpocketing.

## 3.2 Spring 2019: IVE Project

Writing with the reader in mind is a difficult concept, even in the L1, and this concept of a readership examining, enjoying and engaging with their writing seemed alien to the students. Nonetheless, when students initially complained that they did not write to express things even in Japanese let alone in English, we discussed their online activities and communications. As computer majors, they all had viable presences on Twitter and Line, a Japanese social networking system (SNS), and were au fait with the concept of a commenting and liking readership within that context. Therefore, this IVE Project was to provide a transferable skill with the same goal of finding a readership, but this time in English.

> Aki
>
> I like to dance. I'm particularly good at hip hop dance. I have been learning since I was in elementary school. I have no time to dance now. I would like to dance again if I have a chance.
>
> My hobby is to travel. I often travel. I went to Hawaii, Cebu, Hokkaido, Osaka last year. I went to Bali in March this year. Especially because Hawaii is my favorite place, I want to go there for a long time again. But I want to go to countries other than Asia among the students, so I will do my best at savings. By the way, I'm not good at saving money.
>
> We are a family of six. I'm the second girl of four sisters. I love my sisters so much. I always buy souvenirs for my sisters. But recently my sisters are sad in rebellion. My personality is bright, childish and a little of a crybaby. . .

After these initial introductions by Japanese students within their group within the IVEProject, many of the Colombian students commented on information within their Japanese counterparts' introductions, however they did not address the recipients by name, which meant that the Japanese students had to read each comment and decide whether or not it was directed at them, or someone else in the online group. Aki successfully found a comment from a Colombian student called Maria that was directed towards the content of her introduction, as below.

> You are a very tender and dedicated girl, also loving and think of your family, may God keep filling you up to share.
>
> and I know that even if you do not have the time to dance, the moment will come again.
>
> You know what about travel I think it's great that you go out and know and even more if you have the means to do it . . . enjoy life just one and every moment is wonderful.

In response this, Aki read Maria's 383-word introduction, then drew commonalities and differences between their two experiences.

Your age is about the same as my mother. I think it is a great thing to raise two children alone. I have a pity because I have no brothers. But there are sisters!

My hobby is traveling and I would like to get in touch with "Aristo" when I go to Columbia someday. I thought the green desk in front of the hotel receptionist in the photo was cute! It is very cute cat. . .

The blog objective was to write 100 words or more, however, as the students received comments from students in Colombia and read about life there, they naturally wanted to explain about life in Japan and what being Japanese meant to them. The minimum limit of 100 words, rather than a cursory goal, was superseded as the students interacted with their Colombian counterparts and lost awareness of word count. One of the most interesting things to emerge at this point of the IVEProject was this growing awareness of a wider audience-community, who were reading and commenting on the Japanese students' work.

## 3.3 Fall 2019: IVE Project

By engaging with the world *through* English, the goal was for students to develop into articulate, conscientious and responsible adults through self-reflection. For example, in the case of Taro *(see below),* whose ambition was to be a comedian, understanding the implicit nature of Japanese communication versus the more explicit one of English was important in order for him to convey humor in his L2. Rather than becoming disillusioned with this information, Taro sought to reflect on this and incorporated it into his worldview.

Taro

I learned a lot in this class. The frequency of using English simply on a daily basis is increasing, and new words are growing daily by listening to and examining teachers. By learning elegant words and English not Japanese, I have learned very important things for the future. There is still a lot of time, so I strongly want to participate actively so that I can improve it further.

As for the future, I would like to get a job related to television. I have been greatly influenced by watching comedians on TV. My life has become brighter. Not only comedians but also photographers, producers, and all other people who make television will be one for people on the other side of the screen. I want to be a member of that group, and I want to be a person who can give other people energy and hope. I want to be a person who can help people feel a little cheerful when they see me, or even smile a little on my program. That is why I am studying comedians and producers.

Perhaps because of his love of wordplay and nuance in Japanese, Taro's use of the world "elegant" is striking. While at the start of the first PD project, like many of the students in the group, he did not see English in terms of communication, rather as a gate-keeping mechanism for academic or career advancement; his goal to increase happiness through comedic communicative methods overcame this reticence. It was, however, the interactive and diverse nature of the IVEProject that continued to draw him in and Columbian student Antonio's response helped to motivate him further.

> . . .I think it's very good that you learn other languages to communicate with people from other countries, especially English, an almost universal language.
>
> The satisfaction I feel to be able to help other people who come to our country is fantastic.
>
> I encourage you to continue learning, this will also help you fulfill your dream of motivating other people and making them smile in any language. . .

The above interactions indicate the deepening of psychological connections and both students, rather than engage in discordance, made concerted efforts towards understanding and support, demonstrating Hofstede's dexterity within communication, "creative communicators use culture-sensitive, adaptive communication skills to manage the process appropriately and integrate divergent interaction goals effectively to foster constructive productivity and team satisfaction within the system" (2009: 116).

## 3.4 Fall 2019: Questionnaire

As part of the IVEProject, all students across the entire project were asked to create and submit questions about daily life, culture or topics they deemed relevant to a general questionnaire. Once these had been prepared and submitted, they were analyzed and consolidated into a survey format by the coordinators of the IVEProject. All the students then read and completed the survey in their native language, then submitted their answers via the site. With some curiosity, the students examined the data results the following week.

Most of the Colombian students were not impacted negatively by having neighbors who were unmarried, but rather tended to be more exercised if the neighbors were atheist. Results from the Japanese students were opposite, religion was not considered a concern when it came to neighbors, but rather the Japanese cultural concept of becoming a "full member of society" through marriage was considered more important.

Through this survey, the examination of various "potentially divisive issues that . . . lead to 'flaming' on social media rather than seeking to engage with other points of view" (Helm & Acconcia 2019: 22) could be considered from positions of genuine curiosity and objectivity. With respect to these results, both the Japanese students and the Colombians shared the view that the major role of a government with to maintain order in the nation while providing a sustainable environment. Yuma outlines his reflections on the survey below:

> Yuma
>
> I haven't clearly defined my future dreams so I'm very anxious about what to do next. However, I think life is going to be good, so my goal is to think positively. I haven't imagined this for 20 years, but I hope to be happy with a wonderful group of people and treasures. Suddenly, I have recently been living with something like a Japanese proverb that says "kindness calls friends" as my focus. This is a phrase to remember when you get lost in a choice or think you are moving in the wrong direction. For example, if you become a person who is not sloppy with money or time, the people who remain around you will be in the same category. I want to live my life without forgetting this feeling in order to be happy in the future. . .

With respect to his comments, it was interesting to note that his remarks struck a chord with another Japanese student from another university rather than one of his Colombian counterparts. Throughout the semester both students had taken particular care to comment on one another's blogs, and Ryo's response below echoes Yuma's fears for the future.

> I think the pension problem is very serious. If we don't get a pension, savings will become more important. You can make a lot of money, but you can't do that easily, so it's important to save some money.

Rather than communicate about lighter subjects, throughout the semester both students gradually gained psychological closeness when they reflected deeply on topics that had meaning and relevance to their current lives and future existence.

From the imagined authenticity of the WIR self-reflections and to actual discourses of the IVEProject, the changes within the students' writing in terms of Byram's ICC are clear:
- when it came to attitudes, they were able to relativize the Japanese Self whilst valuing the Colombian Other (Aki)
- there were marked increases in their knowledge of how to interact respectfully online in the L2 (Aki, Taro, Yuma)
- they were able to interpret and explore cultural differences in terms of expansion and learning (Taro)
- interpreting the data from the questionnaire provided a sense of discovery and interaction (Yuma)
- critical cultural awareness fostered a journey into self-reflection regarding the future from both individual and societal perspectives (Yuma)

Through the IVEProjects, students were to make the "strange familiar and the familiar strange" (Byram and Feng 2004: 159).

## 4 Conclusions

Although this three-semester long project played a minor part in the lives of the Japanese students, as Pennycook (1994: 64) argues, that what starts small can bring about profound change at a deeper and more meaningful way:

> Once we start to deal with the local, the incommensurable, the disjunctive, within a world in which discourses construct and regulative subjectivities, offering new and old subject positions to ever-changing populations, and once we see culture as constructed and produced within local conditions of power, then the ways in which we approach issues of global relations become very different.

Overall, these results are compelling evidence that the use of virtual exchange can help reluctant learners overcome previous negative experiences in language classes and develop holistically. In the current global pandemic, the importance of technology in communication has moved centerstage and has infiltrated the lives of most people. By utilizing this exponential push to meet demand and the subsequent leaps in creative design and application, virtual exchange programs in SLA education such as the IVEProject offer students a means by which to experience intercultural communication and develop competencies through the lens of technology. In closing, Belz's insights about language and intercultural competence is proleptic, "in the end, becoming interculturally competent may be not so much about adopting the words and interactional norms of the other in his or her language as it is about performing judicious acts of linguistic hybridity in a broadened discursive space" (2003: 92). As the scope of this chapter is limited to the experiences of the Japanese students as they interacted with the Colombian and other Japanese students from another university, how the project impacted the lives of the Colombian students is subject for another study.

## References

Belz, Julie A. 2003. Linguistic perspectives on the development of intercultural competence in telecollaboration. *Language Learning & Technology* 7 (2). 68–99.
Bowell, Pamela & Brian S. Heap. 2001. *Planning process drama*. London: Fulton.
Byram, Michael. 1997. *Teaching and assessing intercultural communicative competence*. Bristol, New York & Ontario: Multilingual Matters.

Byram, Michael, Adam Nichols & David Stevens. 2001. Introduction. In Michael Byram, Adam Nichols & David Stevens (eds.), *Developing intercultural communication in practice*, 1–8. Bristol, New York & Ontario: Multilingual Matters.
Byram, Michael, Bella Gribova. & Hugh Starkey. 2002. *Developing the intercultural dimension in language teaching*. Strasbourg: Council of Europe.
Byram, Michael & Anwei Feng. 2004. Culture and language learning: Teaching, research and scholarship. *Language Teaching* 37 (3). 149–168.
Byram, Michael & Manuela Wagner. 2018. Making a difference: Language teaching for intercultural and international dialogue. *Foreign Language Annals* 51 (1). 140–151.
Darmody, Merike & Tania Daly, T. 2015. *Attitudes towards the Irish language on the island of Ireland*. Dublin: Economic and Social Research Institute (ESRI).
Hagley, Eric. 2020a. Effects of virtual exchange in the EFL classroom on students' cultural and intercultural sensitivity. *Computer-Assisted Language Learning Electronic Journal* 21 (3). 74–87.
Hagley, Eric. 2020b. Linking the world's EFL classrooms: The IVEProject. *Japan Association of Language Teachers: The Language Teacher*. 44 (5). 26–28.
Heathcote, Dorothy. 1991. *Collected writings on education and drama*. In Liz Johnson & Cecily O'Neill (eds.). Evanston: Northwestern UP.
Helm, Francesca & Giuseppe Acconcia. 2019. Interculturality and language in Erasmus+ Virtual Exchange. *European Journal of Language Policy*. 11. 211–233.
Hofstede, Gert Jan. 2009. The moral circle in intercultural competence: Trust across cultures. In. Darla K. Deardoff (ed.), *The SAGE Handbook of Intercultural Competence*. Thousand Oaks, CA: Sage.
Kao, Shin-Mei & Cecily O'Neill. 1998. *Words into worlds: Learning a second language through process drama*. Ablex: London.
Kern, Richard. 2014. Technology as pharmakon: The promise and perils of the internet for foreign language education. *Modern Language Journal* 98. 340–357.
Moen, Roland & Clifford Norman. 2009. Evolution of the PDCA Cycle. In *Proceedings of the 7th ANQ Congress*. Tokyo: Conference Proceeding.
Nagatomo, Diane H. 2012. *Exploring Japanese university English teachers' professional identity*. Bristol, New York & Ontario: Multilingual Matters.
O'Dowd, Robert. 2018. From telecollaboration to virtual exchange: State of the art and the role of UNICollaboration organization in moving forward. *Journal of Virtual Exchange*, 1. 1–23.
O'Dowd, Robert & Breffni O'Rourke. 2019. New developments in virtual exchange in foreign language acquisition. *Language Learning & Technology* 23 (3). 1–7.
Patton, Michael Q. 1990. *Qualitative evaluation and research methods ($2^{nd}$ ed.)*. Newpark, CA: Sage.
Pennycook, Alastair. 1994. *The cultural politics of English as an international language*. Essex: Longman.
Ryan, Stephen. 2009. Self and identity in L2 motivation in Japan: The ideal L2 Self and Japanese learners of English. In Zoltan Dörnyei & Emi Usioda (eds.), *Motivation, Language Identity and the L2 Self*. Bristol, New York & Ontario: Multilingual Matters.
Ushioda, Emi. 2013. Foreign language motivation research in Japan: An 'inside' perspective from outside Japan. In Matthew T. Apple, Dexter Da Silva, Terry Fellner (eds.), *Language Learning Motivation in Japan*. Bristol, New York & Ontario: Multilingual Matters.

Theis, Thomas N. & H.-S. Phillip Wong. 2017. The End of Moore's Law: A New Beginning for Information Technology. *Computing in Science & Engineering*, 19 (2). 41–50.

Thorne, Steven L. 2003. Artifacts and cultures-of-use in intercultural communication. *Language Learning & Technology*7 (2). 38–67.

Thorne, Steven L. 2016. Cultures-of-use and morphologies of communicative action. *Language Learning & Technology* 20 (2). 185–191.

Alberto Andujar, Paloma Mármol Trapote
# Chapter 3
# Annotating appraisal in a mobile telecollaboration project: A linguistic analysis of students' engagement

## 1 Introduction

Telecollaboration processes have evolved and a dapted to the technological options of the moment, starting with the use of e-mail exchange (O'Dowd 2006), going through the use of videoconferencing tools, until reaching the mobile applications of instant messaging (Andujar and Franco-Rodriguez 2020). Its versatile character has made telecollaboration stimulate communicative situations, allowing students to foster not only their communicative but intercultural competence thanks to a greater accessibility anytime and anywhere. This intercultural competence has been widely investigated in the telecollaboration field (see Belz 2003, 2007; Helm 2013; Lewis and O'Dowd 2016; Sevilla-Pavón and Haba-Osca 2017; Ware and O'Dowd 2008) and was considered one of the purposes of foreign language learning by the Common European Framework for Reference (CEFR, 2001). Likewise, the development of different communication skills as well as factors such as student language learning and performance have also been investigated at an early stage of telecollaboration exchanges (see Helm and Guth 2016; O'Dowd 2013; Ware and O'Dowd 2008).

In this context, apart from exploring the learning potential of this virtual exchanges, it seems relevant to explore how students' engagement may shape and determine language learning processes and intercultural development. As Oskoz and Gimeno-Sanz (2019) indicated, this engagement has normally been investigated in "alinguistic terms" (see Belz 2003; Andujar and Franco-Rodríguez, 2020; Andujar and Medina-López 2019) applying a mixed methods methodology based on qualitative and quantitative analysis of interviews or surveys where students self-reported their engagement levels. However, the growing interest in this practice has made researchers explore how students use the language in telecollaboration environments. In other words, how students from different cultural backgrounds employ linguistic choices when they collaborate in these

---

**Alberto Andujar**, University of Almería, Spain, e-mail: alberto.andujar@ual.es
**Paloma Mármol Trapote**, University of Almería, Spain, e-mail: paloma93_2@hotmail.com

https://doi.org/10.1515/9783110727364-004

environments. In this sense, the appraisal theory, "an approach to exploring, describing and explaining the way language is used to evaluate, to adopt stances, to construct textual personas and to manage interpersonal positionings and relationships" (White 2015: para.1) proposed by Martin and White (2005) is being increasingly applied in the telecollaboration field. An example of this application is the study carried out by Oskoz and Gimeno-Sanz (2019) and Oskoz and Gimeno-Sanz (2020). These two manuscripts presented a linguistic analysis of students' engagement in a telecollaboration exchange through computer-mediated communication (CMC). Following this investigation, the present study attempts to replicate the same analysis in a different telecollaboration exchange, this time through the Mobile Instant Messaging (MIM) platform *WhatsApp*. To do so, two discourse-semantic subsystems of the appraisal framework, Engagement and Attitude, will be investigated.

## 2 Engagement and the appraisal theory

To better understand the construct of engagement before introducing the latest studies exploring this construct in telecollaboration environments, a brief introduction to the concepts and notions comprised in the appraisal theory will be presented. Three interacting domains are found within this theory: engagement, attitude and graduation.

First, the concept of engagement is defined by White (1988: 13) as "those resources by which a text references, invokes and negotiates with the various alternative social positions put at risk by a text's meanings" – that is, the linguistic choices that are applying by the speaker respecting to particular statements. Therefore, engagement explores the writer's position as well as the eagerness to recognize different socio-semiotic positions (White 2015). Engagement is manifested in two ways, monoglossic or bare assertions and heteroglossic statements (Martin and White 2005). A speaker/writer produces monoglossic statements by presenting his/her own opinion as a fact, thus, without recognizing any dialogistic alternatives. On the other hand, a speaker/writer produces heteroglossic statements by opening up the dialogue for different opinions. Within heteroglossic statements, Martin and White (2005: 102–117) distinguish two broad categories. Those which are "dialogically expansive – the degree to which an utterance, by dint or one or more of these locutions, actively makes allowances for dialogically alternative positions and voices" which are subsequently divided into entertain and attribution, or those which are "dialogically contractive– the degree to which meanings are directed to excluding certain dialogic alternatives".

Attitude, the second discourse-semantic subsystem of the appraisal theory, analyses feelings as a system of meanings. This dimension offers the resources for social evaluation "providing a concrete and transparent linguistic procedure for revealing how speakers [. . .] re-analyse one's evaluations of other societies, cultures and individuals and one's culture and society" (Belz 2003: 73). According to Martin and White (2005: 42) this dimension has three semantic subsytems: emotions (affect), which deal with the semantic resources used to convey emotional responses; ethics (judgment), which is concerned with the semantic resource deployed to construct attitude towards behaviour; and aesthetics (appreciation), which involves the resources "for construing the value of things, including natural phenomena and semiosis". As Belz (2003) pointed out, the different dimensions of Affect may be decoded as either positive or negative.

The last sub-system, Graduation, which provides a scaling for the values of judgement (Oskoz and Gimeno-Sanz 2020), has not been taken into account in this study as the focus is on how students convey their ideas instead of learners' points of view during the interaction. Broadly speaking, graduation in attitude allows a speaker/writer to transmit greater or lesser degrees of positivity or negativity. In engagement, graduation acts to scale the degree of the speaker's intensity and investment in the utterance.

Taking into consideration these different sub-systems of the appraisal theory, this investigation will annotate students' engagement in a Spanish-American telecollaboration project focusing on the two first sub-systems, engagement and attitude. Particularly, how students engage both with the content provided and with their peers, in terms of their first culture (C1), their second culture (C2), and the topic (T). Before getting to the linguistic annotation carried out in this investigation, the latest studies investigating engagement in telecollaboration environments will be presented to provide a wider picture of this construct in virtual exchanges.

# 3 Literature review

The effects of telecollaborative projects in L2 learners have become the focus of much research in recent years. Lewis and O'Dowd (2016) inspected all studies related to telecollaboration from 1996 to 2015 and Çiftçi and Savaş (2018) evaluated more recent studies, from 2010 to 2015, offering a large review of the effects of telecollaboration. Their findings once again indicated intercultural competence, learner autonomy and second language learning as some of the potential advantages of telecollaboration environments. Recent studies, such as Gimeno-Sanz (2018) and Andujar and Medina-Lopez (2019) corroborated most of these advantages. However, the number of studies exploring students' engagement in these environments is much more limited.

It is worth mentioning several studies which have explored the construct of engagement during the last years. For instance, Oskoz and Gimeno-Sanz (2019, 2020) explored these concepts in a US-Spain telecollaborative encounter. The study attempted to understand to which extend students experience engagement with their own ideas and those of their partners as well as how they expressed their attitude towards their culture and their partners'. The results of the aforementioned investigations indicated that students produced a greater number of heteroglossic than monoglossic statements, which reveals, on the one hand, the interest of L2 students in contributing to dialogic interactions providing different opinions, and on the other hand, that written online forums were dialogic contexts where learners engage with their partners.

However, the results of the aforementioned investigation may lead to further interpretations such as the ones found by Oskoz, Gimeno-Sanz and Sevilla-Pavón (2018) in their telecollaboration project, in which they stated that a low number of monoglossic statements may also indicate a lack of solidarity with their counterparts. The researchers indicated a lower amount of monoglossic statements by L2 learners when discussing about C2 than C1, which suggested a possible lack of confidence to bring conflicting statements about C2. These findings aligned with Oskoz and Perez- Broncano's (2016) study in which students spent more time discussing about their C1 than their C2.

Another very recent and relevant study for this investigation is Farrell and Brunton's (2020) research, which explored online student engagement from a qualitative point of view in an undergraduate Humanities programme. This study, which explored which themes become a cornerstone for successful online student engagement, concluded that there were a series of psychosocial factors that condition the success of the interaction. Factors such as peer community, an engaging online teacher, confidence, lifeload, and course design became relevant elements for student engagement. Despite the limited sample, their findings illustrate further users how to accomplish successful and engaging learning experiences in telecollaboration contexts.

Further relevant investigations into students' engagement have been carried out during the last years such as Vinagre and Corral-Esteban's (2018), in which they investigated students' use of evaluative language to build rapport and encourage collaboration in e-mail messages sent between Spanish and American students. Using the appraisal theory, the authors found more instances of Affect than Judgement or Appreciation markers. These results indicated that participants preferred to express their own opinions before judging their counterparts' behaviour. Although these findings may depend on different factors such as participants, tasks, themes or the virtual environment among others, the results with regard to engagement do not align with those found in Oskoz and Gimeno-Sanz (2020), in which a higher number of Appreciation markers were found.

Among the aforementioned factors which may have an impact on students' engagement, Andujar and Franco-Rodríguez (2020) explored how the use of technology may influence students' behaviour and engagement in a Spanish-American telecollaboration project. A mixed method analysis was carried out in which pre-post measures were used to track students' behavioural, cognitive and emotional engagement with the learning platform. Likewise, students' opinions about the telecollaboration project were also reported. The authors found high levels of cognitive engagement as a result of the interaction and the Mobile Instant Messaging (MIM) platform used in the project was found to be widely accepted by participants.

These mobile applications and devices were found to be a fertile ground for ubiquitous telecollaboration projects such as the aforementioned, which allowed students to connect from different places and "on the go". In mobile telecollaborative encounters, studies such as Andújar and Franco-Rodriguez (2020), Andujar and Medina-López (2019), Pellas (2013), or Kohn and Hoffstaedter (2017) revealed that most participants reported positive attitudes towards MIM learning tools, holding higher levels of engagement and collaborative language learning. In this vein, Andujar and Franco-Rodríguez (2020) concluded that MIM applications "comprise most highly desired features for optimal telecollaboration projects". However, although several researchers have mentioned the distractive nature of mobile devices for language learning purposes (Mehdipour and Zerehkafi 2013; Rambe and Bere 2013), there seems to be an absence of studies exploring whether these challenges may have an impact on students' engagement in mobile telecollaboration projects.

Thus, in order to explore students' engagement levels in telecollaboration exchanges through mobile devices, instead of using self-reported scales of students' engagement, a linguistic analysis of the interaction was carried out. More specifically, this study attempts to examine the extent to which second-language learners in a US-Spain mobile telecollaborative project engage and express their attitudes with different socio-semiotic voices when discussing C1, C2 and T.

# 4 Study

The present study was carried out with 53 students from two different universities, 30 students from Fayetteville State University (USA) and 23 students from the University of Almería (Spain). The telecollaboration project lasted a month and a half; specifically, it began in mid-February and ended in late April, 2019. The group of Fayetteville State University were English native speakers who participated in a course on Spanish culture and civilization, while the group of the University of Almería were Spanish speakers who were taking an English phonetics course. Both teachers requested institutional permission as well as students' permission to accomplish the project. The telecollaboration platform proposed to develop the text-based interaction was the mobile instant messaging service *WhatsApp*. This tool was selected due to the widespread popularity of the application and students' previous knowledge about its use and functionalities. Due to the time difference of both groups, this tool facilitated the interaction, allowing students to communicate with their peers ubiquitously. Participants had a minimum requirement of 2 interactions on the text messaging service per week, in which they had to use English and Spanish language due to the aims of both courses. The telecollaboration project lasted for 6 weeks.

Regarding the tasks used, they were designed taking into consideration the psychopedagogical principle of social constructivism in order for students to co-construct knowledge from the very beginning of the project. In this sense, a series of topics related to class contents were proposed by participants, following the direction of the two teachers responsible for the groups. In addition, the interaction also included different types of tasks such as pre-reading, debates or gap-filling activities among others. Here is an example of a debate task carried out during the first week:

Debate 1 (with peers abroad) Essential information

This assignment normally involves four students: two in favor and two against a given statement. If a group has three students, then one will be in favor and two against the statement. Your peers are assigned by your instructor and the members of each group are listed in a Canvas announcement posted at the beginning of the course. Contact your peers as soon as possible to schedule a meeting time and coordinate who will be in favor and who will be against the statement. Requirements:

–All students in the group should prepare at least three arguments and three counterarguments so that the debate is dynamic and engaging; you may have a few words noted down to remember your points, but reading is not acceptable(i.e. the assignment will be graded with the lowest score in the rubric);learn or review the useful expressions for conversations available in the virtual platform; the duration of the debate must be a minimum of eight and a maximum of twelve minutes of interactive speaking; be a team player, try to support your partner by asking questions or rephrasing her/his words whenever there is a long silence or when something does not seem clear to the group. Likewise, avoid monopolizing the conversation; Make sure that all of you say your name at the beginning of the debate; webcams must be on and faces visible at all times; All participants must record the conversation and upload it here in Canvas. The preferred platforms for the exchange is Jitsi Meet (Links to an external site.);each student's participation will be assessed based on the Debate Rubric.

Chapter 3 Annotating appraisal in a mobile telecollaboration project — 55

– Descripción de la actividad/ Description of the activity – Tema (topic): El uso constante de los teléfonos inteligentes

Afirmación (statement): «Los medios sociales están creando una generación que ha perdido todo sentido de cortesía y la habilidad de estar presente en el momento. Es preocupante que utilicen sus teléfonos constantemente y en cualquier lugar para ver mensajes de texto, Instagram, Facebook, Snapchat, YouTube, o Twitter.»

Tarea (task): Prepara tres argumentos a favor y tres contraargumentos para apoyar orechazar la afirmación; Contacta a tus compañeros de grupo para coordinar una fecha y una hora para el video chat; Graba el video chat.

The tasks and topics varied throughout the project. Among the topics, cultural aspects of each country such as traditions, habits or education, and current issues such as anorexia or feminism were included in the tasks.

Each task involved a minimum interaction of 10 minutes and no time limitation was set for the students. The data collection from this text-based interaction was obtained using the web version of this application service at the end of the project.

For guaranteeing an appropriate development of the interaction, the project was explained to participants in a 45-minute lesson. Both teachers ensured that all participants had access to smartphones and were familiar with this application. Both teacher monitored the possible technical problems as well as any other problems occurring during the project.

# 5 Methodology

This section is devoted to illustrating the methodology employed throughout the whole project. This includes the description of the data collection instruments as well as the procedures, and the way these data have been analyzed.

## 5.1 Data collection instruments and procedures

As this project has been developed in a mobile telecollaborative environment, all participants were required to complete a pre-questionnaire, the Technology Category Adopter Index (Dugas 2005), before starting the project. This questionnaire (TACI) is used to measure students' use of technology. In order to obtain useful data, this scale was adapted to the features of this project, incorporating aspects related to mobile telecollaborative environments with the aim of assessing students' pre-existing knowledge and experience in this type of projects.

This likert scale was divided into questions 1–6 consisting of closed-ended items ranging from "a little" (1) to "A lot" (5). For questions 6–10, Yes / No answers were used, in which "yes" was coded as 1 and "No" as 2. The results obtained allowed the researchers to make hypotheses about whether students' ability to use technologies could have had an impact on the time that students dedicated to the interaction. Thus, a series of questions, previously corrected by e-learning experts and pre-tested, were used to ensure that the questionnaire was understood correctly by the target sample. The data collected in the questionnaire will be subsequently presented under the section "results".

The second data collection instrument used in this study is the text messages produced by participants in the MIM interaction. Once the project was concluded, these data were collected with the Web version of the mobile application, which allows the download of the conversations, which were subsequently converted into a TXT format. Then, these data were analyzed quantitatively following the Appraisal framework to measure students' engagement and attitude.

## 5.2 Data analysis

As the main aim of this case study was to measure the extent to which second language learners engage and express their attitude in a US-Spain mobile telecollaborative project, a mixed methods methodology was applied (Onwuegbuzie and Teddlie 2003). Firstly, learners' postings were subjected to a qualitative analysis following Martin and White's (2005) Appraisal theory. To analyze the discourse-semantic systems of Engagement and Attitude, the element of analysis used by the researchers was the T-unit, that is to say, a "main clause with all subordinate clauses attached to it" (Hunt 1965).

First, researchers made the following categorizations for T-unit: according to its primary focus C1 and/or C2; then general statements related to the topic under discussion (T) without taking into consideration C1 or C2; finally, D was used for instances such as greetings, closing statement or management of discussion. However, this last categorization was excluded from the study as it did not represent student's engagement during the interaction. It should be noted that for the US students C1 makes reference to their own culture and C2 refers to Spanish culture and vice-versa for Spanish students. The following sentence exemplified both the C1 and C2 references.

> Las matrículas en España son caras, **(C1)** quizá no tanto como allí **(C2)**
> (Enrollments in Spain are expensive, (C1) maybe not as much as there (C2))

To examine Engagement, the T-units were coded as either monoglossic or heteroglossic. Regarding the latter, statements were further analyzed into those which were dialogically expansive or those dialogically contractive. Contrary to Vinagre and Corral (2018), Oskoz and Gimeno-Sanz (2020) considered lexical items such as " I believe", "in my opinion" and "I think" as markers belonging to Expanding strategies, and more exactly to the sub-category of Entertain. It should be pointed out that an utterance can have more than one Engagement marker. In order to better understand the classification carried out following the appraisal theory, Table 3.1 shows examples of expanding and contracting strategies found in the chat-based conversation.

**Table 3.1:** Expanding and contracting strategies in the chat-based conversation. (Based on Oskoz, Gimeno-Sanz, and Sevilla-Pavon 2018).

| Engagement | | | |
|---|---|---|---|
| | | **Expanding** | |
| | | | **Examples** |
| Attribute | Acknowledge | Reporting verbs such as *say, believe, think, report, state . . .* ( X said . . ., X believes . . ., according to X, in X's view) | Ismael, the writer, says that . . . / el escritor Ismael dice As said in the article /como el articulo dice |
| | Distance | The authorial voice overtly distance from a reported proposition when they explicitly disagree with them by means of subset of the reporting verb as *claim* and by the use of "scare" quotes. | They said it was going to be impossible . . . but I believe everything was possible/ Ellos dijeron que va a ser imposible [. . .] pero yo creo que todo es posible. |
| Entertain | | Modal auxiliaries (*may, might, could, must, etc.*) Modal adjuncts (*perhaps, probably, etc.*) Modal attributes (*it's possible that . . ., it's likely that . . . etc.*) Circumstances of the in my view type, and via certain mental verb/attribute projections (*I think, I believe, I'm convinced that, etc.*) Some types of "rhetorical" or "expository" questions | In my opinion . . . / Mi opinión es que . . . / I believe that . . . / Yo creo que . . . It seems interesting, more options should be offered/ Parece interesante se deberían ofrecer mas opciones It could influence many people/ podría influir a muchas personas Probably, it's very late/ probablemente es muy tarde |

**Table 3.1** (continued)

| Engagement | | | | |
|---|---|---|---|---|
| | | | **Expanding** | |
| | | | | **Examples** |
| | | | *Contracting* | |
| Disclaim | Deny | | Negation resources: *no, didn't, never* | Nowadays we don´t think about that/ Hoy en en dia todo eso no lo pensamos<br>I've never heard of her/ nunca he oido hablar de ella |
| | Counter-expectation | | It is typically conveyed though conjunctions and connectives such as *although, however, yet* and *but*, by certain adverbials as *surprisingly* and adjunct such as *even, only or just*. | They said it was going to be impossible . . . but I believe it's possible/ Ellos dijeron que va a ser imposible [. . .] pero yo creo que todo es posible.<br>On the other hand, my sister in-law/ Por otro lado, mi cuñada . . . |
| Proclaim | Concur | | This is conveyed via locutions such as<br>*of course, naturally, unsurprisingly, admittedly, obviously*, etc. | I agree with you/ Estoy de acuerdo contigo<br>Sure, it also depends on the possibilities/ Claro! también depende de las posibilidades |
| | Pronounce | | Authorial emphasis ( the truth/ the facts of the matter is/are . . ., I content that . . ., you must agree that . . . )<br>Intensifiers such as really, indeed, etc.<br>Stress properly placed on speech. | There are songs I really like/ hay canciones que realmente me gustan<br>The truth is that . . . /La verdad es que . . . |
| | Endorse | | Verbs such as *show, prove, demonstrate, find*. | Studies show that . . . /los estudios demuestran que . . .<br>As you said, it's a film . . . como has dicho es una pelicula . . . |

Following Gimeno-Sanz and Oskoz's (2020) study, this investigation will also divide the sub-category of Attribute, Acknowledge, and Distance into Acknowledge of external sources, Acknowledge of classmates, Distance of external sources, and Distance of classmates. Likewise, the subcategories of Endorse and Counter-expectation were also divided into Endorse of external sources, Endorse of classmates, Counter-expectation of external sources, and Counter-expectation of classmates. The following excerpt shows an analysis of the Engagement domain:

> Well with regard to the first question **(T > expand > attribute > knowledge classmate)**, I believe that **(T > expand > entertain)**, university campus prepare people for real life **(T > monoglossic)** but **(T > contract > disclaim > counter)** not as much as we need **(T > contract > disclaim > deny)**
>
> Bueno respecto a la primera pregunta **(T > expand > attribute > knowledge classmate)** opino que **(T > expand > entertain)** si que los campus preparan a las personas para la vida real **(T > monoglossic)** pero **(T > contract > disclaim > counter)** no tanto como necesitamos **(T > contract > disclaim > deny)**

As for the domain of Attitude, researchers examined whether the T-units expressed positive or negative emotions and decided whether each one represented Affect, Judgement or Appreciation. Likewise, each T-unit can have more than one attitudinal resource, as the following example illustrates:

> In my country reggaeton is fashionable **C1 > judgment + >normality +.** It is a type of music I personally don´t like **T > affect > unhappiness > antipathy** because is sexist **T > judgment – > propriety -**
>
> En mi pais está de moda **C1 > judgment + >normality +** el reggaeton. Muisca que personalmente no me gusta **T > affect > unhappiness > antipathy** porque es machista **T > judgment – > propriety -**

This second example shows an analysis of two T-units combining both Attitude and Engagement:

> I believe that **(T > expand > entertain)** Merida is stronger **T > judgment + > capacity +** and independent. **T > judgment + > tenacity + (T > monoglossic)**. Although **(T > contract > disclaim > counter)** I also like **T > affect > happiness > affection** Mulan and Tiana because they are strong. **T > judgment + > capacity + (T > monoglossic)**
>
> Creo que **(T > expand > entertain)** Merida es más fuerte **T > judgment + > capacity +** y independiente. **T > judgment + > tenacity + (T > monoglossic)** Aunque **(T > contract > disclaim > counter)** también me gusta **T > affect > happiness > affection** Mulan y Tiana porque ellas son fuertes **T > judgment + > capacity + (T > monoglossic)**

# 6 Results

This section is devoted to providing an overall account of the results obtained in relation to the aims of this investigation. As aforementioned, this study attempted to explore students' engagement through an analysis of the text of the chat interaction as well as investigate students' use of the language within the appraisal framework during the telecollaboration project.

Before getting to the results of the analysis, the information collected in the TACI questionnaire will be presented. As shown in Figure 3.1, the mean score for items 3,4,5 and 6 revealed that students were active Internet users as well as heavy users of chat-based communication tools.

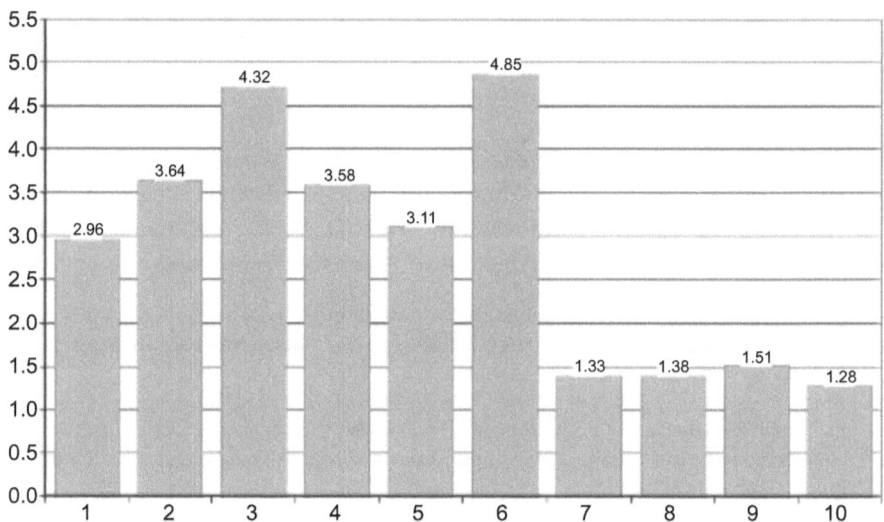

**Figure 3.1:** Results of the Technology Category Adopter Index.

The numbers of the horizontal axis correspond with the following questions:
1. Are you familiar with ICT tools?
2. Do you use virtual environment for your studies?
3. Do you use Internet for your study?
4. Do you use char communication tools at your university?
5. Are ICT tools used for the study at your university?
6. Do you use Internet in your private life?
7. Have you ever used WhatsApp or any mobile instant messaging tool before?
8. Have you ever participated in a telecollaboration project?
9. Have you ever participated in an online language exchange?
10. Have you ever practiced eTandem before

The fact that students were already familiarized with this type of communication tools may have had a positive effect on students' level of engagement. Regarding their previous experience in telecollaboration environments and eTandem exchanges there was, however, a difference between American and Spanish students. American students have had positive experiences with it while for Spanish students it was the first time. This may also have influenced the engagement of those students who were not familiar with this type of interaction.

As for the construct of engagement, the overall analysis of the information collected through the web version of the application is shown in Table 3.2.

**Table 3.2:** Monoglossic vs Heteroglossic statements.

| Culture | Monoglossic | Heteroglossic | Total number of T-units |
|---|---|---|---|
| C1 | 104 (71.72%) | 40 (28.27%) | 144 |
| C2 | 10 (25.64%) | 28 (74.35%) | 38 |
| T | (2297; 47.42%) | (4022; 63.6%) | 6319 |

Results indicate that learners produced a total of 6.501 T-units that were monoglossic or heteroglossic for T, C1 and C2. Learners produced a higher number of heteroglossic statements (4.090; 62.91 %) than monoglossic statements (2.411; 37.08%). With regard to T, C1 and C2, there is a significant unbalance. The total of students' statements focused on T (6319) were found in a higher amount for C1 (4022; 63.6%) than for C2. (2297; 47.42%). In any case, the results indicate a strong preference for T.

Focusing on heteroglossic statements, learners produced a slightly higher quantity of expanding (2.112; 51.63%) than contracting (1978; 48.36%) statements. Students mostly use expansive statements (see Figure 3.2) when addressing the topic (T) under discussion (2062; 50.41%), followed by C1 (26; 0.635) and C2 (24; 0.58%). In the same way, students use more contracting statements to address T (1960; 47.92%) than C1 (15; 0.36%) or C2 (3; 0.07%).

With regard to expanding statements, Entertain has obtained the highest results (2009; 49.11%) while Attribute had the lowest results (103; 2.51%) which suggests that students present their own opinions to keep the conversation going while taking into account their counterparts' views or outside sources in a somewhat mitigated way. Students' statements show that learners have a higher preference for Entertain (see Figure 3.3), particularly for T (1959; 47.87%), followed by C1 (26; 0.63%), and C2 (24; 0.58%). Within Attribute, learners dedicated the total number of statements to T (103; 2.51%) as they did not make reference to either C1 or C2 in this domain. Learners formed this domain by

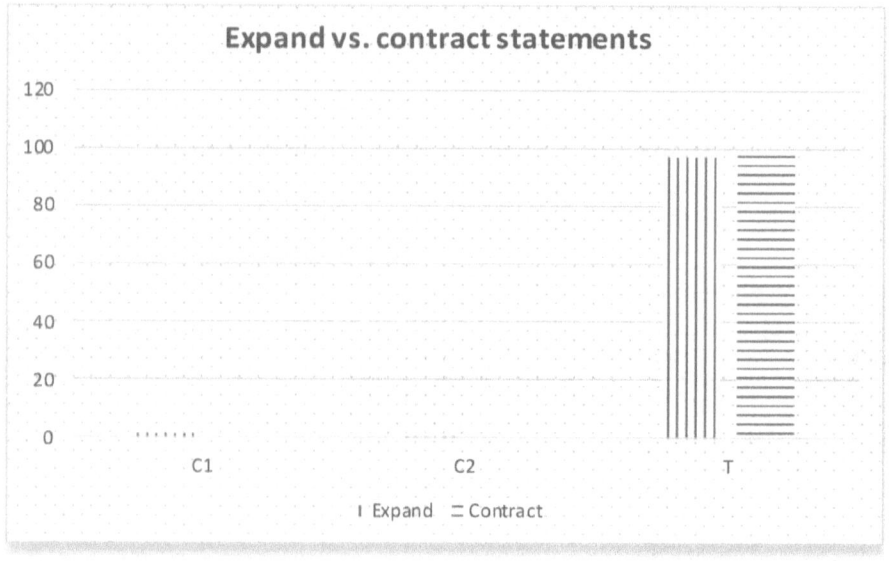

**Figure 3.2:** Expand and contract statements in C1, C2 and T.

outside information based on videos, reading or external voices (96; 2.34) and by acknowledging classmates' contributions (7; 0.17%).

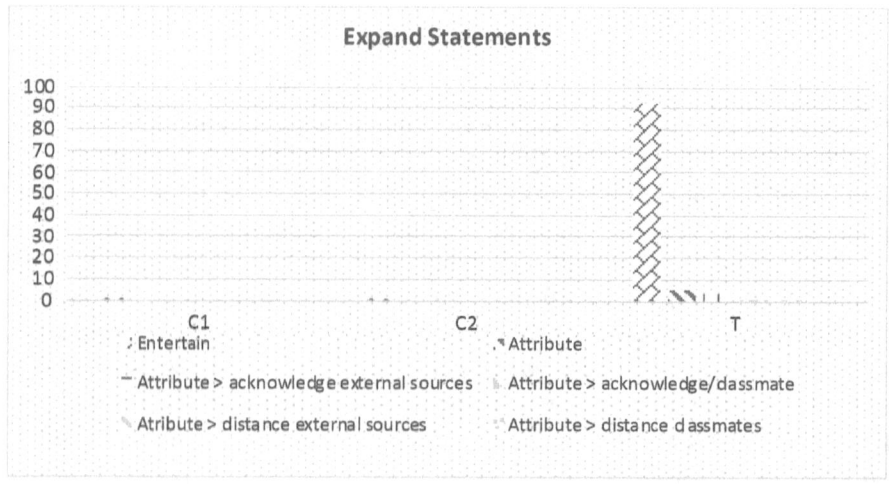

**Figure 3.3:** Expand statements in C1, C2 and T.

With regard to contracting statements, students tended to use more Disclaim (1487; 36.35%) than Proclaim (489; 11.95%) discourse markers (see Figure 3.4). Students mostly used these discourse markers when addressing T (1477; 36.11% vs. 483;11.80%). Within the Disclaim categories, Deny was more prevalent (834, 20.39%), followed by Counter classmates (433; 10.58%) and Counter external source (222; 5.42%). This category was used mainly with regard to T (828; 20.24%, 433; 10.09%, and 216; 5.28% respectively). As for the category of Proclaim, students used more frequently Pronounce discourse markers (257; 6.28%), followed by Concur (206; 5.03%) and Endorse classmates and external source (26; 0.63). This category was also created in with respect to T.

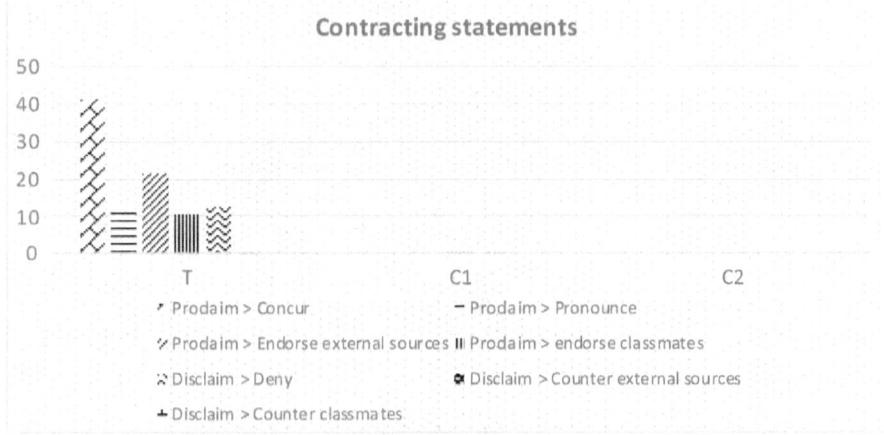

**Figure 3.4:** Contracting statements in C1, C2 and T.

With regard to the second aim of this research – how L2 learners utilized attitudinal markers (Affect, Judgment and Appreciation) when discussing their own culture (C1), the L2 culture (C2) and the topic under discussion (T) – the total number of Attitudinal markers in heteroglossic statements have been analyzed.

Students produced 4.090 heteroglossic statements, out of which 883 were Attitudinal markers. The most common ones were Appreciation (403; 45.63%), followed by Affect (322; 36.46%) and Judgement (158; 17.93%) (See Figure 3.5). When comparing C1, C2 and T in these categories, it can be appreciated that students produced most of the attitudinal markers making reference to T. The results also show a high preference for positive rather than for negative markers in the following markers: Appreciation + > Appreciation – (319; 36.12% > 84; 9.51%) and Affect + > Affect – (245; 27.74% > 77; 8.72%). The markers for Judgment show a balance

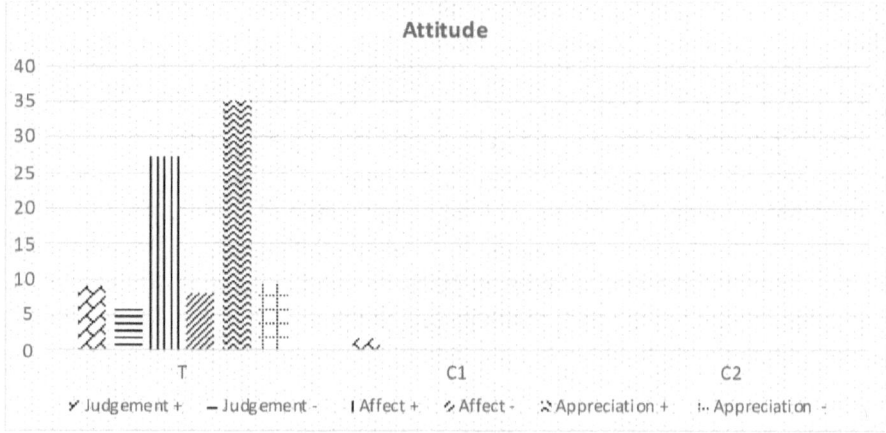

**Figure 3.5:** Contracting statements in C1, C2 and T.

result, although with a positive tendency as well, Judgement + (82; 9.28%) and Judgement − (60; 6.79%).

A detailed analysis of the subsystems that composed the domain of attitude was carried out. First, we focus on Appreciation (see Figure 3.6). It has obtained the highest results (403; 45.63%). In relation to T, the most common category was Quality + (132; 14.95%), followed by Impact + (102; 11.55%) and Valuation + (66;

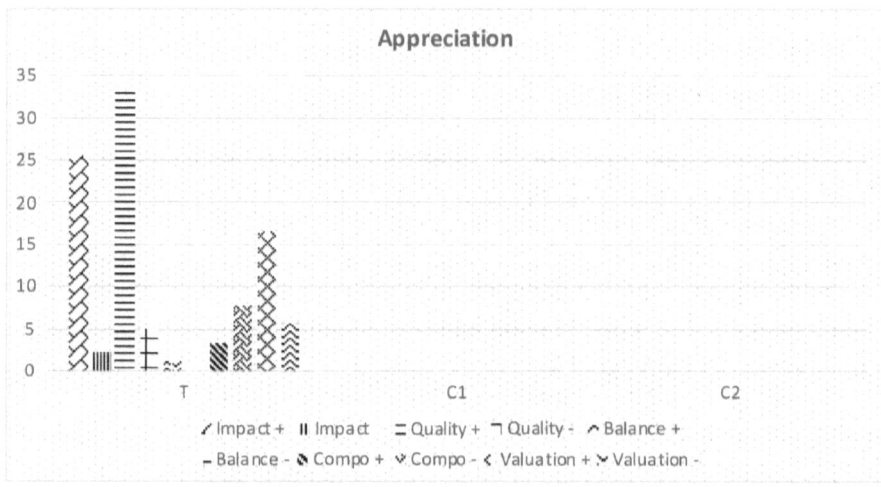

**Figure 3.6:** Appreciation markers in C1, C2 and T.

7.47%). The least common appreciation markers were Balance, either positive or negative (6; 0.67% and 1; 0.11%, respectively).

Regarding Judgment, there is a balance between positive and negative values regarding T (See Figure 3.7), although with a slight tendency to positive ones (82; 9.28%+ > 60; 6.79%). The most common category is Capacity + (43; 4.86%), closely followed by Capacity − (29; 3.28%) and Normality + (24; 2.71%). The least common appreciation markers were Veracity + (1; 0.11%), followed by Property + (4; 0.45%). Concerning C1, the only aspect registered is that of Normality + (16; 1.81%).

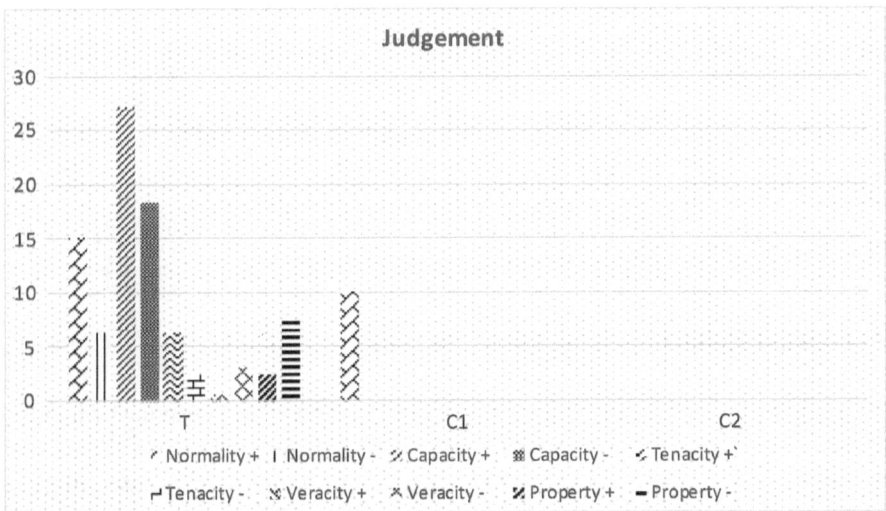

**Figure 3.7:** Judgement markers in C1, C2 and T.

The last subsystem of Attitude, Affect, has registered a total of 322 t-units (36.46%). Learners used more positive affective values than negatives (245; 27.74% and 77; 8.72%) with regard to T (See Figure 3.7). It we take a closer look at the subcategories of Affect, the most common one was Affection (298; 33.74%), distantly followed by Antipathy (29; 3.28%), Misery (24; 2.71%) and Desire (18; 2.03%).

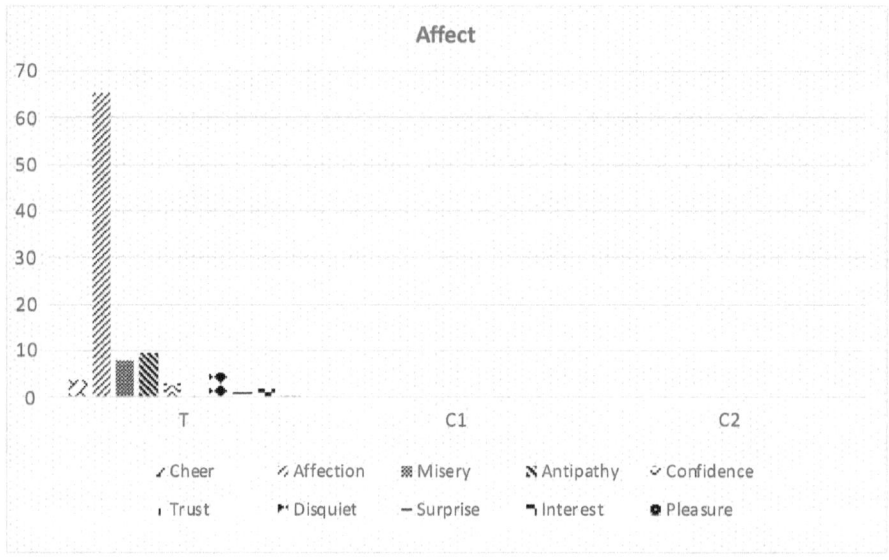

**Figure 3.8:** Affective markers in C1, C2 and T.

# 7 Discussion

With regard to the results of this investigation, the higher presence of heteroglossic than monoglossic statements indicates that interactions via WhatsApp become an environment where students exchange opinions and share different points of view. These results align with Oskoz and Gimeno-Sanz (2020) and Oskoz et al., (2018), in which the importance of these telecollaboration environments as a dialogical space was pointed out. However, this study, in comparison with the aforementioned ones, has obtained a larger amount of monoglossic statements, which suggests that the majority of students would also have established solidarity with their partners, in line with Kozar (2014).

Within heteroglossic statements, this study corroborates Oskoz and Gimeno-Sanz (2020), Oskoz et al., (2018) and Oskoz and Pérez-Broncano (2016), which suggested that L2 learners produced more expanding than contracting statements. However, the results show a very small difference between the two, so we could speak of a balanced use between both factors, which, according to Ryshina Pankova (2014), is necessary for learners to engage in argument development. The results obtained in relation to C1, C2 and T will be commented below.

With regard to C1, students focused on Entertain and, to a lesser extent on, Counter, and Deny resources to give their opinions. This suggests that students feel comfortable presenting their own perceptions and opinions (entertain) about their own culture, but they also challenged the different opinions, by denying and/or countering prior utterances about C1. Similarly, for C2 the students have expressed their opinions in a mitigated way through Entertain resources.

The results obtained in relation to T corroborated those obtained by Oskoz and Gimeno-Sanz (2020) about the students' balance use of expanding and contracting statements. This balance, on the one hand, leads to engagement in argument development (Ryshina Pankova 2014) and, on the other hand, shows the relevance of the issues being discussed in line with Mei's (2006) research, since students make use of a wide range of discourse markers to give their opinions and therefore, open a dialogic place with different semiotic voices. The strong preference for T found in this investigation supports Oskoz and Gimeno-Sanz's (2020) claims which indicated that T could be that dialogic place in which L2 students feel secure to provide strong and conflicting opinions (Oskoz and Gimeno-Sanz 2020). This reinforces O'Dowd's (2016) idea of approaching telecollaboration projects in an interdisciplinary way, as well as the need to organize the project contents to avoid falling into routine cultural issues. In addition, as Oskoz and Gimeno-Sanz (2020) suggested, students may feel more comfortable when discussing T, as they provide facts (monoglossic), express their own perceptions and support their viewpoints in other voices (expanding). These results, however, should be addressed with caution. The fact that students focused the majority of their comments on T suggests that the chosen topics have not caused the mutual enrichment of cultural aspects, which is generally linked to these telecollaborative exchanges. This at the same time demonstrates the importance of topic selection in this type of virtual exchanges.

Regarding the second aim of this study, the results indicated that students turned their attention to evaluating phenomena and expressing their own feelings and emotions rather than judging their partners behavior. These results support Oskoz and Gimeno-Sanz's (2020) findings but differed from Vinagre and Corral's (2018) study in which L2 learners used more Affect markers. Moreover, participants mostly used positive language in the three subcomponents. This tendency, as Vinagre and Corral (2018) indicated, may be encouraged by the students' endeavor "to portray and attractive personal identity" in order to create a friendly and confidence atmosphere based on mutual collaboration. What is more relevant of these results is that, these attitudinal markers have been only addressed when discussing T, differing from those in Oskoz and Gimeno-Sanz (2020) and Oskoz and Pérez-Broncano's (2018), in which learners produced them mostly related to C1.

As for Appreciation, similarly to Oskoz and Gimeno-Sanz's (2020) results, the most used markers were Impact and Quality, within the subcategory of

Reaction. This emphasized that L2 students focused on making an evaluation of the effect and value of the practices generated in the topic. As for the category of Affect, learners employed more Affection markers within the category of Happiness, which illustrates that L2 learners tended to express their own emotional reactions when discussing the different topics. These results differed from those in Vinagre and Corral (2018) and Oskoz and Gimeno-Sanz (2020), in which the most commonly used markers were Desire and Misery, within the subcategories of Inclination and Unhappiness, respectively. Finally, with regard to judgment, this study corroborates Oskoz and Gimeno-Sanz (2020) and Vinagre and Corral's (2018) findings which indicated that L2 learners were inclined to use more markers of Social esteem (Normality, Capacity and Tenacity) than Social Sanction (Veracity and Propriety).

# 8 Conclusion

This investigation confirms that mobile telecollaborative encounters, through instant messaging services like WhatsApp, are a dialogic space, which allows L2 students to recognize and interact with different socio-semiotic perspectives. In this sense, this research broadens the scope of telecollaboration projects, offering a ubiquitous alternative for telecollaboration through Mobile-assisted Language Learning (MALL).

The question, however, no longer focuses on whether we should engage foreign language students in this type of virtual exchanges but how to create environments which provide multiple subjectivities and perspectives for true dialogue. The purpose of this study was to examine the extent to which L2 students engage in an intercultural exchange when discussing their own culture (C1), the L2 culture (C2) and the topic under discussion (T). Yet, despite the controversial themes proposed, the cultural exchange was not explicit, as students focused mostly on discussing the topics.

This research, therefore, has a number of pedagogical implications. On one hand, to move beyond the exchange of information with respect to T and bring an explicit intercultural exchange, it seems necessary to include conversation topics about cultural aspects that may make students reflect and analyze deliberatively the issues in relation to C1 and C2. To do so, it will be also required to provide students with external and previous readings before every interaction so that students can move beyond the information exchange. Another possibility would be to give more specific questions to be addressed which would allow to provide scaffolding for their reflections in the discussions. On the other hand, it seems convenient that the language teachers involved in the telecollaboration project monitor the interaction regularly in order to improve the deficiencies that arise in the communication process. Moreover, the tasks should include very specific guidelines regarding the type of interaction that is expected, as well as discourse strategies so that the students, in addition to giving their points of view, can counter, distance or endorse opinions. In other words, if the assignment did not ask students to engage in discussions and "arguments," participants will not probably do so.

This study also presents a number of limitations that need to be considered. First, the small sample size prevents us from generalizing the results of this investigation. Second, examining which types of discursive markers were used by both groups separately, as well as those used in their mother tongue and in the foreign language when discussing C1, C2 and T, would provide a more detailed picture of the dialogic activity of both groups. Third, students' reaction to conversation topics was not examined, which would have been interesting in order to observe how the topic influenced the use of affective, either positive or negative, markers. It would have been advantageous to know how various factors such as conversation topics, the age of the participants or the means by which the intervention is carried out can positively or negatively affect engagement. In any case, as observed in this investigation, instant messaging services such as WhatsApp, which have the potential to connect classes from different places and at different times, allow the generation of authentic dialogical environments.

# References

Andujar, Alberto & Cristóbal Medina-López. 2019. Exploring new ways of eTandem and telecollaboration through the WebRTC protocol: Students' engagement and perceptions. *International Journal of Emerging Technologies in Learning*. 14(5). 200–217. https://doi.org/10.3991/ijet.v14i05.9612

Andujar, Alberto & Jose Franco-Rodriguez. 2020. WhatsApp and Jitsi to Foster Student Engagement in an American-Spanish Telecollaboration Exchange. In Alberto Andujar (ed.), *Recent Tools for Computer-and Mobile-Assisted Foreign Language Learning*, 60–78. Hershey, PA: IGI Global. https://doi.org/10.4018/978-1-7998-1097-1.ch003

Belz, Julie A. 2003. Linguistic perspectives on the development of intercultural competence in telecollaboration. *Language Learning & Technology*. 7(2). 68–99. https://www.lltjournal.org/item/2431 (accessed 11 November 2020)

Belz, Julie A. 2007. The development of intercultural communicative competence in telecollaborative partnerships. In Robert O'Dowd (ed.), *Online intercultural exchange: An introduction for foreign language teachers*, 127–166. Clevedon: Multilingual Matters.

Council of Europe. 2001. *Modern Languages: Learning, Teaching, Assessment. A Common European Framework of Reference*. Cambridge: Cambridge University Press. https://rm.coe.int/16802fc1bf (accessed 11 November 2020)

Çiftçi, Emrullah Yasin & Perihan Savaş. 2018. The role of telecollaboration in language and intercultural learning: A synthesis of studies published between 2010 and 2015. *ReCALL*. 30(3). 278–298. https://doi.org/10.1017/S0958344017000313

Dugas, Cheryl. A. 2005. Adopter characteristics and teaching styles of faculty adopters and nonadopters of a course management system. Unpublished doctoral dissertation, Indiana State University, Terre Haute, IN.

Farrell, Orna & James Brunton. 2020. A balancing act: a window into online student engagement experiences. *International Journal of Educational Technology in Higher Education*. 17. 1–19. https://doi.org/10.1186/s41239-020-00199-x

Gimeno-Sanz, Ana. 2018. Learner expectations and satisfaction in a US-Spain intercultural telecol- laboration project. *Bellaterra Journal of Teaching & Learning Language & Literature*. 11(3). 5–38. https://doi.org/10.5565/rev/jtl3.776

Helm, Francesca. 2013. A dialogic model for telecollaboration. *Bellaterra Journal of Teaching & Learning Language & Literature*. 6(2). 28–48. https://doi.org/10.5565/rev/jtl3.522

Helm, Francesca. 2015. The practices and challenges of telecollaboration in higher education in Europe. *Language Learning & Technology*. 19(2). 197–217. http://llt.msu.edu/issues/june2015/helm.pdf

Helm, Francesca & Sara Guth. 2016. Telecollaboration and language learning. In Fiona Farr & Liam Murray (eds.), *The Routledge handbook of language learning and technology*. Oxfordshire, England: Routledge. https://core.ac.uk/download/pdf/78855027.pdf

Hunt, Kellogg. W. 1965. A synopsis of clause-to-sentence length factors. *The English Journal*. 54(4). 300–309. https://doi.org/10.2307/811114

Olga, Kozar 2014. Discursive practices of private online tutoring websites in Russia. *Discourse (Abing- don)*. 36(3). 354–368. https://doi.org/10.1080/01596306.2013.871238

Kohn, Kurt & Petra Hoffstaedter. 2017. Learner agency and non-native speaker identity in pedagogical lingua franca conversations: Insights from intercultural telecollaboration in foreign language education. *Computer Assisted Language Learning*. 30(5). 351–367. https://doi.org/10.1080/09588221.2017.1304966

Lewis, Tim & Robert O'Dowd 2016. Online intercultural exchange and foreign language learning: A systematic review. In Robert O'Dowd & Tim Lewis (eds.), *Online intercultural exchange: Policy, pedagogy, and practice*, 21–66. New York, NY: Routledge.

Martin, James R. & Peter R. White 2005. *The Language of Evaluation. Appraisal in English*. New York, NY: Palgrave.

Mehdipour, Yousef & Hamideh Zerehkafi 2013 Mobile learning for education: Benefits and challenges. International Journal of Computational Engineering Research. 3(6). 93–101. https://bit.ly/38QDhk9

Mei, Wu Sieu. 2006. Creating a contrastive rhetorical stance: Investigating the strategy of problematization in students' argumentation. *RELC*. 37(3). 329–353. https://doi.org/10.1177%2F0033688206071316

Mei, Wu Sieu & Desmond Allison. 2005. Evaluative expressions in analytical arguments: Aspects of appraisal in assigned English language essays. *Journal of Applied Linguistics*. 2(1). 105–127. https://dx.doi.org/10.1558/japl.v2.i1.105

O'Dowd, Robert. 2006. The use of videoconferencing and e-mail as mediators of intercultural student ethnography. *Internet-mediated intercultural foreign language education*. 86. 86–120. http://hdl.handle.net/10125/69621

O'Dowd, Robert. 2013. Telecollaborative networks in university higher education: Overcoming barriers to integration. The Internet and higher education. 18. 47–53. https://doi.org/10.1016/j.iheduc.2013.02.001

O'Dowd, Robert. 2016. Emerging trends and new directions in telecollaborative learning. *CALICO Journal*. 33(3). 291–310. https://doi.org/10.1558/cj.v33i3.30747.

Onwuegbuzie, Anthony J. & Charles Teddlie. 2003. A framework for analyzing data in mixed methods research. In Abas Tashakkori & Charles Teddlie (eds.), *Handbook of mixed methods in social and behavioral research*, 351–383. Thousand Oaks: Sage.

Oskoz, Ana & Olimpia Pérez-Broncano. 2016. What did you say? How did you say it? Linguistic choices in online discussions. *Foreign Language Annals*. 49(4). 772–788. https://doi.org/10.1111/flan.12240

Oskoz, Ana, Ana Gimeno-Sanz & Ana Sevilla-Pavón. 2018. Examining L2 Learners' Use of Engagement Strategies in Telecollaborative Written Interactions. In Birthe Mousten, Sonia Vandepitte, Elisabet Arnó & Burce Maylath (eds.), Multilingual Writing and Pedagogical Cooperation in Virtual Learning Environments, 200–220. Hershey, PA: IGI Global. https://doi.org/10.4018/978-1-5225-4154-7.ch008

Oskoz, Ana & Ana Gimeno-Sanz. 2019. Engagement and Attitude in Telecollaboration: Topic and cultural background effects. *Language Learning & Technology*. 23(3). 136–160. http://hdl.handle.net/10125/44700

Oskoz, Ana & Ana Gimeno-Sanz. 2020. Exploring L2 Learners' engagement and attitude in an intercultural encounter. *Language Learning & Technology*. 24(1). 187–208. https://doi.org/10125/44716

Pellas, Nikolaos & Ioannis Kazanidis 2013. On the value of Second Life for students' engagement in blended and online courses: A comparative study from the Higher Education in Greece. *Education and Information Technologies*. 20(3). 445–466. https://doi.org/10.100710639-013-9294-4

Rambe, Patient & Aaron Bere. 2013. Using mobile instant messaging to leverage learner participation and transform pedagogy at a South African University of Technology. British Journal of Educational Technology. 44(4). 544–561. https://doi.org/10.1111/bjet.12057

Ryshina–Pankova, Marianna. 2014. Exploring academic argumentation in course-related blogs through engagement. In Geoff Thompson & Laura Alba (eds.), *Evaluation in context*, 281–302. Philadelphia, PA: John Benjamins. https://doi.org/10.1075/pbns.242.14rys

Sevilla-Pavón, Ana & Julia Haba-Osca 2017. Learning from real life and not books: A gamified approach to Business English task design in transatlantic telecollaboration. *Ibérica, Revista de la Asociación Europea de Lenguas para Fines Específicos*. (33). 235–260. http://hdl.handle.net/10550/58528

Vinagre, Margarita & Avelino Corral. 2018. Evaluative language for rapport building in virtual collaboration: An analysis of Appraisal in computer-mediated interaction. *Journal of Language and Intercultural Communication*.18(3). 335–350. https://doi.org/10.1080/14708477.2017.1378227

Ware, Paige & Robert O'Dowd 2008. Peer feedback on language form in telecollaboration. *Language Learning & Technology*. 12(1). 43–63. http://128.171.57.22/bitstream/10125/44130/12_01_wareodowd.pdf

White, Peter. 1998. *Telling media tales: The news story as rhetoric*. (PhD), The University of Sydney, Sydney, Australia.

White, Peter 2015. Introductory tour through appraisal theory. http://www.grammatics.com/appraisal/AppraisalGuide/Framed/Frame.htm. (Accessed 20 November 2020)

Carolin Fuchs, Bruce Tung, Bill Snyder
# Chapter 4
# Learner appropriation of genre in a US-China virtual exchange

## 1 Introduction

Connecting language student teachers with language learners to support linguistic interaction with expert speakers receiving pedagogical training is not a new concept (e.g., Belz & Müller-Hartmann 2003). Moreover, a growing body of research has focused on genre in relation to telecollaboration (Cunningham 2019; O'Dowd et al. 2020; Rampazzo & Aranha 2019), either as a pedagogical tool or as a learning outcome. However, work in this area is still limited, and the use of student teachers as pedagogical support interacting indirectly with learners in virtual exchanges has not been explored extensively.

In this paper we explore Chinese English as Foreign Language (EFL) learners' appropriation of written genres (Bartholomae 1986) in technology-based reading and writing tasks designed for them by student teachers in the US. We focus on the genres of an academic statement of purpose (SOP) and a business letter (BL). Mastery of these genres was part of helping EFL learners develop *professional competence* (Hyland 2004) as part of their course requirements. We understand the term 'appropriation' as "assembling and mimicking" the language of a specialized discourse, and "finding some compromise between idiosyncrasy, a personal history, and the requirements of convention" (Bartholomae 1986: 22). Appropriation in different forms may reflect different levels of development. Wu (2019: 128) makes use of a Vygotskian distinction between *mimicry* (blind copying; pseudo-learning), *emulation* ("recognition of the goal but . . . inability to understand the means;" partial learning), and *imitation* ("ability to understand how the means is used to accomplish the goal;" true learning), which can represent stages of a learning process.

This virtual exchange was part of a larger multi-site project (Fuchs et al. 2017), which aimed to connect language student teachers at a private graduate institution in the US with institutions in South Africa and Cyprus in Phase I, and with China in Phase II, the focus of this paper. In Phase II, the US-based

---
**Carolin Fuchs**, Northeastern University, USA, e-mail: c.fuchs@northeastern.edu
**Bruce Tung**, American University of Central Asia, Kyrgyzstan, e-mail: tung_b@auca.kg
**Bill Snyder**, Soka University, Japan, e-mail: snyder@soka.ac.jp

https://doi.org/10.1515/9783110727364-005

participants designed writing tasks to be implemented with EFL learners in China. This exchange was mediated by the design requirements provided by the student teachers' instructor in the US and the EFL teacher in China. Our research question is as follows: How were academic and business writing genres appropriated by EFL learners based on the pedagogical support provided by the US participants?

## 2 Literature review

### 2.1 Language learner-expert speaker constellations in telecollaboration

Prior research has demonstrated the potential of connecting language learners with language student teachers to support their linguistic interactions with expert speakers receiving pedagogical training (Belz & Müller-Hartmann 2003). Benefits for student teachers include identifying errors and providing corrective feedback through conducting a video analysis of their interactions with the learners (Lenkaitis 2020; Lenkaitis et al. 2020). In addition, student teachers can profit from mediated practices when designing tasks for implementation (Fuchs et al. 2017).

At the same time, Dooly (2011) calls for further investigation of how learners and teachers interpret and engage with tasks (as plans and as outcomes) especially in telecollaboration. Her analysis of interactional data from Spanish and Czech primary students revealed a discrepancy between the teacher's evaluation of students being off-task versus the students' actual engagement and persistence throughout the process. Against the backdrop of task appropriation, our paper focuses on learner outcomes in this type of virtual exchange, especially as they relate to written genres.

### 2.2 Genre and genre pedagogy

Genre pedagogy has been of increasing interest in the teaching of English for academic and specific purposes over the past 30 years (Hyon 2018; Wu 2019). Genres can be seen as schemata that expert writers have developed that allow them to approach the production of texts in specific contexts. In this sense, genres are socio-cognitive constructs. Genres are used to do things with language; they are purposeful. Genres are also conventional, which allows us to recognize them across contexts. At the same time, they are flexible and can vary in unpredictable ways and change over time (Johns 2008).

Genre pedagogy aims to help learners develop genre schemata. There are two main approaches to genre pedagogy. The first and more common one focuses on acquisition of specific genres through the use of models and templates that guide learners in developing mastery, and the second focuses on raising awareness of genres structures in relation to contextual factors that influence them. Johns (2008) argues for the use of the genre awareness approach with novice learners, feeling it is more likely to prepare learners to "cope with an unpredictable future" (239).

There are other concerns regarding the first approach that focuses on the acquisition of particular genres. Specifically, there is a concern that the use of exemplars might promote mimicry rather than more advanced mastery of genres (Johns 2008; Wu 2019), especially for students who see the models as showing them how to write their text rather than as imperfect cases demonstrating how they might approach the task (MacBeth 2010).

## 2.3 Genre in telecollaboration

Recently, a growing body of studies has focused on genre in relation to telecollaboration (Cunningham 2019; O'Dowd et al. 2020; Rampazzo & Aranha 2019), either as a pedagogical tool or as a learning outcome. For example, focusing on synchronous spoken business discourse, Cunningham (2019) found that telecollaboration enabled groups to navigate oral interview stages. He concluded that genre-based pedagogy can help learners demonstrate attention, link existing and new knowledge, and create meaningful connections between different topics (see also Cunningham & Vyatkina 2012). In our exploration of how learners acquire genre structures based on the pedagogical support provided through the virtual exchange by the US participants, we attempt to unpack some of the multiple layers of task appropriation by participants.

# 3 Method

## 3.1 Participants

There were two sets of focus groups. One group included ten applied linguistics/Teaching English to Speakers of Other Languages (TESOL) students enrolled in two different sections of a first-semester TESOL Methods course (with

57 student teachers) at a private graduate institution in the US. These ten student teachers were divided, grouped, and participated as Team A, Team B, and Team C in this study. The other focus group consisted of 49 EFL learners in China who performed different reading and writing tasks designed by the US teams. The EFL learners were from five different cohorts of the freshmen class in the International College at a public university in China, with IT/telecommunications as their intended major. They were enrolled in an Intercultural Communications (IC) course taught by Author 2, a Chinese-American novice teacher who, at the time, was also a part-time graduate student at the US institution. While Author 2 had completed a course in the use of technology in language education, he had not yet taken the Methods course the US participants were enrolled in. In addition, the IC course he was teaching was largely focused on developing oral communication skills and did not include an explicit writing focus.

## 3.2 Task for US participants

US participants in the Methods course were instructed to design, implement, and assess a technology-based reading and writing task (which accounted for 30% of their grade) for Author 2's EFL learners in China (see Fuchs et al. 2017). A writing task was chosen because it matched the course syllabus in the US and would be relatively straightforward to implement.

Teams negotiated with Author 2 a short, collaborative writing task (see Appendices A-D for examples) that included pre-writing, drafting, and revision stages (Brown 2007). They also included a step-by-step lesson plan for Author 2 (e.g., Appendix A), a description of the target student population and teaching context, and a rationale for choosing a specific technology tool for the writing task by making reference to the relevant literature introduced in class (Pegrum 2009). Teams focused on making their tasks authentic for the EFL learners, "to prepare them for the complex experiences and interactions in real life" (Team C, Final Task). Teams were also asked to grade the EFL learners' outcomes and make revision suggestions for the task in a final presentation. Our focus for this study is on the SOP and BL writing tasks.

Author 2 provided guidance to the US students in this negotiation regarding making the tasks feasible for the Chinese EFL context and interesting for the EFL learners. Much of Author 2's specification of the tasks was negotiated throughout the task design process–prior to task implementation–based on technology and time restrictions. He especially made the US participants aware of what technological resources were available in the Chinese context. Direct telecollaborative interactions between the US teams and the EFL learners were limited to giving and receiving scores and feedback upon completion of the tasks.

## 3.3 Tasks for EFL learners

Each EFL cohort met once a week for 90 minutes for Author 2's IC course. Technology in the classroom was limited to a PC and a projector; internet connectivity was unavailable in the classroom or dormitory. Each cohort was given the option to choose their preferred task from a list of six tasks created by the US teams; two different tasks were selected in most cohorts and administered simultaneously over a period of two weeks. Tasks were chosen by the EFL learners that best suited their interests and were completed as in-class and homework assignments based on instructions provided by Author 2 and handouts prepared by the US teams. Table 4.1 provides an overview of the tasks chosen by the EFL learners in the five cohorts (see Appendices A-D).

**Table 4.1:** Participants (EFL learners and US teams), tasks, and tools used.

| EFL Cohort (focus group size) | Learners who completed task | Task | Tools Used | US Team |
|---|---|---|---|---|
| 1 (12) | 2 | SOP | Email, MS Word | Team A |
| | 8 | BL | Email, Blog | Team C |
| 2 (17) | 3 | SOP (peer reviewed) | Email, MS Word | Team A |
| | 13 | BL | Email, Blog | Team C |
| 3 (4) | 4 | SOP | MS Word | Team B |
| 4 (6) | 6 | BL | Email, Blog | Team C |
| 5 (10) | 10 | BL | Email, Blog | Team C |

As shown in Table 4.1, not all students completed the tasks. Thirty-seven EFL learners completed Team C's BL task, which proved to be the most popular one. The nine students who chose the SOP task were those who were planning to study abroad.

## 3.4 Procedure

The group data presented are from a previously unanalyzed subset of a larger set of data (see Fuchs et al. 2017). This exploratory case study shares characteristics of ethnography in line with a sociocultural framework for telecollaboration studies (Dooly & O'Dowd 2012) and for academic discourse (Flowerdew 2002). Authors 1 and 2 were participant-observers in the study (Richards 2003). Author 3, a teacher-educator in Japan, was affiliated with the school in the US at the time. Data collection included students' writing, which were supplemented by emails and Google Groups posts by US students, and Authors 1 and 2. Data analysis focused on EFL student writings and US teams' tasks and was supported by information from participant-observer emails and instructor notes.

For the EFL writings, Authors 1 and 2 independently analyzed each of the data sets, i.e., students' first drafts. In their analyses, the authors focused on task compliance elements (Tedick & Mathison 1995), which had been generated by US teams to grade students' writings. First, for the SOPs, Authors 1 and 2 looked for "effective" and "strong" use of transition words, "clear and effective topic sentences," and "strong supporting sentences and relevant information." Second, for the BL task, Authors 1 and 2 used Team C's BL writing rubric (Appendix D), and discrepancies were resolved after discussion. Furthermore, the two Authors generated additional categories (e.g., *expressing emotions, sharing personal information*) which were not part of Team C's grading rubric or the task design but emerged during a round of open coding. Finally, the two Authors analyzed the feedback provided by US teams to the EFL learners.

# 4 Results

## 4.1 Learner appropriation of the SOP task

The objective for Team A's SOP task was to provide students with information needed to write a strong Statement of Purpose for graduate schools in the US, and to provide the students with practice in writing an SOP. However, for both SOP tasks, there appeared to be a mismatch between the EFL learners' appropriations of the genre in contrast to the rather prescriptive nature of the writing genres assigned by Teams A and B.

Team A's guidelines (Appendix A) as well as Team C's rubric (Appendix D) could be described as prescriptive in that they had traditional Western-style writing features ("effective topic sentence" and "strong use of transition words").

Yet, the new categories identified by the Authors (*expressing emotions, sharing personal information*), which may traditionally be considered inappropriate for this academic genre, occurred in the learner texts, e.g., "from the bottom of my heart," "the motherland," "reverberate like thunder," "I am always tireless pursuit of higher standard for improve the ego's," "I think I could add glory of your university."

Some learners focused more on who they were as applicants versus the school they were applying to. In addition, some of the writings did not match typical structures for these genres. For instance, Bryan began his SOP with his childhood fascination with TVs (first paragraph) and his previous college education (second paragraph) before getting closer to the purpose at the beginning of the third paragraph ("My goals are to major in electrical engineering and get the degree M.S."). Finally, at the end of the fourth and final paragraph, he stated that "[a]ttending the [US institution] will give [him] a well-round[ed] education and experience to help fulfill [his] goals."

When evaluating the same SOPs, Authors 1 and 2 used Team A's guidelines in Appendix A to calculate the frequency of the desired features (transitions, topic sentences, supporting sentences) and produced contrasting results. In addition, for transitions, Author 2 scored based on the commonly used words/phrases that he taught his students; then, he consulted Purdue OWL (https://owl.purdue.edu/) and the University of Wisconsin's Writing Center (https://writing.wisc.edu/) websites, and added additional words or phrases from their pages to the criteria. For topic sentences, Author 2 only counted the body paragraphs, not introductions.

It was part of the US teams' assignment to provide feedback on learner products. Team A responded to the SOPs that were received on time with inserted comments, which focused on some organizational aspects but primarily on surface-level grammar corrections, as shown in Katherine's SOP example in Table 4.2. Furthermore, some corrections by the US student teachers were unclear, unnecessary (1, 4, 5, 6), or incorrect (2, 3).

This outcome was similar to what was received by other students. For instance, Ron received the following corrections on his paper: "Delite" (sp); "I'm a major in medicine" (word order); "I would get" (future tense); "study medicine hard" (phrasal verb); compound sentence structure (and); "very excellent" (superlative); word choice (subject). Other discursive aspects ("avoids personal feelings – emotions that are not relevant to the purpose of the essay") remained unaddressed in Team A's feedback.

The EFL learners were also asked to provide peer feedback and to integrate peer feedback into their final drafts; however, Author 2 had had limited time to provide training on how to effectively do this. Moreover, as shown in the example

**Table 4.2:** Team A's feedback on student writing.

| Original sentence (Kathrine) [emphasis added] | Team A's Correction |
|---|---|
| 1. It is <u>a very important part of</u> studying. | very necessary in |
| 2. I <u>am an applied</u> telecommunications major and will get my Bachelor's degree from [name of Chinese university], which is one of the famous telecommunication universities in China, next summer. | Maybe there is an error. Instead:applied Delete [comma]. |
| 3. Thank you for your time <u>and</u> attention <u>in reviewing</u> my application. | To pay to reading |
| 4. I know that your [name of US school] is famous for your engineering around the world,so I <u>can</u> learn the most advanced technology in your [school],<u>and</u> that is the most important reason why I look forward to becoming a member of you | could .Also, |
| 5. <u>A second reason is that</u> | The |
| 6. In the future,I <u>want</u> to make contribution to world and human beings | would |

from the peer review of Katherine's paper in Appendix B, her peer was only able to answer the first three questions. Questions 4 and 5 asked the peer reviewer to leave text-specific comments, which either points to an overestimation of the language learners' proficiency levels or to a practice that learners were not comfortable doing. Likewise, other students also did not answer all the questions, possibly due to the complexity of the task.

Team B provided a rubric (Appendix B) with components that included content, organization, discourse, syntax, mechanics, and vocabulary; however, they were unable to provide scoring or feedback because the cohort that chose their task did not submit on time. With regard to the BL task outcome, Team C used their rubric to rate the 37 EFL learners.

## 4.2 Learner appropriation of the BL task

The purpose of Team C's writing tasks was to give students the opportunity to analyze and compare formal and informal writing tasks (business letter and blog post) and to "learn appropriate language and format to use for specific writing genre" (Excerpt of Handout 1 in Appendix C). The BL task aimed to improve EFL learners' accuracy in formal writing and to provide "opportunities to think about how [they] can practice and use English outside of the class using the Internet" (Excerpt of Handout 1 in Appendix C).

With regard to task outcome, Team C used their rubric (Appendix D) to rate the 37 EFL learners, as summarized in Table 4.3:

**Table 4.3:** Team C's rubric-based ratings of EFL learners' BLs.

| Point range (out of 12) | Number of students |
| --- | --- |
| 10–11 | 9 |
| 7.5–9.5 | 13 |
| 5–7 | 8 |
| No rating (late submission) | 7 |

Approximately one third of the 21 students who received a score were in the mid-to-low range, while about one third received the highest scores.

While Team C's grading rubric for this BL assignment was based on three categories (format and organization, elements, grammar usage and spelling), it is unclear how the US team weighted these in their grading with points out of 12. Moreover, there were multiple ways to interpret what the students produced, which led to divergent scores from the US teams and the Authors. These results raise the question about the consistency of the 'appropriation' of the writing tasks by participants, especially against the backdrop of linguistic backgrounds and experiences, EFL learner interests, student teacher preparedness, and the time limits for EFL instruction in China of two lessons per group task. For instance, time limitations did not allow for in-depth preparation for the task or the peer review. In the BL task, it was not specified if the letter should have been written for a Western travel agent, but it did include a very specific letter template (Appendix C). Some students followed the template closely to the point of including typographical guidance provided in the template such as bracketing. The EFL learners received from Team C an elaborate feedback list of errors they had made, ranging from formality to subject-verb agreement, verb forms, starting a sentence, punctuation, and spelling (Appendix E).

## 5 Discussion

Our research question asked how the EFL learners appropriated the genres they were asked to produce based on the pedagogical support provided by the US student teachers. The findings of our analysis show that the EFL learners did make use of the models and guidance provided by the US student teachers and filtered through their instructor in their written products. And the evaluations by the US student teachers indicate that the EFL learners were successful in doing so. Team C gave a substantial majority of the business letters they evaluated scores of 7.5 or higher on a scale of 12, suggesting that the students had successfully met the criteria for the task.

But this leaves open the question of how the EFL learners made use of the supports provided and whether this use represented true learning. The EFL learners' products show some evidence of mimicry, or blind copying (Wu 2019), such as their maintenance of typographic markers like brackets taken from the BL guidance. Such copying reflects a lack of understanding of how the elements of genre structure help achieve the writing goal (Wu 2019) and possible overreliance on the models provided (MacBeth 2010), suggesting that the EFL learners' writing in these cases was responsive to the prompt but not necessarily purposeful (Johns 2008).

However, adherence to models and guidelines was not always the case. Both Author 1 and Author 2 noted the EFL learners' creativity in the SOP responses, where they generally did not copy the model provided. Such cases may represent efforts reflecting emulation or imitation, which would show that the writing was at least purposeful, aiming at achieving a particular goal, and possibly reflecting an understanding of how genre elements would help in achieving the goal.

A number of factors may have affected the EFL learners' ability to effectively imitate the genres they were asked to produce. These factors include the length and indirect structure of the virtual exchange; the nature of the models and guidance provided; the ability level of the students in relation to the tasks; and possibly, the technologies used in the tasks themselves.

During the task implementation phase, EFL students had two weeks to complete the task. Most approaches to teaching genre involve longer periods of instruction because of the complex nature of genre (Johns 2008). What we see in the EFL learners' products is a baseline showing their starting points in mastering the genres, with the variation among them reflecting individual differences in their language ability and other aspects of genre awareness.

The US student teachers and the EFL learners did not interact directly, except at the end of the exchange when feedback was provided to the EFL learners.

Bartholomae (1986) reminds us that students "have to appropriate (or be appropriated by) a specialized discourse, and they have to do this as though they were easily or comfortably one with their audience" (9). Due to multiple levels of appropriation, this virtual exchange not only produced unique or "invented" (Bartholomae 1986) discourse structures, but also amplified the issue of audience awareness in that it was not clear who the EFL learners were writing for: their teacher, their peers (in the case of peer review), or the US teams (where they were graded)?

The tasks provided to the EFL learners reflected a traditional approach to teaching genre, using models and guidance to promote the acquisition of specific genres. Models used for teaching genre are generally incomplete facsimiles, meant to focus learners' attention on particular aspects of intended goals, and leaving other aspects unremarked on (Johns 2008; MacBeth 2010; Wu 2019). The tasks generated by the US teams were prescriptive and emphasized language features, which may have led the EFL learners to focus on these in their writing.

An additional factor influencing the effectiveness of the models and guidance provided to the EFL learners may have been the levels of experience of the US student teachers and the novice EFL teacher in China. Teaching writing to English learners and using teacher and peer feedback in a complementary fashion were one of many foci of the Methods course. Yet, Team A's "incorrect" corrections point to the need for a tailored discussion to underline that feedback should be text-specific, relevant, clear, should not appropriate the text, and must allow for students a way to revise in response to the feedback (Goldstein 2006).

The EFL learners' level of ability in English affected their choices of and completion of tasks. Author 2 noted that he may have overestimated his students' ability to complete the tasks they were asked to do. A number of students decided not to engage in the SOP task when they saw the models provided, and many of the students who did the SOP task were not able to complete the peer review of the task. Learners bring limited cognitive resources to any language task (Schmidt 2001) and may only be able to focus on aspects of any task that are most easily within their grasp and may ignore others or abandon the task altogether.

Finally, the technologies used in this virtual exchange may have had an impact on the EFL learners' performance. The US teams were working to fulfill goals set by their instructor regarding designing technology-based tasks while creating goals for the EFL learners. An integral part of the tasks designed by US teams was the integration of a suitable technology tool. As Thorne (2003) has argued, "individual and collective experience is shown to influence the ways students engage in Internet-mediated communication with consequential outcomes for both the processes and products of language development" (p.38; see also Thorne 2016). While limited tool accessibility and different cultures-of-use can be a challenge for telecollaboration (Fuchs 2019), it is unclear what impact the learners' familiarity with the respective technology choices may have had on their task appropriation or performance.

There are a number of ways in which the design of virtual exchange presented here could be changed which might allow learners to more clearly demonstrate higher levels of appropriation of genre, most importantly increasing the length of the task implementation phase. Most models of genre pedagogy are designed for semester length courses that focus specifically on teaching writing. But the six-week workshop described in Wu (2019) or using the six genre awareness activities described in Hyon (2017) over a 6- to 8-week period could be the bases of longer exchanges. A longer virtual exchange with a more explicit process-genre pedagogy focus would give learners more time to analyze varying models, understand how non-linguistic factors, such as audience, influence genre performance, and work through multiple cycles of performance and feedback.

# 6 Conclusion

This paper describes a telecollaboration involving US-based student teachers designing genre writing tasks for Chinese EFL learners. The results of this study show that mediated virtual exchanges involving student teachers designing tasks for the learners, even if brief, can result in successful task completion. Provided with models and pedagogical guidance, learners can produce genre-specific texts as required. The extent to which this performance is dependent on mimicry of models rather than emulation or imitation is something which needs to be determined with further research.

It is apparent that several factors contributed to the differences between expected outcomes and actual outcomes of the tasks involved. Time constraints, pedagogical approach, limited experience with the writing genres and learning contexts, limitations on technology that could be used in the classroom in China, and possible differences in cultures-of-use for different tools all impacted language learning in this virtual exchange. And yet, as Kramsch (2009) has observed, while "language instruction strives to develop communicative competence as exchange of information and communicative tasks," students, like these EFL learners did, actively create a language learning experience of their own through their appropriation of the tasks they are presented with. It would be valuable to look at the learner experience of virtual exchanges like this one, marked by complexity and indirect interaction, in order to understand how they saw their appropriation of the tasks and what they learned from them.

It would also be worth exploring the student teachers' appropriation of the role of task designer and how that was affected by mediation. A line of research on task design in the early 2000s (Bygate 1999, 2000; Johnson 2000, 2003; Samuda 2005) points to a need to explore the relationship of task design to task implementation, a project we are currently undertaking with the data from this exchange.

## Appendix A: Team A Guidelines: SOP Assignment

| Stage | Sequence/Procedure | Time |
|---|---|---|
| Pre-Class | – The EFL Teacher will divide the class into several small groups. Students of the same major (i.e., English, IT, Communications) will be in the same group.<br>– Each student will be assigned the website of a specific program at a specific university.<br>– A list of questions will be given to each student. | 5 minutes |
| Pre-Class | – For homework, students log on to the website that they have been assigned and collect answers to the reading questions. | |
| Stage 1 | – Each student in the group will have visited a different website. Therefore, each student will have different answers to the questions. Students share answers they have collected and choose the university that sounds the most interesting. | 6 minutes |
| Stage 2 | – One student from each group announces to the entire class which university and which program they have chosen. The student briefly explains their choice. | 3 minutes |
| Stage 3 | – Teacher explains that they will be beginning to write Statements of Purpose during the class. | 1 minute |

(continued)

| Stage | Sequence/Procedure | Time |
|---|---|---|
| Stage 4 | – Students work in their small groups and brainstorm answers to the question: "What kind of information about yourself should be written in a Statement of Purpose?"<br>– We expect students to give answers like:<br>  i. My career goals<br>  ii. My academic background and academic achievement<br>  iii. My personality | 5 minutes |
| Stage 5 | – Students are given a sheet containing questions for a reading and an example of a well-written Statement of Purpose.<br>– Students read the Statement of Purpose and answer the questions, which focus on the following areas:<br>  i. the general meaning of each paragraph<br>  ii. topic sentences<br>  iii. supporting sentences | 10 minutes |
| Stage 6 | – Students read example of poorly-written paragraph of SOP<br>– They compare the strong SOP (which they read in the previous stage) and the weak SOP (which they are given in this stage). They are asked to explain why one SOP is much better than the other one. | 5 minutes |
| Stage 7 | – Working in groups, students compare answers. We hope to hear answers like:<br>  i. strong use of transition words in the good SOP vs. poor use or no use of transition words in the weak SOP<br>  ii. clear topic sentences in the strong SOP vs. vague topic sentences in the weak SOP<br>  iii. strong supporting sentences relevant information in the strong SOP vs. weak supporting sentences and irrelevant information in the weak SOP | 5 minutes |
| Stage 8 | – Teacher leads a review of the following:<br>  i. the effective use strong use of transition words<br>  ii. clear and effective topic sentences<br>  iii. strong supporting sentences and relevant information | 10 minutes |

(continued)

| Stage | Sequence/Procedure | Time |
|---|---|---|
| Ten-minute break. | | |
| Stage 9 | – Using the model SOP as an example, and incorporating information from Stage 8, the students work alone and write one good supporting paragraph for their own SOP. | 20 minutes |
| Stage 10 | – Teacher explains that the students will be doing a peer critique of the paragraph that their partner has written.<br>– Teacher hands out a checklist to guide the students' critique<br>– Students trade paragraphs. | 3 minutes |
| Stage 11 | – Working alone, the students read their partner's paragraph and write down notes for giving a constructive critique. | 7 minutes |
| Stage 12 | – Students work in pairs and give feedback on their partner's paragraph. | 8 minutes |
| Stage 14 | – Teacher explains the homework assignment: Write a full statement of purpose.<br>– Teacher will provide the students with a written document detailing the assignment, the word limit, and a checklist of dos and don'ts.<br>– Teacher will then answer any questions that the students may have about the assignment. | 7 minutes |

# Appendix B: Team A's Homework Part 2: Peer Critique of Katherine's Paper

Instructions: Read through your partner's draft. Answer the following five questions. Track changes on his/her draft.
1. What part(s) of the SOP interest you the most? Explain why.
   The part which is interested me the most is that the reason why she fits for that school.Because this part can show her characteristic.
2. Is the body paragraph formula stated clearly? (Body paragraph formula: Strong topic sentence; evidence and explanation; smooth transition to next point)
   Maybe.Some are clear,but some are not.
3. Where do you feel you would like more detail or explanation?

About why she likes that school. Her reason is too simple.
4. What parts do you find unclear, confusing, or underdeveloped? Mark each point with a question mark in the margin, then write a note to the writer about your concerns.
5. Mark any grammatical, mechanical, and/or spelling errors you find. If you're not sure, mark them and explain what you think is the problem.

# Appendix C: Excerpt of Team C's Handout 1: Overview of Overall Task

### Purpose of the tasks

The reading and writing tasks provided here will give you the opportunities to analyze and compare formal and informal writing tasks (business letter and blog post). You will learn appropriate language and format to use for specific writing genre. The reading tasks will improve your scanning and skimming skills. It will also help you improve the skill of guessing difficult words from surrounding context. The business letter writing task will help you improve your accuracy and blog post writing will help you improve your writing fluency. These reading and writing tasks will also give you opportunities to think about how you can practice and use English outside of the class using the Internet.

### Team C's Handout 3: Business Letter Assignment

Congratulations! You have won the Lonely Planet Dream Vacation Contest. Your prize is an all-expenses-paid, one-week vacation to the country of your choice! Now is your chance to have the vacation you've always dreamed of, without worrying about the cost.

There is only one requirement for you to receive your prize – you must write a formal business letter to a travel agent at our company, Lonely Planet. In this letter, you will be requesting that your agent create a personalized travel itinerary for you, and you will describe your dream vacation.

In this letter, you will explain:
- **First paragraph:** Where exactly you want to go (country, city name), and an explanation of why this is your dream destination.

- **Second paragraph:** What kinds of activities you most want to do (outdoor, indoor, art, museums, food, general tourism, etc.), and why these activities appeal to you.
- **Third paragraph:** Any personal restrictions (dietary restrictions like allergies or vegetarianism, physical handicap, can't ride a bike, hate walking, etc.)
- Your general "speed" (like to have a lot of time at each place, like to have as many activities in one day as possible, etc.)
- Any other general information that you think would be helpful for your travel agent

In order to receive your paid vacation, your letter should be an exemplary, properly formatted business letter that follows the guidelines we provide below. Make sure to check your letter for spelling and grammar mistakes, and make sure to use formal language (do not use casual, colloquial language).

DEADLINE:
You must submit your letter to your travel agent and to your class teacher by **e-mail** on the assigned date, by 6 o'clock pm.
    Please refer to the following page for the letter format.

Components of a Business Letter:
1. **Letterhead.** This should carry the company's address and the name of the person who writes the letter.
2. **Date.** Include the date so that the letter will be kept for future reference.
3. **Recipient's Name and Address.** Add the address of the person you're sending the letter to. His/her position (travel agent) should be mentioned.
4. **Salutation.** Use a proper salutation. Addressing the recipient by name is preferred. Use the person's title (Mr. Mrs. Ms. or Dr.) with either a first name or a last name, but not both. Using a last name is more formal. (Use a partner's name.)
5. **Body.** This is the portion where you introduce and explain the purpose of the letter. Be brief and succinct; remember that this is a business letter for a purpose.
6. **Closing.** Use the correct form of leave-taking. "Yours sincerely" and "yours cordially" are the widely used forms of leave taking.
7. **Signature.** Leave space for your signature below the closing. Type your name below where your signature would go, with your contact information below.

**[Your Name]**
[Street • City • State • Zip Code]
[Phone # • Email]

[Date today]

[Recipient's Name]
[Company Name]
[Address]
[Address]

Dear [Recipient's name or title]:

[SUBJECT]

Sincerely,

[Sign here]

[Your name]
[Your e-mail]

# Appendix D: Team B's Grading Rubric

| Category | 1 | 2 | 3 | 4 |
|---|---|---|---|---|
| **Format and Organization** | The writer demonstrates a lack of understanding of the correct form for a business letter. The letter lacks two or more essential parts. | The writer shows a vague understanding of correct forms. However, a business letter may lack an essential part. | The writer uses the correct form for a business letter, and omits only minor elements. A business letter contains the six essential parts: heading, inside address, salutation, body, closing, and signature. | The writer uses the correct and complete form for a business letter containing the six essential parts: heading, inside address, salutation, body, closing, and signature. |
| **Elements** | Most parts of the letter are incomplete or incorrect. The writer does not state the purpose for writing. The writer does not use formal language or else uses it inconsistently. Important or essential details are omitted. | More than one part of the letter may be incomplete or incorrect. The writer states the purpose of the writing, but not necessarily at the beginning. The level of language is inappropriate. One or more important details may be missing. | One part of the letter may be incomplete or incorrect. The writer states the purpose of the letter. The body contains courteous, formal language and all the necessary details. | Each part is complete and correct. The writer briefly but clearly states the purpose of the letter or memo. The body contains courteous, formal language and all the details that the audience will need. There are no extraneous details. |
| **Grammar, Usage and Spelling** | The letter is difficult to understand because of errors in mechanics, usage, grammar, or spelling. | There are several errors in mechanics, usage, grammar, or spelling. Some hinder comprehension. | There are minor errors in mechanics, usage, grammar, or spelling. | There are few or no errors in mechanics, usage, grammar, or spelling. |

# Appendix E: Team C's Summative BL Feedback for EFL Learners

| | |
|---|---|
| **Proofreading** | Proofreading – reading it again to check for mistakes. You should proofread all your writing before you give it to the teacher. Let us practice all together correcting sentences that you wrote! <br> Activity: <br> Each group will look at one slide about a common mistake that the class made in the business letters. Correct your slide with your group, and write down the corrections. |
| **Spelling** | Spelling mistakes are the easiest to make and also the easiest to correct! <br> Always proofread for spelling mistakes. <br> Examples: <br> 1: I would like to visit Frence. <br> 2: I want to go to German. <br> 3: This place is very attrative to me. <br> 4: I am curioused about the ocean. <br> 5: The ervironment is very good here. <br> 6: Because there is a beactiful country! <br> 7: The last thing is, if it's possible,I want to spend 80% of the travle time in forest. |
| **Subject-Verb Agreement (and missing verb)** | Make sure the SUBJECT and the VERB match. <br> Make sure each sentence has a main verb. <br> Examples: <br> 1. Outdoors is my favorite activities. <br> 2. If the waiter take tips, how much should I give? <br> 3. Many old buildings in the UK. <br> 4. It also because I have watched many movies. <br> 5. I want to there. |
| **Formality (Language)** | For a business letter, you must use polite language <br> Use MODAL (I would, could you, NOT I want) <br> Use FULL words (do not instead of don't) <br> Examples: <br> 1. I want to go to a city in Germany <br> 2. Let me introduce you to why do I want to go to Austria <br> 3. Can you make me a good plan to go to this country? <br> 4. I want to tell you which place I love. <br> 5. Thank you again, god bless you. |

(continued)

| | |
|---|---|
| **Starting a sentence** | Do not start a sentence with a conjunction (and/but). Use another word (also/however). If you use and/but, put a comma (,) before the conjunction.<br>So: I want to jump, and I want to swim.<br>NOT: I want to jump. And I want to swim.<br>INSTEAD: I want to jump. Also, I want to swim.<br>Examples:<br>1. And I want to taste more seafood there.<br>2. I want to visit Japan to eat sushi. And I want to see the tall buildings.<br>3. I want to go to Canada. Because the scenery is beautiful in Canada.<br>4. I think I am very healthy. But I can't ride a bike.<br>5. I want to go to America. Because I like American culture and city life. |
| **Punctuation (? . ; ')** | After a short form, you must put a PERIOD.<br>(Mister = Mr., NOT Mr)<br>After a title (like Mr.), you use the full name or last name (Mr. Smith OR Mr. John Smith)<br>Examples:<br>1. Dear Mr B.<br>2. Mr Travel Agent Smith |

# References

Bartholomae, David. 1986. Inventing the University. *Journal of Basic Writing*, 5 (1). 4–23.
Belz, Julie & Andreas Müller-Hartmann. 2003. Teachers as intercultural learners: Negotiating German-American telecollaboration along the institutional fault line. *The Modern Language Journal* 87 (1). 71–89. https://doi.org/10.1111/1540-4781.00179 (accessed 2 March 2021).
Brown, Henry Douglas. 2007. *Teaching by principles: An interactive approach to language pedagogy* (3rd ed.). Pearson Education.
Bygate, Martin. 1999. Task as context for framing, reframing, and unframing of language. *System* 27 (1). 33–48.
Bygate, Martin. 2000. Introduction to special issue: Tasks in language pedagogy. *Language Teaching Research* 4 (3). 185–192.
Cunningham, Joe. 2019. Telecollaboration for content and language learning: A genre-based approach. *Language Learning & Technology* 23 (3). 161–177. http://hdl.handle.net/10125/44701 (accessed 2 March 2021).
Cunningham, Joe & Nina Vyatkina. 2012. Telecollaboration for professional purposes: Towards developing a formal register in the foreign language classroom. *Canadian Modern*

Language Review/La Revue Canadienne des Langues Vivantes 68. 422–450. https://doi.org/10.3138/cmlr.1279 (accessed 2 March 2021).

Dooly, Melinda. 2011. Divergent perceptions of tellecollaborative language learning tasks: Task-as-workplan vs. task-as-process. *Language Learning & Technology* 15 (2). 69–91. http://dx.doi.org/10125/44252 (accessed 2 March 2021).

Dooly, Melina & Robert O'Dowd. (eds.). 2012. *Researching online foreign language interaction and exchange: Theories, methods and challenges*. Peter Lang.

Flowerdew, John. 2002. Ethnographically inspired approaches to academic discourse. In John Flowerdew (ed.), *Academic Discourse*, 235–252. Routledge.

Fuchs, Carolin, Bill Snyder, Bruce Tung & Yu Jung Han. 2017. The multiple roles of the task design mediator in telecollaboration. *ReCALL* 29 (3). 239–256. https://doi.org/10.1017/S0958344017000088 (accessed 2 March 2021).

Fuchs, Carolin. 2019. Critical incidents and cultures-of-use in a Hong Kong–Germany Telecollaboration. *Language Learning & Technology* 23 (3). 74–97. http://hdl.handle.net/10125/44697 (accessed 2 March 2021).

Goldstein, Lynn. 2006. Feedback and revision in second language writing: Contextual, teacher, and student variables. In Ken Hyland & Fiona Hyland (eds.), *Feedback in second language writing: Contexts and issues*, 185–205. Cambridge University Press.

Hyland, Ken. 2004. *Genre and second language writing*. University of Michigan Press.

Hyon, Sunny. 2017. Using genre analysis to teach writing in the disciplines. In John Flowerdew & Tracey Costley (eds.), *Discipline specific writing: Theory into practice*, 77–94. Routledge.

Hyon, Sunny. 2018. *Introducing genre and English for specific purposes*. Routledge.

Johns, Ann. 1997. *Text, role, and context*. Cambridge University Press.

Johns, Ann. 2008. Genre awareness for the novice academic student: The ongoing quest. *Language Teaching* 41 (2). 237–252. https://doi.org/10.1017/s0261444807004892 (accessed 2 March 2021).

Johnson, Keith. 2000. What task designers do. *Language Teaching Research* 4 (3). 301–321.

Johnson, Keith, 2003. *Designing language teaching tasks*. Palgrave Macmillan.

Kramsch, Claire. 2009. *The multilingual subject*. Oxford, UK: Cambridge University Press.

Lenkaitis, Chesla. 2020. Recorded video meetings in virtual exchange: a new frontier for pre-service teacher reflection. *Journal of Virtual Exchange* 3. 39–58. https://doi.org/10.21827/jve.3.35750 (accessed 2 March 2021).

Lenkaitis, Chesla, Shannon Hilliker & Kayla Roumeliotis. 2020. Teacher Candidate Reflection and Development Through Virtual Exchange. *IAFOR Journal of Education*, 8 (2), 125–139.

MacBeth, Karen. 2010. Deliberate false provisions: The use and usefulness of models in learning academic writing. *Journal of Second Language Writing* 19. 33–48. https://doi.org/10.1016/j.jslw.2009.08.002 (accessed 2 March 2021).

O'Dowd, Robert, Shannon Sauro & Elana Spector-Cohen. 2020. The role of pedagogical mentoring in virtual exchange. *TESOL Quarterly* 54 (1). 146–172. https://doi.org/10.1002/tesq.543 (accessed 2 March 2021).

Pegrum, Michael. 2009. *From blogs to bombs: The future of digital technologies in education*. UWA Publishing.

Rampazzo, Laura & Solange Aranha. 2019. Telecollaboration and genres: a new perspective to understand language learning, *Journal of Virtual Exchange* 2. 7–28. https://doi.org/10.21827/jve.2.35637 (accessed 2 March 2021).

Richards, Keith. 2003. *Qualitative inquiry in TESOL*. Palgrave Macmillan.

Samuda, Virginia. 2005. Expertise in pedagogic task design. In Keith Johnson (ed.), *Expertise in second language learning and teaching*, 230–254. Palgrave Macmillan.

Schmidt, Richard. 2001. Attention. In Peter Robinson (ed.), *Cognition and second language instruction*, 3–32. Cambridge University Press.

Tedick, Diane & Maureen Mathison. 1995. Holistic scoring in ESL writing assessment: What does an analysis of rhetorical features reveal? In Diane Belcher & George Braine (eds.), *Academic writing in a second language: Essays on research and pedagogy*, 205–230. Ablex Publishing Corporation.

Thorne, Steven. 2016. Cultures-of-use and morphologies of communicative action. *Language Learning & Technology* 20 (2). 185–191. http://dx.doi.org/10125/44473 (accessed 2 March 2021).

Thorne, Steven. 2003. Artifacts and cultures-of-use in intercultural communication. *Language Learning & Technology* 7 (2) 38–67. http://dx.doi.org/10125/25200 (accessed 2 March 2021).

Ware, Paige & Claire Kramsch. 2005. Toward an intercultural stance: Teaching German and English through telecollaboration. *Modern Language Journal* 89 (2). 190–205. https://doi.org/10.1111/j.1540-4781.2005.00274.x (accessed 2 March 2021).

Ware, Paige & Robert O'Dowd. 2008. Peer feedback on language form in telecollaboration. *Language Learning & Technology* 12 (1). 43–63. https://www.lltjournal.org/item/2616 (accessed 2 March 2021).

Wu, Zhiwei. 2019. Understanding students' mimicry, emulation, and imitation of genre exemplars: An exploratory study. *English for Specific Purposes* 54. 127–138. https://doi.org/10.1016/j.esp.2019.02.002 (accessed 2 March 2021).

Kaishan Kong
# Chapter 5
# "Zoom" in and speak out: Virtual exchange in language learning

Due to the unprecedented challenges caused by COVID-19, virtual learning has become the new normal in education. Like many other subjects, the discussion of language education has shifted from if we should adopt virtual learning to how we could make virtual learning effective for language learners (Bailey and Lee 2020; Bao 2020; Rose et al. 2020). Besides virtual classes delivered by teachers, virtual exchange between language learners is also worth discussing, with increasing light shed on its advantages, challenges, design, implementation and integration in curriculum design (Egbert 2020; Guillén et al. 2020; Lomicka 2020). This study examines two American students' virtual exchange meetings with native speakers from China and discusses the benefits from this virtual exchange program in two areas: language development and learner autonomy.

## 1 Literature review

### 1.1 Virtual exchange in the foreign language classroom

There are many terms to describe the use of technology to support language education, to name a few, Computer-assisted Language Learning (CALL), Computer-mediated Communication (CMC), Online Language Learning (OLL), technology-mediated tasks, and virtual exchange. Some terms cover a broader field while others underscore specific class activities. The collection of terminology unfolds decades of discussion, exploration and research on the effectiveness of technology in language education.

This chapter focuses on virtual exchange in particular. According to O'Dowd (2020: 477), "virtual exchange is a well-known pedagogical approach in foreign language (FL) education which involves engaging classes in online intercultural collaboration projects with international partners as an integrated part of their educational programmes". Similar to other terms listed above, virtual exchange can take place in asynchronous and synchronous arrangements, which means

---

**Kaishan Kong,** University of Wisconsin-Eau Claire, e-mail: KONGK@uwec.edu

https://doi.org/10.1515/9783110727364-006

that the students can exchange via instant messenger or video conferencing tools like Zoom while both online at the same time, or they can alternate response to each other via emails without being present at the same time.

In particular, O'Dowd (2016) summarized two principal models of virtual exchange in foreign language education: e-tandem and intercultural telecollaboration approaches. E-tandem is an online version of the tandem language learning model, defined as "face-to-face exchanges between two learners with different L1s, each trying to learn the other's language" (Chung et al. 2005: 52). The telecollaboration model is distinguished from e-tandem mainly in its emphasis on intercultural communicative competence. In other words, the focus on language exchange is more salient in E-tandem, while telecollaboration emphasizes a broader competence in intercultural communication through collaborative projects online. Virtual exchange is not limited to communication with native speakers; nonetheless, it is an inclusive, fluid and overarching umbrella to include, but not limited to, these two models.

The virtual exchange project under discussion in this chapter does not strictly fit in either one of the two models; rather, it is somewhere in between because it is both for language support (e-tandem) and it stimulates intercultural communicative competence (telecollaboration model). More details will be explained in the research context.

## 1.2 Theoretical support of virtual exchange

Virtual exchange, as a form of computer-assisted language education, has been examined from an interactionalist or sociocultural perspective, both of which underscore the importance of interaction and reciprocal support from learners in second language acquisition. From the interactionalist perspective, second language acquisition is accomplished through a learner's interaction with others who may modify their speech to meet the learner's communicative and learning needs. Informed by Long's Interaction Hypothesis, researchers consider virtual exchange as a platform where interlocutors employ language resources and communicative strategies to express ideas, to make clarifications, to "prevent a communicative impasse or to remedy an actual impasse that has arisen" (Ellis and Barkhuizen, 2005: 167). Over the past two decades, a multitude of studies on both asynchronous exchange and synchronous exchange exhibited similar successful learning outcomes in meaning negotiation as in a traditional face-to-face exchange (Blake 2011; Sotillo 2000; Yanguas 2010). Sauro (2009) reported metalinguistic feedback on virtual exchange and its positive effect on grammatical accuracy; Oskoz (2009) and Lee (2008) both identified learners' linguistic improvement through various virtual exchange activities in their research results. Virtual exchange activities designed based on an interactionalist view allow students to engage in meaningful negotiation with their peers or with more expert interlocutors (advanced learners or native speakers) and activate their agency to direct the conversational flow based on their need.

From the sociocultural perspective, learning develops through interaction with others and is impacted by the social and cultural environment. Inspired by Vygotsky's sociocultural theory (Vygotsky 1978), sociocultural linguists accentuate two major constructs in language learning: mediation and internalization (Lantolf 2006; Swain et al 2010). Mediation is considered as a carrier of knowledge; it connects learners with the outside world through various forms, such as tangible artifacts and abstract concepts. Internalization is the process of learners' appropriation of symbolic artifacts in communicative activity and covert them to mediate mental activity (Lantolf 2006; Sung and Poole 2017). Through mediation and internalization, learners can transfer knowledge from others to themselves. Sociocultural perspective underscores the essential value of scaffolding, a metaphorical term for support and assistance, from a more advanced learner; thus, promotes the notion of Zone of Proximal Development (ZPD), depicting the difference between what a learner can accomplish alone and with they can accomplish with an expert's help.

Numerous studies have addressed the virtual exchange of various forms through a sociocultural lens. One line of research has focused on learners activating their agency to develop sociocultural competence while building intercultural relationships. Some studies (e.g., Darhower 2008; Dooly 2011; Jin 2013) addressed learners' role as social and cultural participants to engage in building a learner-centered community to foster their target language proficiency; other studies with a focus on pragmatic perspective (e.g., Belz 2007; Kinginger and Belz 2005) supported the notion that virtual exchange may benefit learners' development in their awareness of and competence in culturally appropriate language use. In the meanwhile, some researchers (e.g., Basharina 2007; Kramsch and Thorne 2002) warned against the discrepancies in social and cultural genres of communication between virtual exchange partners. Such discrepancies could lead to communication breakdown rather than ensuring understanding development. In sum, virtual exchange provides a platform for learners' social and cultural engagement; they use language as a tool to mediate learning and provide support to each other. Interaction, reflection and knowledge internalization made the virtual exchange a potential pedagogy to expand learners' world views and sociocultural competence (Helm 2016).

## 1.3 Benefits and characteristics of virtual exchange

The interactionalist and the sociocultural perspectives do not contradict each other; on the contrary, both perspectives recognize that virtual exchange is an active process where interaction propels improvement. After a review of literature on virtual exchange or other terms that refer to the same concept, two major benefits can be summarized: language improvement and learner autonomy.

Language improvement in various areas has been discovered from existing studies. For instance, Sotillo (2000) reported ESL learners' syntax and lexicon complexity development. Several other studies (Kabata and Edasawa 2011; Priego 2011) shared a similar finding attributed to immediate feedback, error corrections, noticing, and self-corrections that happen via virtual exchange. Some scholars argue that because virtual exchange entails some advantages that a traditional classroom lacks, such as "learners' time management needs and technological preferences" (Kawaguchi and Di Biase 2009: 288), virtual exchange may make the learning experience more enjoyable in addition to successful language learning. In particular, when a language learner conducts virtual exchange with a native speaker, the novice learner is exposed to both authentic use of the target language and authentic intercultural communication.

Furthermore, learner autonomy is becoming more prominent in the realm of language learning through virtual exchange. In Benson's (2013) definition, learner autonomy involves three levels: control over learning management, control over cognitive processes, and control over learning content. Concerning virtual exchange in language education, this control is more necessary and valuable. Especially in virtual exchange with native speakers, although many virtual exchange tasks are structured, learners are encouraged to stretch their potential, get adjusted to the discomfort level, and learn to take risks in a nonjudgmental context (Jin et al. 2008). Resorting to a dictionary, requesting repetition and clarification, employing circumlocution are among the measures taken by learners to take control of their own learning.

Virtual exchange "puts the responsibility of organizing what is to be learned into the hands of the learners themselves and lends itself to a more diverse range of learning styles" (Jin et al. 2008: 17). In other words, virtual interaction with peers, regardless of native speakers or peer learners, awakens learner's sense of agency and motivates them to find solutions to avoid and remedy any communication impasses. When virtual exchange occurs with native speakers, learning authentic cultural knowledge and being able to understand a native speaker may also account for students' enhanced learner autonomy and motivation.

In summary, virtual exchange is a pedagogical practice using technology to connect learners. This review section has addressed the value of virtual exchange

and its theoretical support in second language acquisition. Most studies conducted in this area focus on English language learning, but research on learners of historically less commonly taught languages such as Chinese is limited (Diao 2014; Jin 2017; Wang and Vasquez 2012). Diao (2014) revealed increased linguistic awareness among American students after using Weibo (a social network app) to interact with local peers while study abroad in China; Jin (2017) concluded four affordances of using WeChat (a social network app) for virtual exchange. These studies provided valuable insights towards the facilitation of virtual exchange in Chinese as a Foreign Language (CFL) education, yet they both studied the effectiveness of asynchronous social network systems in the context of study abroad. In the broader realm of CFL teaching and learning, more studies produced from diverse teaching contexts and investigating various formats of virtual exchange will construct a fuller picture of CFL development. To fill a void in this line of research, this chapter investigates a virtual exchange program in a beginning college-level CFL class in the United States. The study seeks to answer the following questions:
1. In what way(s) does virtual exchange enhance learners' language development?
2. In what way(s) does virtual exchange enhance learner autonomy?

# 2 Research

## 2.1 Context of the study

This study was situated in a college-level beginning Chinese class. Due to COVID-19, this class was delivered in a hybrid model, where students had two synchronous meetings and two asynchronous sessions each week. Intercultural Talk (IT) was a 10-week long language exchange program through virtual exchange between one CFL learner and an international student from China who is a Chinese Native Speaker (CNS). The CFL learners were students in the Chinese class, and the CNSs were volunteers who wanted to practice English, interact with domestic students and use this opportunity to fulfill the service-learning requirement on campus.

The dyad arrangement was consistent during the semester, which meant that they did not change partners during the program. The topics covered in the IT program included: self-introduction, family, visiting friends, invitations and hobbies. These topics aligned with the discussion chapters in the Chinese class, reflecting its integration in the curriculum design so as to create rich and productive learning experiences (Liddicoat and Scarino 2013). The purpose of this program was two-fold, enabling students to provide linguistic support to each other and to establish an intercultural peer relationship. The CFL students received individualized support to improve their Chinese and learn Chinese culture through talking with a peer; the CNSs were able to make friends with the local community and practice English skills.

A weekly IT routine included: (1) the professor publicized the IT tasks by Monday, (2) CFL students made an appointment with their IT partner (CNS) to meet for a synchronous virtual exchange to complete the tasks, (3) CFL students submitted their IT reflection report by Sunday night. Each IT meeting included interview questions and cultural comparison tasks related to the topic of that specific week (Appendix). They were designed to elicit productive language output (González-Lloret 2020) in a knowledge-building process (Swain 2000), elicit/provide feedback, and reflect on the virtual exchange. Students were required to record and submit four virtual exchange meetings during the semester, respectively in the $3^{rd}$ week, $6^{th}$ week, $9^{th}$ week and $12^{th}$ week. The purpose was for the instructor to observe the progression of the interaction and the language use.

The class consisted of seven students, and this was their first semester of Chinese language class in college. Although all seven students participated in the research, this chapter will present two students' data. Student #1 (S1) was a male student with zero Chinese language and cultural background. Student #2 (S2) was a female student who had studied Chinese for two years in high school but was placed in the beginning class after a placement test in college.

## 2.2 Data collection and analysis

This exploratory study adopted three sets of data to address the research questions: (1) recorded IT meetings, (2) CFL students' weekly IT reflections, (3) CFL students' video presentations over these ten weeks. It is worth noting that the video presentations via FlipGrid (an online social learning website) were assigned after each IT virtual exchange meeting. The topics of the FlipGrid videos aligned with those of the IT project. The purpose of assigning the FlipGrid presentation after their IT meeting was for the learners to firstly have a chance to improve their language through virtual exchange, then they had a chance to apply the knowledge back in a video presentation. The students felt more confident in this presentational assignment after they had a chance to practice with and receive feedback from their IT partners. These video presentations were valuable data to identify students' language improvement over the semester.

To answer the first research question on learners' language development, I examined two aspects: (1) the number of words and grammar mistakes produced by the participants in their FlipGrid videos. Since the two focal participants were at the beginning level of Chinese class, some common grammar mistakes included: misuse of words, incorrect word order and inaccurate conjunctions. (2) Lexical richness, employing a type-token ratio (TTR) to document learners' variety of vocabulary in the spoken text transcribed from their FlipGrid video presentations. "The TTR is the number of different words used (types) divided by the total number of words (tokens)" (Tarone and Swierzbin 2009: 85). The closer the TTR ratio is to 1, the greater the lexical richness of the segment. To answer the second research question on learner autonomy and motivation, I closely examined the weekly IT reflections to collect self-reported evidence, as well as analyzed the recorded IT meetings to identify moments when learners demonstrated autonomous learning.

## 2.3 Results

This section will describe three results: (1) the number of words and grammar mistakes produced by the participants in their FlipGrid videos, (2) the participants' TTR, and (3) the participants' IT reports and feedback.

### 2.3.1 Increased length in video productions

It was obvious that both participants' vocabulary increased drastically in their videos. S1 and S2 each produced 17 words in their first video, but they each produced over 100 words in the seventh video. Table 5.1 showed the specific types and tokens in each participant's production. Compared with S2 who already came in with some Chinese background, S1, without any background, was showing a higher number of words and a greater improvement.

**Table 5.1:** The participants' TTRs shown in types/tokens.

|    | 1<br>Say hi and self-introduction | 2<br>Introduction of someone else | 3<br>My family picture | 4<br>My friend | 5<br>Dinner invitation | 6<br>My weekend | 7<br>My hobbies |
|----|-----|-----|-----|-----|-----|-----|-----|
| S1 | 12/17 | 19/25 | 57/100 | 90/129 | 49/74 | 60/104 | 80/160 |
| S2 | 16/17 | 18/23 | 37/62 | 54/81 | 48/68 | 42/76 | 70/145 |

As shown in Figure 5.1, both participants' increase in the total number of words was noticeable from video 1 to video 4, and then both showed a drop in the number of words in video 5 before picking up again. It could be because of the participants' fatigue during mid-term when video 5 was assigned. It could also be explained by the type of the task. Video 1 to Video 4 were all about personal information and about friends, which were very familiar and predictable topics; however, video 5 required the participants to create a verbal invitation, which was a new and unfamiliar language function to the beginners. Then video 6 and video 7 were back to talking about self, so the participants might feel more comfortable and were able to produce more words, which could account for the increased tokens (total number of words).

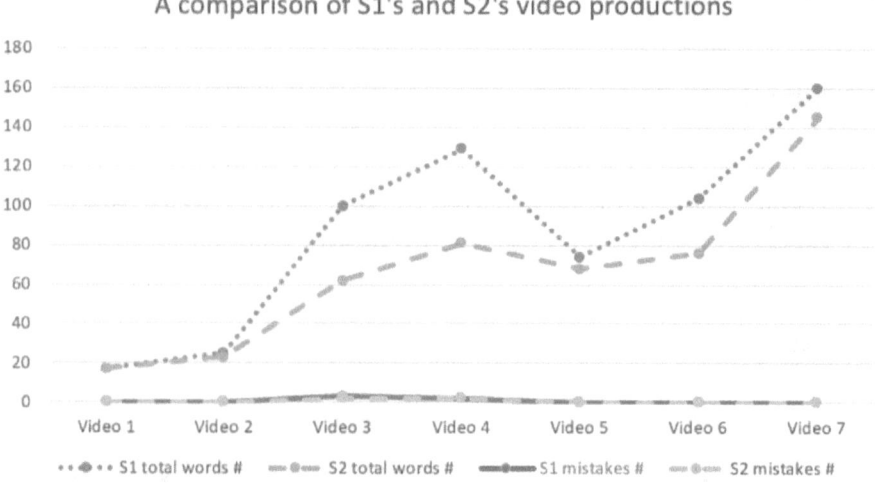

**Figure 5.1:** A comparison of S1's and S2's video productions in the number of words and mistakes.

When analyzing the participants' grammar mistakes in their videos, I noticed that they both made mistakes in videos 3 and 4. In video 3 (my family picture), S1 made three mistakes, all of which were the misuse of verbs. S2 made two mistakes, one on a verb misuse and the other on the word order. In video 4 (my friend), S1 made two mistakes of inaccurate conjunctions. S2 made one mistake of word misuse. Despite the grammar mistakes, it was salient that the participants' vocabulary soared considerably in their videos, in comparison to the first two videos. From reading the participants' IT reflections in those two weeks, they both reported a great conversation with their IT partners and learned many new words from their IT partners. The increased number of mistakes, compared with video 1 and video 2, could be explained that the participants were taking greater risks to apply what they had learned from their IT talks in their video productions.

Chapter 5 "Zoom" in and speak out: Virtual exchange in language learning — 105

## 2.3.2 TTR trend

The TTR evaluates lexical richness; the closer the TTR ratio is to 1, the greater the lexical richness of the segment. In other words, if the TTR is 1, it means that every word in the text is different without any repetitions. Figure 5.2 showed that both participants' TTR did not increase steadily from video 1 to 7; nonetheless, it was insufficient to conclude that the learners' language did not develop. A holistic view of Table 5.1, Figures 5.1 and 5.2 unfolded that although the TTR did not increase considerably, the length of production and variety of words did drastically improve. For instance, both participants only produced 17 words in their video 1 presentation. The content was self-introduction including name, nationality and profession. Although TTR was quite high, they did not use many words in total. On the other hand, their TTR was lower in video 7, but they produced more than 100 words in the video. S1's vocabulary grew from a total of 17 words in video 1 to a total of 160 words in video 7, among which 50% were different words. Moreover, S1 used 90 different words in a total of 129 words in video 4, which was quite impressive for a beginner.

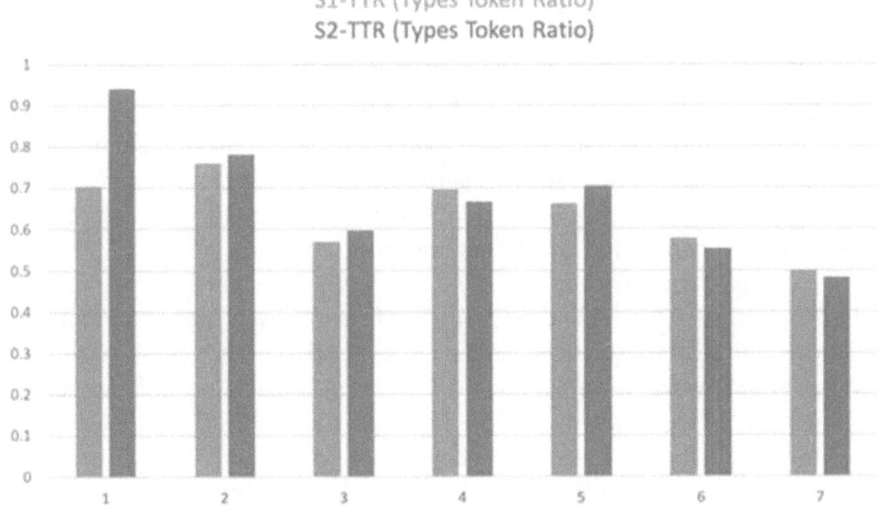

**Figure 5.2:** A comparison of both participants' TTRs.

### 2.3.3 Self-reported benefits from the IT program

Both participants provided extremely positive feedback on their weekly IT meetings. Some repeated comments included: *I absolutely loved it, I really enjoyed the talk*, and *My partner helped me say . . ..* Three specific benefits were summarized from both participants:

(1) Both participants reported that their IT partners helped them improve pronunciation, correct grammar mistakes and expand their vocabulary. For example, S1 said "Jim helped me with my pronunciation of family and how to say that there are five people in my family" in IT report #5, and said "my partner tried to help me figure out the name for my dad's job" in IT report #6. These aligned with the video productions where both participants adopted some new words (not from their textbook) in their videos.

(2) Both participants reported that the cultural knowledge that they learned from their IT partners made them more curious and more motivated in learning this language. S2 wrote in her IT report #6, "One takeaway I have from this talk is that even though there are a lot of cultural differences, there are also a lot of similarities. I enjoyed this talk a lot". S1 gave a specific example in his IT report #8,

> I learned that dating in China is a lot like dating in the US, but schools forbid you from dating. People do the same activities on dates as they do here, going to the movies, eating dinner, etc. I feel that I know my partner better and I'm getting more confident in speaking Chinese. My partner did an outstanding job helping me.

Every week, both participants reported their enjoyment of making cultural comparisons with specific examples. One particular activity was teaching each other popular slang in their native language. Watching their recorded IT sessions lent support to the dynamic and excitement from both parties.

(3) Virtual change with native speakers considerably enhanced the participants' confidence. S2 wrote in report #4, "The interview went well. I could understand everything he was saying even though he spoke quickly. I felt very nervous and was afraid I would mess up, but he complimented me on my pronunciation. I felt very proud of myself afterwards". Similarly, S1 wrote in his IT report #8, "Every time I talk with him, I am surprised by how well he understands what I say in Chinese. It motivates me to keep learning. It was a good talk". Their enhanced motivation was shown in the length of videos as discussed above; in particular, I noticed that S1, the participant with no Chinese background, embedded more and more Chinese in his last four IT reports, almost 100% Chinese in the last report. Since the participants were allowed to write the IT reports in English, it was a pleasant surprise to see S1's motivation to use the target language to write his reflection, which was a sign of risk-taking.

## 3 Discussion

Informed by interactionist and socioculturalist theories, virtual exchange focuses on structuring interaction in order to facilitate meaningful negotiation with peer learners, native speakers or to provide authentic experiences of intercultural communication with speakers of other languages (Dooly 2017; O'Dowd 2020). Numerous studies have documented how a learner's language develops as a result of virtual exchange (Lee 2008; Oskoz 2009; Sauro 2009). A consensus is that the interactive feature of virtual exchange engages learners to receive input, feedback and opportunities to produce modified output. The design of the virtual exchange tasks in this study manifested the intentional structure of interactivity and sociocultural exchange. The interview activity engaged the learners to conduct a meaningful conversation and negotiated meanings on familiar topics; the cultural comparison tasks propelled the learners to share authentic experiences in an effective and culturally appropriate way. The participants reported a great degree of enthusiasm and engagement in cross-cultural comparison topics, such as dating, popular hobbies, and slang. The weekly IT tasks began with some guiding questions and the participants were able to prepare beforehand, which helped to lower their anxiety. As the conversation continued in the IT meeting, the participants were required to create follow-up questions. It created a soft-landing experience and allowed the participants to experience a process in comprehending, manipulating and producing language (Zhang and Luo 2018). Although the recorded IT sections showed some mistakes in the participants' language use, it was clear that both partners focused on the meaning and the language use in an authentic way, which fit in the pursuit of effective online learning.

Findings in this study echoed Lee's (2008) conclusion that exposure to authentic use of language and scaffolding from their partners provided a constructive environment for corrective feedback and language development. Lee's study examined how form-focused corrective feedback was negotiated among 30 participants in Spanish learning through virtual exchange. She discovered many incidents where experts assisted their partners with both lexical and syntactical explanations to help them increase accuracy; similar evidence was identified in this study. The participants' reflection and increased lexicon complexity in this study supports the value of peer scaffolding. When traditional face-to-face interaction was interrupted due to an unprecedented pandemic, virtual exchange has offered an alternative solution and easier access to interact with speakers of the target language (Jin 2017), and provided a platform for a multitude of input and a fount of opportunities for students to "produce language, engage in communication, and receive useful timely feedback" (González-Lloret 2020: 261).

Further, in Kawaguchi and Biase's (2009: 299) study on five students' Japanese language development through virtual exchange, the authors also employed types and tokens to measure language development, and the results indicated that all participants "uniformly increased cumulative word type with each session". A similar result emerged from the finding in this study. For example, from video 3 to video 7, both participants produced a significantly increased number of words, and their TTRs ranged from 50% to 80%. Especially for S1, despite zero background in Chinese, his progress was even more noticeable than S2. The reflective reports from both participants repeatedly mentioned that the native speakers provided more vocabulary choices for them, corrected their language use to be more authentic, and modeled alternative ways of expressing the same idea. The support and scaffolding from native speakers identified in the finding of this study were what Jin (2017: 11–13) referred to as "authentic meaning-focused communication" and "linguistic resources and multiliteracies" in her study to take an in-depth look at the digital affordances from virtual exchange via WeChat (one of the most popular digital social networking systems in China) between native speakers and Chinese language learners. Also similar to Jin's (2017) finding, this study found that each participant might have differing benefits from virtual exchanges with native speaking partners due to their proficiency level. For example, S1 as a total beginner benefitted greatly from vocabulary exposure and ample examples from the native speaker; by contrast, S2 who had some prior knowledge in Chinese, reported that her greatest benefit was noticing and learning how the native speakers spoke differently from the textbook. Regardless, virtual exchange with native speakers in this project provided them with a rich repertoire of authentic language use and linguistic resources.

Moreover, the interactionalist and socioculturalist features of virtual exchange in this study showed an enhancement of both participants' learner autonomy. In line with Benson's (2013) definition of learner autonomy involving three levels of control: over learning management, over cognitive processes and over learning content, findings in this study showed that the two participants gradually developed their ability to take charge of their learning and directing their attention to linguistic input. From the recordings of virtual exchange meetings, it was noticeable that the two participants strictly followed the prompts on the worksheet without much spontaneous discussion in the first two meetings; however, in the next two recorded meetings, the participants were adjusted to the discomfort level (Jin et al. 2008) and took risks to apply the language in conversation as well as directing the conversation to topics of their interest. For instance, S1 asked the partner to teach him new words and modeled after the partner's speaking; S2 requested repetition and clarification to ensure understanding. What the participants did was an increased exercise of their learner agency and ability to direct the conversation flow to benefit their learning (Chapelle 2008). When interacting with a peer in an authentic cross-cultural environment, the participants felt the individualized attention from their partner and the freedom to decide what they wanted to learn (Benson 2013; Tseng et al. 2020). Along with the elevating sense of freedom, the participants raised their linguistic awareness and gradually learned to take control over their learning.

In addition, the pleasure of conversing on everyday topics when both partners could bring in their unique sociocultural experiences helped to foster learners' integral motivation and confidence, which ultimately also contributed to enhanced learner autonomy. As noted in the literature, interaction in a sociocultural environment can foster intercultural competence, integrative motivation, learner confidence and empathetic exchanges (González-Lloret 2020; O'Dowd 2020; Payne 2020). In this study, multiple data sources (the recorded meetings, participants' positive feedback in their reflection, and the fact that they even wrote the reflection in the Chinese language) all pointed to the same direction, that the two participants became more confident as a language learner, more curious about Chinese culture, and more motivated to continue learning the language.

Two particular elements could be identified in this study. The first catalyst was from cultural knowledge building. As explained in the context of this study, the dyads were given tasks to compare cultures. S1 had no prior background in the Chinese language or culture, and S2 had a little language background; therefore, interacting with a peer from the target culture helped to expand their knowledge horizon. They found common values as well as different cultural references, which inspired them to explore more. A second incentive was being understood by their IT partners. If it were in a traditional classroom, opportunities for such direct and personalized interaction would be limited. This would add to the value of virtual exchange, "not a simple replacement of face-to-face" but offering tremendous opportunities for cultural stimulation, and "for self-paced language production and comprehension" (Kawaguchi and Di Biase, 2009: 301). As the participants' motivation grew, they gradually pushed themselves to initiate conversations and raise questions that were unique to their own learning needs. As they were taking more risks, they were more engaged and were understood by their native-speaking partners; therefore, their confidence grew, and it led to enhanced learner autonomy.

## 4 Conclusion

This study presented findings in a virtual exchange program in a college-level beginning Chinese class, with a focus on two participants' data. The results showed that although these two participants had varied language backgrounds, they both benefited from the virtual exchange program with their partners who were native speakers of Chinese. The benefits were reflected in their language development and learner autonomy. Regarding language development, interaction allowed the native speaker to provide scaffolding to the learner, including vocabulary exposure, error corrections and authentic language use; as a result, there was a significant increase in the number of words and lexical richness in the participant's language production. In the meanwhile, the cross-cultural interaction through the virtual exchange program in this study cultivated learner autonomy within the learners. In particular, the fact that they were able to converse with a native speaker and be understood, along with sharing cultural knowledge, considerably increased their confidence and motivation. The two participants stretched their potential and gradually took control of the learning content by raising questions of their interests, taking risks to produce more language and writing reflection reports in the target language. Despite the small scale of this study, the findings in this study did resonate with findings in some previous studies to support the benefits of virtual exchange with native speakers.

Admittedly, there were several limitations in this study. The data sample was limited; only one tool (TTR) was used to analyze the language development, and the learner autonomy was analyzed through self-reports. These limitations also suggest future research opportunities. It would be significant to examine all students' data in this cohort to gain a more generalizable conclusion; secondly, more tools could be adopted to analyze participants' linguistic complexity; and finally, a survey could be adopted to shed a more nuanced light on learner autonomy.

Virtual exchange has tremendous pedagogical potential in language learning and learner autonomy. To achieve these goals, instructors need to judiciously consider the learning goals, practicality and clear instructions as well as thoughtful scaffolding such as providing training and feedback. Using ZOOM or other conferencing tools for virtual exchange is no longer an uncharted territory; rather, the discussion focus should shift from technical tools to the design of virtual exchange programs. Regardless of what tools to be used, a sound virtual exchange program will enable learners to, as the title suggests, zoom in and speak out, meaning they can immerse themselves in a more focused learning environment and produce greater language output.

# Appendix: A sample worksheet for one of the Virtual Exchange meetings

**Topic: Visiting friends**

**Task 1: Interview in Chinese.**
Interview the following questions:

| Questions问题 [wèntí] | Answers 回答[huídá] |
|---|---|
| - 你平常喜欢喝茶还是喝咖啡? <br> - 你喜欢看中国电影还是外国电影? <br> - 你喜欢听谁的歌? <br> - 你喜欢去朋友家玩儿吗? <br> - 你昨天晚上做了什么? <br> - 你今天晚上做什么? <br> - 你喜欢跳舞还是唱歌? <br> - 你的好朋友是谁? <br> - 你喜欢你的好朋友吗?为什么? <br> - 你喜欢美国大学[American university]吗?为什么? <br> - Add 3 extra questions.加三个问题 | |

**Task 2: English interview**
- Create some questions for your IT partner to find out what Chinese hosts normally offer for the guests to drink or eat. Is it common to bring gifts? If so, what are some good gifts and what are some inappropriate gifts?
- Share some information about your culture with your partner so they can learn something from you too.
- Identify 2–3 similarities/differences between Chinese and American culture regarding hosting and visiting friends.

**Task 3: Submit IT reflection report (You may complete this report in English, Chinese or both)**
- What extra questions in Chinese did you raise for your partner?
- Provide specific examples of language support that your IT partner offered to you.
- What cultural comparisons (2–3 similarities/differences) did you identify?

Did you have a pleasant IT talk? Do you plan to meet again in the future?

## References

Bailey, Daniel & Andrea Lee. 2020. Learning from experience in the midst of covid-19: Benefits, challenges, and strategies in online teaching. *Computer-Assisted Language Learning Electronic Journal* 21 (2). 178–198.

Bao, Wei. 2020. COVID-19 and online teaching in higher education: A case study of Peking University. *Human Behavior and Emerging Technologies* 2 (2). 113–115.

Basharina, Olga. 2007. An activity theory perspective on student-reported contradictions in international telecollaboration. *Language Learning & Technology* 11 (2). 82–103.

Belz, Julie. 2007. The development of intercultural communicative competence in telecollaborative partnerships. In Robert O'Dowd (ed.), *Online intercultural exchange An introduction for foreign language teachers*, 127–166. Clevedon, UK: Multilingual Matters.

Benson, Phil. 2013. *Teaching and researching: Autonomy in language learning*. New York: Routledge.

Blake, Robert. 2011. Current trends in online language learning. *Annual Review of Applied Linguistics* 31. 19–35.

Chapelle, Carol. 2008. Technology and second language acquisition. *Annual Review of Applied Linguistics*, 27, 98–114.

Chung, Yang-Gyun., Barbara Graves, Mari Wesche & Marion Barfurth. 2005. Computer-mediated communication in Korean-English chat rooms: Tandem learning in an international language program. *The Canadian Modern Language Review* 62 (1). 49–86.

Darhower, Mark. 2008. The role of the linguistic affordances in tellecollaborative chat. *CALICO Journal* 26 (1). 48–69.

Diao, Wenhao. 2014. (Dis)engagement in Internet linguistic practices among sojourners in China. In Shuai Li & Peter Swanson (eds.), *Engaging language learners through technology integration: Theory, applications, and outcomes*, 162–180. Hershey, PA: IGI-Global.

Dooly, Melinda. 2011. Divergent perceptions of tellecollaborative language learning tasks: Task-as-workplan vs. task-as-process. *Language Learning & Technology* 15 (2). 69–91.

Dooly, Melinda. 2017. Telecollaboration. In Carol Chapelle & Shannon Sauro (eds.), *The handbook of technology in second language teaching and learning*, 169–183. Hoboken, NJ: Wiley-Blackwell.

Egbert, Joy. 2020. The new normal?: A pandemic of task engagement in language learning. *Foreign Language Annals* 53 (2). 314–319.

Ellis, Rod & Gary Barkhuizen. 2005. *Analysing learner language*. Oxford: Oxford University Press.

González-Lloret, Marta. 2020. Collaborative tasks for online language teaching. *Foreign Language Annals* 53 (2). 260–269.

Guillén, Gabriel, Thor Sawin & Netta Avineri. 2020. Zooming out of the crisis: Language and human collaboration. *Foreign Language Annals* 53 (2). 320–328.

Helm, Francesca. 2016. Facilitated dialogue in online intercultural exchange. In Robert O'Dowd & Tim Lewis (eds.), *Online intercultural exchange: Policy, pedagogy, practice*, 150–172. London/New York: Routledge.

Jin, Li. 2013. Language development and scaffolding in a Sino-American telecollaborative project. *Language Learning & Technology* 17 (2). 193–219.

Jin, Li. 2017. Digital affordances on WeChat: Learning Chinese as a second language. *Computer Assisted Language Learning* 31 (1–2). 27–52.

Jin, Li, Tony Erben, Ruth Ban, Robert Summers & Kristina Eisenhower. 2008. Using technology for foreign language instruction: Creative innovations, research, and applications. In Tony Erben & Iona Sarieva (eds.), *CALLing all foreign language teachers: Computer-assisted language learning in the classroom*, 13–35. Larchmont, NY: Eye on Education.

Kabata, Kaori & Yasuyo Edasawa. 2011. Tandem language learning through a cross-cultural keypal project. *Language Learning & Technology* 15 (1). 104–121.

Kawaguchi, Satomi & Bruno Di Biase. 2009. Aligning second language learning and computer-assisted language learning: Networking the language class, tandem learning and e-movies. *International Journal of Learning* 16 (10), 287–302.

Kinginger, Celeste & Julie Belz. 2005. Socio-cultural perspectives on pragmatic development in foreign language learning: Microgenetic case studies from telecollaboration and residence abroad. *Intercultural Pragmatics* 2 (4). 369–421. https://doi.org/10.1515/iprg.2005.2.4.369 (accessed 3 November 2021).

Kramsch, Claire & Steven Thorne. 2002. Foreign language learning as global communicative practice. In David Block & Deborah Cameron (eds.), *Globalization and language teaching*, 83–100. London, UK: Routledge.

Lantolf, James. 2006. Sociocultural theory and second language learning: State of the art. *Studies in Second Language Acquisition* 28 (1). 67–109.

Lee, Lina. 2008. Focus-on-form through collaborative scaffolding in expert-to-novice online interaction. *Language Learning & Technology* 12 (3). 53–72.

Liddicoat, Anthony & Angela Scarino. 2013. *Intercultural language teaching and learning*. West Sussex: Wiley-Blackwell.

Lomicka, Lara. 2020. Creating and sustaining virtual language communities. *Foreign Language Annals 53* (2). 306–313.

O'Dowd, Robert. 2016. Learning from the past and looking to the future of online intercultural exchange. In Robert O'Dowd & Tim Lewis (eds.), *Online intercultural exchange: Policy, pedagogy, practice*, 273–298. London/New York: Routledge.

O'Dowd, Robert. 2020. A transnational model of virtual exchange for global citizenship education. *Language Teaching* 53 (4). 477–490.

Oskoz, Ana. 2009. Learners' feedback in online chats: What does it reveal about students' learning? *CALICO Journal* 27 (1). 48–68.

Payne, Scott. 2020. Developing L2 productive language skills online and the strategic use of instructional tools. Foreign Language Annals, 53 (2), 243–249. http://doi.org/10.1111/flan.12457 (accessed 3 November 2021).

Priego, Sabrina. 2011. Helping each other: Scaffolding in electronic tandem language learning. *International Journal of Technology, Knowledge & Society* 7 (2). 133–152.

Rose, Heath, Jim McKinley & Nicola Galloway. 2020. Global Englishes and language teaching: A review of pedagogical research. *Language Teaching*.1–33.

Sauro, Shannon. 2009. Computer-mediated corrective feedback and the development of L2 grammar. *Language Learning & Technology* 13 (1). 96–120.

Sotillo, Susanna. 2000. Discourse functions and syntactic complexity in synchronous and asynchronous communication. *Language Learning & Technology* 4 (1). 82–119.

Sung, Ko-Yin & Fredrick Poole. 2017. Investigating the use of a smartphone social networking application on language learning. *JALT CALL Journal* 13 (2). 97–115.

Swain, Merrill. 2000. The output hypothesis and beyond: Mediating acquisition through collaborative dialogue. In James Lantolf (ed.), *Sociocultural theory and second language learning*, 97–114. Oxford, UK: Oxford University Press.

Swain, Merrill, Penny Kinnear & Linda Steinman. 2010. *Sociocultural theory in second language education: An introduction through narratives*. Bristol, UK: Multilingual Matters.
Tarone, Elaine & Bonnie Swierzbin. 2009. *Exploring learner language*. Oxford: Oxford University Press.
Tseng, Wen-Ta, Hao-Jyuan Liou & Hsin-Chin Chu. 2020. Vocabulary learning in virtual environments: Learner autonomy and collaboration. *System*, *88*, 102190.
Vygotsky, Lev. 1978. *Mind and society: The development of higher mental processes*. Cambridge, MA: Harvard University Press.
Wang, Shenggao & Camilla Vasquez. 2012. Web 2.0 and second language learning: What does the research tell us? *CALICO Journal 29* (3). 412–430.
Yanguas, Inigo. 2010. Oral computer-mediated interaction between L2 learners: It's about time. *Language Learning & Technology 14* (3). 72–79.
Zhang, Yumei & Shaoqian Luo. 2018. Teachers' beliefs and practices of task-based language teaching in Chinese as a second language classrooms. *Chinese Journal of Applied Linguistics 41* (3). 264–287.

**Culture and virtual exchange**

Anna Nicolaou, Ana Sevilla-Pavón
# Chapter 6
# Developing intercultural communicative competence in ESP contexts through virtual exchange: An ecological perspective

## 1 Introduction

In today's fast-paced, global world, being capable of communicating effectively and appropriately with people hailing from different cultures is of utmost importance. In language teaching, the ability to use the language in "socially and culturally appropriate ways" (Byram, Gribkova, and Starkey 2002: 7), has been gaining recognition and "foreign language ability, global awareness, and intercultural communication skills are increasingly acknowledged as essential dimensions of productive participation in the emerging economic, civic, political and social arenas of the 21st century" (McCloskey 2012: 49). Therefore, intercultural competence, which encompasses the amalgamation of the aforementioned competences, has come to be one of the most prevailing objectives in language learning. Intercultural Communicative Competence (ICC) was defined by Byram in 1997 as follows: "[I]intercultural communicative competence in a foreign language classroom consists of a conceptual framework of four interrelated components: knowledge, skills of discovery and interaction, attitudes and critical awareness".

The view that language and culture are interconnected has been supported by many linguists advocating that "language does not exist apart from culture, that is, from the socially inherited assemblage of practices and beliefs that determines the texture of our lives" (Sapir 2004: 221), or that language interaction is critical to how culture evolves between groups at all levels (Levy 2007).

---

**Acknowledgements:** Acknowledgements are due to the Spanish Ministry of Science, Innovation and Universities for funding the research project VELCOME: Virtual exchange for learning and competence development in EMI classrooms (Ref: RTI2018-094601-B-100), for the period 2018–2021, which has supported this research study.

---

**Anna Nicolaou,** Cyprus University of Technology, e-mail:anna.nicolaou@cut.ac.cy
**Ana Sevilla-Pavón,** IULMA/Universitat de València, e-mail: Ana.M.Sevilla@uv.es

https://doi.org/10.1515/9783110727364-007

Fantini and Richards (1997) noted that exposure to more than one language, culture and world view encourages the development of the awareness, attitudes, skills, and knowledge that will enable us to effectively participate and empathise with others in a local or global context. With this in mind, Intercultural Communicative Competence has found a collocation in Second Language Acquisition (SLA) and Foreign Language (FL) learning as it has emerged in an era marked by increased mobility and digital connectivity whereby an extension to Communicative Competence in L2 instruction was necessary in order to emphasise that "in order to communicate, language learners not only need grammatical skills and knowledge but also social knowledge about how and when to use utterances appropriately" (Chun 2015: 7) across cultures (Bennett 2011). Byram, Holmes, and Savvides (2013) refer to the 'cultural turn' that language teaching and learning has experienced with the emergence of new social contexts as a result of globalisation, Information and Communications Technologies (ICT), and increased migration. These new circumstances have made it clear that communicative language teaching is not sufficient in teaching communication and interaction to people who speak different languages or to people who use a shared lingua franca. Intercultural communicative competence has, therefore, come into place to indicate that along with societal appropriateness, speakers in the new global and remarkably digitised era should also be aware of both their own culture and the culture of others and therefore develop their cultural awareness.

However, it is well acknowledged by linguists and practitioners that in language learning environments, the development of intercultural communicative competence (Lee and Markey 2014) or international understanding (Kramsch 1995) is not ensured unless educators intentionally proceed with curricular and co-curricular efforts (Deardorff 2006). Therefore, educators have exhibited an interest in adding a cultural dimension in language pedagogy in both conventional and technology-enhanced language learning contexts. The latter have attracted the attention of many educators in the last decades who have acknowledged the opportunities for optimising 'languaculture' (Risager 2005) learning through the affordances of technology. One approach that has been developed as a pedagogical paradigm in the last years in order to foster SLA and ICC is 'virtual exchange' or 'telecollaboration' (Godwin-Jones 2019), which has been defined as the engagement of groups of learners in online intercultural interactions and collaboration projects with partners from other cultural contexts or geographical locations as an integrated part of their educational programmes" (O'Dowd 2018: 1). Virtual exchange has been implemented in various contexts and "various models of telecollaboration have emerged, with diverse learning objectives, involving different typologies and configurations of participants, and utilizing a range of languages and modalities of language use" (Helm 2013: 28). In the field of second language (SL) and foreign language (FL) learning, virtual exchange has been frequently framed as 'intercultural telecollaboration' and has been mostly specified by sociocultural perspectives of foreign language education (O'Dowd 2018) which aspire to enhance the learning experience of SL/FL learners by providing them with opportunities for interaction and communication with others who speak the same language (Chun 2015). Virtual exchange projects reported in the literature have documented numerous gains with respect to the aforementioned and other goals, focusing mainly on the enhancement of language skills (Guth and Helm 2010), as well as to cultural learning and critical cultural awareness (O'Dowd 2011). These learning goals have been achieved through virtual exchanges mainly embedded in language learning courses or teacher education programmes. However, in view of supporting higher education institutions' efforts to provide their students with rich intercultural experiences while at home, there is a growing need for internationalisation of the curriculum through curricular design connected to a specific discipline, ensuring the development of global skills through meaningful interaction and intercultural learning (Beelen and Jones 2015). With this in mind, there is an increasing demand for content-based virtual exchange projects which engage learners of a particular course of study other than foreign language (O'Dowd 2016). This echoes a content-based instruction (CBI) approach to language learning which has become increasingly valued at all levels of schooling and in higher education (Wesche 2010) as it successfully amalgamates discipline-specific knowledge, the use of authentic language material, and the addressing of students' various needs (Yuan and Yu 2008).

## 2 Content-based ESP learning and virtual exchange

"Content-based instruction (CBI) is an umbrella term referring to instructional approaches that make a dual, though not necessarily equal, commitment to language and content-learning objectives" (Stoller 2008: 1163). Brinton, Snow, and Wesche (2003) have identified the three prototype models of CBI to be theme-based, sheltered, and adjunct courses with theme-based courses being the most common. Theme-based CBI courses involve the selection of topics or themes which are relevant to the learner's academic and cognitive needs and interests. These themes are used in order to place new language in context and provide an anchor for skill and language-based learning and practice (Brinton 2012; Brinton, Snow, and Wesche 2003). In this context, theme-based CBI can be linked to English for Specific Purposes (ESP) teaching, as ESP learners are brought together in the common pursuit of expanded language proficiency in a specific domain. The evolution of ESP curricula has emerged as a result of the increased need to utilise language "in real communication" (Ngan 2011: 91). Orr notes that, "ESP is taught as a tailor-made language package to specific communities of learners with highly specialized language needs" (2002: 2). Similarly, CBI communities of learners, despite being more diverse, are also related by means of content (Brinton 2012). The two approaches also share the aspect of internationalisation in their scope and their aspiration to engage their communities of learners in authentic and meaningful uses of language (ibid) while addressing their specialised language needs which are more and more complex in a world that is becoming increasingly digitised and interconnected. In view of "the need to update English as foreign language training to the current global context of its users" (Candel-Mora 2015: 27), "ESP teachers have to help their students deal with global communicative practices online in all their complexities" (White 2007: 235) in their respective fields (Jooste and Heleta 2017). To that end, virtual exchange can be employed as an effective pedagogy towards that direction, particularly because intercultural and global competences seem to have remained a secondary objective in the context of ESP learning until recently.

Virtual exchange embedded in CBI ESP learning environments is scarce in the literature even though there has been a growing presence of projects focusing on both "language and content learning experiences" (Hoskins and Reynolds 2020: 179) in the last years. This is probably due to the fact that educators have acknowledged the need to engage learners in authentic discourse and the production of different types of writing beyond "the genre of personal conversation and in particular self-presentation in telecollaborative exchange" (O'Dowd 2016: 3). One interesting project implemented at the intersection of CBI and ESP is reported by Guariento, Al-Masri and Rolinska, (2016), who implemented an exchange between the University of Glasgow and the Islamic University of Gaza. The project was a dual telecollaboration as it involved an exchange between Science and Technology students and an exchange between Biomedical students. The exchanges were embedded in subject-specific ESP courses and involved peer-review and mentoring telecollaboration between the students, who were enrolled in similar disciplines. The two projects, which aimed at enhancing learners' general academic development, communication skills, cross-cultural awareness, as well as specialist knowledge, among others, received positive evaluations by the students. In addition, an inter-disciplinary virtual exchange was implemented between students in Finland and Poland (Háhn and Radke 2020). In this exchange, language students at a university in Finland were paired with Polish students specialising in information and communications technology and tourism management. The exchange focused on the promotion of both linguistics and tourism and involved the co-creation of multimedia content. As the authors note, the students acknowledged both the opportunity to interact in an authentic context and the intercultural collaboration that the project involved towards the creation of promotional videos which were the main outcome of the exchange. A different project is reported by Walker and vom Brocke (2009), who implemented eGroups, a project-based bilingual exchange between students of German at a university in New Zealand and students of Social Sciences at a university in Germany. The project aimed at fostering authentic communication and meaningful, content-based language use in an intercultural context. The authors emphasise the importance of pedagogical design in technology-rich higher educational contexts aiming at shifting to more learner-centred instructional approaches. They also underline the undoubtful potential of user-generated content environments.

Many initiatives that have attempted to integrate content-based language learning and intercultural learning in online collaborative projects were embedded in the field of business communication. Two projects reported from the field of business communication or business English are reported by Koris and Vuylsteke (2020) and Kovačić, Bubaš, and Orehovački (2012) respectively. The former underlines the importance of aligning teaching approaches, course objectives, and learning processes prior to the initiation of the project while the latter highlights the use of collaborative web tools, such as wiki and Google Docs, for completing assignments. The areas of Business and Economics have also found a fertile ground for implementing content-related virtual exchange projects. One such example is reported by Lindner (2016). This specific exchange was designed at the intersection of Global Virtual Teams (GVT), Foreign Language Education (FLE), and Virtual Exchange (VE). Students of Business and Economics at German and Czech universities collaborated towards the completion of business-related tasks in an effort to become prepared for the interconnected, global professional contexts in which they will probably function in their future employment. The author concludes that telecollaboration projects implemented in the fields of Business and Economics are "an experiential approach to ESAP that provides students with valuable situated practice for a workplace scenario that they will very likely encounter in the future" (2016: 154). Another project which emerged from a partnership between business schools in Spain and the Netherlands is reported by Ferreira-Lopes and Rompay-Bartels (2020). The authors explored the teachers' challenges and solutions during the implementation of the intercultural virtual collaboration (IVC) project. Among the challenges reported was the alignment of institutional courses, schedules, and grading systems. In this study, the authors emphasise the potential of inter-institutional partnerships towards making virtual collaborations more authentic. Earlier, Cunningham and Vyatkina (2012) had attempted the partnering of learners of German with German-speaking professionals aspiring to develop the learners' professional spoken register. The aspect of authenticity is emphasised in this study as it aimed at engaging students in authentic online conversations by simulating learning scenarios that resembled future working contexts. Finally, a recent project reports on a virtual exchange between students of Economics in Poland enrolled in business courses and students majoring in Technological Studies in Tunisia enrolled in an entrepreneurship course. The project aimed at enhancing students' linguistic and digital skills, teamwork, and self-confidence while at the same time raising their awareness about the different entrepreneurial ecosystems in the two countries (Cheikhrouhou and Marchewka 2020). Among the benefits of the study, was the opportunity for real life cross-cultural communication despite the challenges and misunderstandings in the exchange.

From the review of different virtual exchange projects, there seems to be a growing interest in embedding online international collaborations in content-based educational settings. This can be attributed to the view that professionals in various spheres need to be competent in communicating and interacting with people from different cultural backgrounds in an era marked by increased multilingualism, interculturality and globalisation (Aguilar 2018). The reviewed studies demonstrate that virtual exchange can indeed go beyond "the genre of personal conversation" (O'Dowd 2016: 3) and can be implemented in contexts which are relevant to the learners' academic and future professional needs, offering thus an internationalised, authentic learning environment. With this in mind, the present study reports on the Business English Intercultural (BEGIN) virtual exchange project and aims at contributing to the discussion about the implementation of content-based virtual exchange projects embedded in university ESP courses.

## 3 The BEGIN virtual exchange project

This study aims at examining the affordable opportunities of technology to develop tertiary education English for Specific Purposes (ESP) students' intercultural communicative competence and discipline-specific language learning through a virtual exchange project. Specifically, the study aims at exploring the possibility of using technology tools as a location of real-life communication and interaction among university students studying similar ESP courses at two distant tertiary institutions, the Cyprus University of Technology (CUT) in Cyprus and the University of Valencia (UV) in Spain.

The BEGIN project was implemented in 2016–2017 as part of a compulsory Business Management course at CUT and as part of an International Business course at UV. The ESP model adopted in both universities reflects *Theme-based CBI* courses which involve the selection of topics or themes of specific interest and relevance to the learners. "The theme of each unit serves to contextualize new language that is presented and provides the point of departure for skill- and language-based instruction and practice" (Brinton, Snow, and Wesche, 2003: 4). The project adopted English as a Lingua Franca (ELF) configuration and was aligned with the two university courses' curricula at the two institutions which revolved around the areas of international business, management, entrepreneurship, and innovation. The educational intervention aimed at integrating culture in the two aforementioned courses and the development of critical skills of utmost importance in the students' future personal lives as well as their prospective professional careers. Intercultural encounters, whether physical or virtual, are very likely in the 21st century, which is characterised by a remarkable growth in ICT and increased migration. The highly competitive world we live in presents people, especially younger ones, as well as older people adapting (or not) in the workforce, with new challenges in everyday life and at the workplace.

The BEGIN project design was based on the current needs of students as citizens in a society that calls for enhanced competence in dealing with diverse groups of people both at personal and at professional level, and specifically in the spheres of business, management, entrepreneurship, and innovation. The project involved ESP learners in synchronous and asynchronous communication and collaborative completion of tasks via various Google applications, such as Google+ Communities, Hangouts, Gmail, Google Forms, and Google Drive, as illustrated in Figure 6.1. Target competences of the BEGIN project included intercultural communicative competence as defined by Byram (1997), as well as discipline-specific language learning in the Business Management and International Business domains.

The project was completed by 78 participants over the course of one semester, from September to December, during which participants interacted asynchronously on a weekly basis on the aforementioned platforms. In addition, they interacted synchronously in pairs or small groups (each pair was made up of participants from the two universities participating in the project). These synchronous interactions were carried out through Hangouts videoconferencing and took place at the beginning of the project, halfway through the project, and at the end of the project. The first synchronous meeting helped participants get to know each other and break the ice, as well as solve several problems

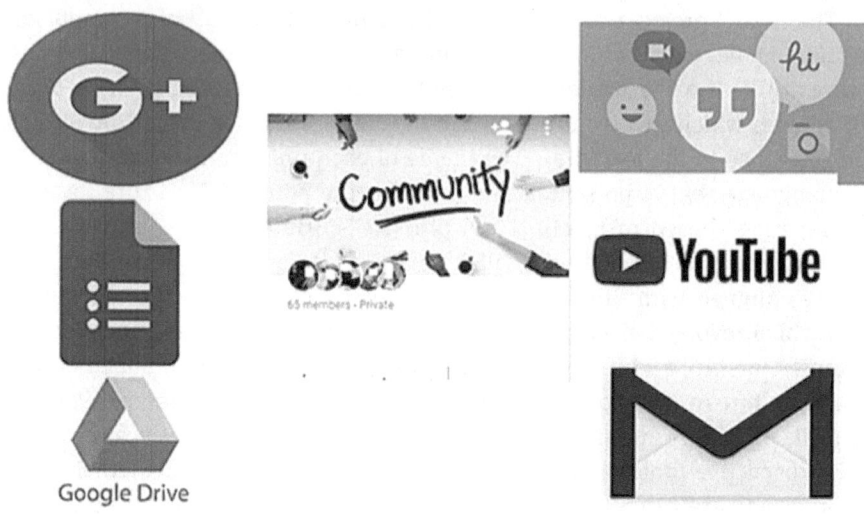

**Figure 6.1:** Overview of applications used in the BEGIN project. Source: the authors.

collaboratively by discussing the scenarios listed in Table 6.1 and coming up with possible solutions by following the steps summarised in Table 6.2:

**Table 6.1:** List of business scenarios used in the BEGIN virtual exchange project for collaborative problem solving. Source: adapted from Sevilla-Pavón and Nicolaou (2019).

| List of BEGIN virtual exchange project's problem-solving scenarios |
|---|
| 1  "A US publishing company collaborating with a French architectural firm" |
| 2  "An angry customer checks in at a hotel and loses something of value" |
| 3  "Several colleagues get stuck in the office lift on the top floor of the building on a Friday evening and the emergency alarm does not work, there is no signal for their mobile phones and they need to choose only eight objects with which to survive the weekend". |
| 4  "Misunderstandings between a German and a Chinese company during a business trip: high-context vs. low-context cultures" |
| 5  "Brand blurring and stretching: presenting your new product, the (new) brand name, the packaging, the positioning strategy, and a promotional idea to raise brand awareness" |
| 6  "Culture shock on the subway: an Italian businessperson on a business trip to the US" |

**Table 6.2:** Summary of the steps followed when collaboratively solving the business scenarios of the BEGIN virtual exchange project. Source: adapted from Sevilla-Pavón and Nicolaou (2019).

| BEGIN virtual exchange project's problem-solving scenarios: STEPS |
| --- |
| 1  Writing the title of the scenario. |
| 2  Identifying and describing the problem. |
| 3  Thinking of possible explanations why the participants are facing this situation, what went wrong and what each of the participants could have done in order to avoid this situation. |
| 4  Suggesting hypothetical solutions to the problem (giving two or three possible solutions). |
| 5  Evaluating the proposed solutions and selecting the best alternative (choosing the proposed solution which would best solve the problem). |

Meanwhile, the second synchronous meeting helped students organise their work for the completion of their final collaborative assignment: an entrepreneurial idea in the form of a product, service or initiative aimed at addressing a gap in the market and being appealing to the consumers of both the context of the Cypriot culture and the Spanish culture. Students had to consider the aspects of market segmentation, innovation, feasibility, marketability, competitive advantage, and cost. The participants' final collaborative output had to be completed in groups and presented in the form of a digital story and a business pitch supported by audiovisual resources such as PowerPoint or Prezi presentations. Apart from the multimedia outputs, participants were required to collaborate towards the production of a business plan and an investor's report. Table 6.3 summarises the steps of the main virtual exchange task:

**Table 6.3:** Summary of the steps followed when collaboratively working on the main task of the BEGIN virtual exchange project. Source: adapted from Sevilla-Pavón and Nicolaou (2019); Nicolaou (2020).

| BEGIN virtual exchange project's main task: STEPS |
| --- |
| 1  Reading the scenario and brainstorming ideas in their groups about the new product (a good, service, app, a hybrid, an initiative). |
| 2  Brainstorming on the structure of their story. The students from the Cypriot university focused on the pricing strategy, distribution, promotion, advertising, product launch and sales promotion, competing products or technologies, and strategies, such as packaging, branding and guarantee. The students from the Spanish university focused on market research, business plan, introduction of the team and type of company, design, features and consumer benefits, and feasibility. |

**Table 6.3** (continued)

| BEGIN virtual exchange project's main task: STEPS |
|---|
| 3  Composing and exchanging scripts providing peer feedback to each other. |
| 4  Producing and sharing digital stories and delivering business pitches. |
| 5  Adopting the role of a strategic investor, evaluating the innovative products and elaborating an investor's report. |
| 6  Assessing their own and their peers' digital stories by exchanging review comments and by filling in assessment sheets. |
| 7  Participating in a fictitious business fair and receiving awards for best digital story and business pitch. |

figures 6.2 and 6.3 show examples of some of the students' entrepreneurial ideas, which were presented as digital stories. The first example shows a screenshot of the digital story about "Passionate Travellers App". It was an app developed by BEGIN project participants in order to assist travellers with orienting themselves, providing them with multilingual information. As for the second example, it has to do with a digital story about another group's entrepreneurial idea, "WardrApp", which consists in an application that can assist consumers in making cost-effective and fashionable choices while being at home.

**Figure 6.2:** Example 1 of an entrepreneurial idea presented in the form of a digital story by BEGIN project participants: Passionate Travellers App. Source: the authors.

Chapter 6 Developing intercultural communicative competence in ESP — 127

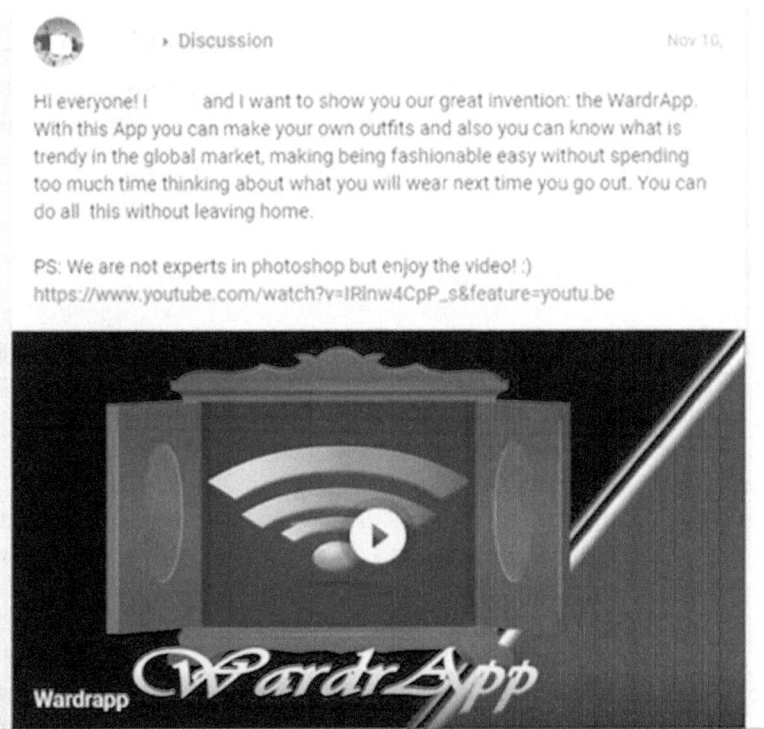

**Figure 6.3:** Example 2 of an entrepreneurial idea presented in the form of a digital story by BEGIN project participants: WardrApp. Source: the authors.

The project's tasks (Nicolaou and Sevilla-Pavón 2017; Sevilla-Pavón and Nicolaou 2019; Nicolaou 2020; Sevilla-Pavón and Nicolaou 2020) were structured based on Salmon's five-stage model for online collaborative learning (2013) and included introductory tasks during the 'Access and Motivation' stage, ice-breaking tasks during the 'Socialisation' stage, and sharing experiences, discussions around stereotypes, cross-cultural business and globalisation during the 'Information Exchange' stage. The project implied sustained interaction and collaborative work throughout the five stages. The most challenging stage of the project, the 'Knowledge Construction' stage, involved the global business scenarios problem-solving task, the elaboration of various business-related documents – such as a business plan -, and the digital storytelling task. This was followed by evaluation and reflection tasks in the 'Development' stage, as well as during all the previous stages. Through the various tasks and activities, learners were required to adopt a global mindset situated at simulated business settings in which they might find themselves in their future professional careers. The task sequence was supported by both universities' institutional ESP syllabi in terms of concepts and lexis pertaining to the areas of entrepreneurship, corporate social responsibility, innovation, marketing, product development, promotion and advertising, as well as financing start-ups, and investment (Nicolaou 2020).

## 4 Theoretical framework

The BEGIN project adopted a socio-constructivist approach with an ecological perspective. The socio-constructivist aspect of the project was reflected in the learner-centred, task-based approach that was followed. The tasks were designed in such a way to promote collaborative inquiry and the social construction of knowledge (Nicolaou and Sevilla-Pavón 2016). "An ecological approach aims to look at the learning process, the actions and activities of teachers and learners, the multilayered nature of interaction and language use, in all their complexity and as a network of interdependencies among all the elements in the setting, not only at the social level, but also at the physical and symbolic level" (van Lier 2010: 3). The project was a redesigned version of a previous one, and in its new form it aspired to offer students a dynamic learning context that would be rich in affordances (Sevilla-Pavón and Nicolaou 2017; Nicolaou 2020). According to Gibson's theory of affordances (2014), an affordance is the possibility of an action on an object or environment. This affordance is directly perceptible by the organism; therefore, the meaning of the objects in the environment is directly apparent to the agent acting in it. To exemplify the affordances, Gibson used examples, such as "a substance such as an apple as *eat-able*, an object such as a stone as *throw-able* . . . In each case, the affordance property is possessed by a bearer relative to a specific organism or class of organisms" (Scarantino 2003: 950). The BEGIN project, in its redesigned form, was informed by Gibson's theory and the ecological theory (van Lier 2004) applied in CALL settings (Dey-Plissonneau and Blin 2016) and was designed in such a way that affordances of developing intercultural communicative competence, as well as enhancing discipline-specific linguistic skills, would be optimised in the virtual exchange. Through the structure of the virtual exchange project and particularly the design of tasks, there was an effort to make such affordances perceptible and therefore acted upon by learners (Hoven and Palalas 2011). In addition, the project was viewed with a holistic perspective; therefore, relationships between learners, teachers, artefacts, materials, departments, institutions and networks were explored (Nicolaou 2020).

Therefore, within an ecological perspective, the BEGIN project was implemented in a context (ESP courses) which was compatible with learners' interests and academic needs. Tasks and expected outcomes (artefacts) revolved around themes that were aligned with students' academic curricula. Surrounding contextual elements were also considered, namely the two institutions' internationalisation policies, the resources provided at each, the technological infrastructure, as well as corresponding class schedules. In addition, since this project was designed with a lingua franca configuration, the students' levels of English were taken into consideration. The instructors pursued comparable linguistic and academic levels of students in order to enhance reciprocity and mutuality, meaning that students with similar English and general academic levels were paired together. Moreover, additional scaffolding was deemed important and was hence provided to the students. Finally, with a view towards establishing rapport, interdependence and connection among students, the BEGIN project required a number of collaborative tasks with frequent synchronous exchanges, followed by regular reflective work (Nicolaou and Sevilla-Pavón 2017; Nicolaou 2020; Sevilla-Pavón and Nicolaou 2020). All these elements, namely the institutional context, participants, resources, institutions' provisions and constraints, technological tools, networks, linguistic proficiency, task structure and sequence, themes, timetabling, and artefacts comprised the elements of the virtual exchange project's ecosystem.

# 5 Methodology

## 5.1 Settings and procedure

The methodological approach adopted for the BEGIN project was strongly informed by the principles of Design-Based Research (DBR) (Brown 1992; Collins 1992), "a methodology designed by and for educators that seeks to increase the impact, transfer, and translation of education research into improved practice" (Anderson and Shattuck 2012: 16). DBR can, thus, be understood as an emerging educational paradigm situated in a real educational context where an intervention takes place. It consists in continuous cycles of design, enactment, analysis, and redesign for the development of practical design principles, patterns or grounded theorizing (Anderson and Shattuck 2012; Brown 1992; Collins 1992). The fact that design-based research places a strong emphasis on the context of learning and on how the constituent parts of educational ecosystems form a whole (Blyth 2009) rendered this a suitable methodology for this particular project.

## 5.2 Data collection and research instruments

In line with DBR, the BEGIN project involved a mixed-methods methodological approach with a wide array of data collected by means of pre- and post-intervention questionnaires and focus group interviews with learners. In addition, data were triangulated with learners' reflective papers. Specifically, a pre-intervention questionnaire was designed for the purposes of this study and was administered to students during the 'Access and Motivation' stage of the project in the form of an online survey. The pre-intervention questionnaire collected data pertaining to the students' cultural awareness via 13 Likert scale items which aimed at identifying the students' level of cultural awareness. A post-intervention questionnaire was also designed for the purposes of this study and was administered to students during the 'Development' stage of the project, upon completion of all virtual exchange tasks. The post-intervention questionnaire aimed at collecting data pertaining to any measurable changes in the students' levels of cultural awareness after participating in the BEGIN educational intervention. Therefore, the Cultural Awareness section with the 13 Likert-scale items that appeared in the pre-survey also appeared in the post survey in the same, identical form.

Additional data were gathered by means of focus group interviews with student participants upon completion of all telecollaborative activities. Several focus group interviews were conducted with randomly created groups of four to five participants. A teaching assistant led, and audio recorded the interviews, which were then transcribed for their analysis. Their goal was to involve students in an in-depth reflection and discussion on emerging themes pertaining to the virtual exchange project. Among other themes, the development of cultural awareness was discussed along with the development of discipline-specific knowledge. A sample of the questions discussed in the focus group interviews is shown in the following table:

**Table 6.4:** Sample of the BEGIN virtual exchange project's focus group interview questions. Source: Sevilla Pavón and Nicolaou, (2019); Nicolaou (2020).

| Questions for the BEGIN virtual exchange project's focus group interviews |
|---|
| 1  Describe your experience participating in the BEGIN virtual exchange project as part of your English for Specific Purposes course at the University. Have your expectations from the project been satisfied? |
| 2  What issues have arisen from your work with foreign students through virtual exchange? What has gone smoothly and what has been challenging in this work? What has been the greatest difficulty? |

**Table 6.4** (continued)

| Questions for the BEGIN virtual exchange project's focus group interviews |
|---|
| 3   When interacting with your foreign partners, how did you ensure that communication was effective? How did you overcome problems/difficulties in working with distant partners from abroad? |
| 4   What have you learned from this virtual exchange (about yourself, your foreign partners, other cultures, your university degree, entrepreneurship, society)? |
| 5   How has your participation in this virtual exchange changed the way you view other cultures/ethnicities? |
| 6   How has your participation in the virtual exchange activities affected your . . .<br>. . . language skills?<br>. . . digital (technology) skills?<br>. . . relationship with your fellow students?<br>. . . relationship with your teacher?<br>. . . knowledge and skills relating to your degree? |
| 7   What was the role of technology in this project? How has technology helped? What were you able to do/achieve in this project thanks to technology? |
| 8   Is there anything you would add/change in this project? (tasks, digital tools, time spent, duration) |

Data were triangulated with students' reflection papers which were assigned at the beginning, middle, and end of the project. Reflection papers required students to individually describe their feelings about the project and how these evolved over its different phases, the challenges they faced, the perceived benefits of the project, the domain-specific skills they developed, and whether this project had changed their views and attitudes towards other cultures and ethnicities. Participants wrote their reflection papers after they had each of their three synchronous meetings and submitted them through the Moodle platforms of their respective universities. They were analysed qualitatively using the NVivo software, following Thematic Analysis (TA). "Thematic analysis (TA) is a method for identifying, analyzing, and interpreting patterns of meaning ("themes") across qualitative data" (Clarke and Braun 2017: 297). TA helped identify the specific themes which emerged in the students' writings and enabled researchers to compare those themes with the ones identified in the discussions.

## 5.3 Participants

Seventy-eight (N=78) university students participated in the BEGIN project, which has been described in detail in section 3. Forty-five (N=45) students were enrolled in the Business Management course at CUT and thirty (N=33) students were enrolled in the International Business course at UV. The participants from both countries were between 18 and 25 years of age and their English proficiency level was between B1 (intermediate) and B2 (upper intermediate) according to the Common European Framework of Reference for Languages (CEFR Council of Europe 2001; 2018). For the purposes of this study, data analysis refers to the development of the participants' intercultural awareness and discipline-specific knowledge using findings from both quantitative and qualitative data.

Out of the 78 students who participated in the BEGIN project, 72 students completed the pre-intervention questionnaire, 45 from CUT and 27 from UV. The post-intervention questionnaire was completed by 67 students, 40 students from CUT and 27 from UV. The qualitative data gathered from the two questionnaires were analysed in IBM SPSS Statistics, version 5.[1] The analyses which were performed include frequencies, Cronbach's alpha reliability test, as well as Wilcoxon matched-pairs signed-ranks test. In addition, 41 students participated in the focus group interviews, 31 from CUT and 10 from UV. Finally, numerous reflection papers were collected from students at both universities. For the purposes of this study, data will be reported from the students' final reflection papers, 22 from CUT and 28 from UV. Qualitative data from both the focus group interviews and the final reflection papers were analysed using NVivo,[2] version 11. The qualitative analysis involved the coding of data in different categories, as well as the creation of annotations and memos corresponding to the categories.

# 6 Results and discussion

This section will present and discuss the results of the quantitative and qualitative data analysis. The first part will demonstrate the results pertaining to the development of students' intercultural communicative competence while the second part

---

[1] SPSS stands for Statistical Package for the Social Sciences and is a software package used to manage and analyse quantitative data, produced by SPSS Inc. and acquired by IBM in 2009.
[2] NVivo is a computer software package for qualitative or unstructured data analysis produced by QSR International.

will present the results related to the enhancement of their discipline-specific knowledge.

## 6.1 Intercultural communicative competence

The pre- and post-intervention questionnaires[3] included a section labelled "Cultural Awareness" which comprised 13 questions that indicated attitude towards other cultures on a 7-point Likert scale, where 1 meant 'Completely Disagree' and 7 meant 'Completely Agree'. The 13 questions of this part of the questionnaire were completed by student participants prior to the BEGIN intervention and upon its completion, 14 weeks later. As mentioned earlier, between the two questionnaires students interacted asynchronously on a weekly basis (on their online forum, etc.) and they also had three synchronous meetings (via videoconference on platforms such as Google Hangouts). These questions aimed at measuring the students' levels of cultural awareness before and after the intercultural intervention and to note any changes in these levels.

A Cronbach's alpha reliability test was used as a measure of internal consistency so as to determine how closely related the 13 items were as a group. The analysis indicated a high level of internal consistency for the scale with the specific sample (0.894). A reliability coefficient of .70 or higher is considered acceptable in most social science research studies. Table 6.5 shows the reliability of the set of thirteen questions (items):

**Table 6.5:** Cronbach's Alpha in items measuring cultural awareness.

| Cronbach's Alpha | N of Items |
|---|---|
| .894 | 13 |

In order to analyse the pre and post data in the specific part of the questionnaire, a non-parametric Wilcoxon matched-pairs signed-rank test was carried out in SPSS. The mean score of the set of 13 questions was compared with 56 matched pairs of students. Pairs were matched based on the students' dates of birth which they had indicated in the demographics section of both the pre- and post-intervention questionnaires. The respondents' birthday date was

---

[3] This questionnaire can be found at: https://roderic.uv.es/handle/10550/66409

selected as the criterion to ensure the reliability of the results through same-individual pre-treatment/post-treatment comparisons. The Wilcoxon signed rank test determined the existence of statistically significant differences (p=0,014) between the pre and post data with regard to the whole set of thirteen items for the students who participated in the intervention and whose dates of birth were matched. Table 6.6 demonstrates the mean scores in the thirteen items included in the 'Cultural Awareness' section of the questionnaire prior to students' participation in the virtual exchange project and upon completion of their participation:

**Table 6.6:** Wilcoxon signed rank test for comparison between pre- and post-intervention data.

| Mean After-Mean Before | N | Mean Rank | Sum of Ranks |
| --- | --- | --- | --- |
| Negative Ranks | 20[a] | 22,80 | 456,00 |
| Positive Ranks | 34[b] | 30,26 | 1029,00 |
| Ties | 2[c] | | |
| Total | 56 | | |

The Wilcoxon signed rank test presented in Table 6.7 demonstrates the significance between the mean scores found, as the p-value is lower than 0.05:

**Table 6.7:** Difference between pre and post-intervention data.

| | Mean After – Mean Before |
| --- | --- |
| Z | −2.470[b] |
| Asymp. Sig. (2-tailed) | **0.014** |

a. Wilcoxon signed-rank test.
b. Based on negative ranks.

Qualitative data were collected upon completion of the BEGIN project in order to perform an in-depth examination of the students' opinions about the project. In this paper, the qualitative data are represented using CUT or UV to indicate the student's university followed by a number given to each participant in order to replace his/her name for the purposes of anonymity. The students' comments gathered from the focus group interviews and reflections papers indicate that the virtual exchange project was positively received by the students and that despite challenges, such as difficulty to coordinate collaborative tasks, meeting deadlines, and utilising multimodal technologies, the experience was perceived by most students as conducive to the development of knowledge of other cultures. These comments confirmed the students' feelings (as 60% of the students "completely agreed" with that statement) of having been closer to other cultures thanks to the project which they reported in the post-questionnaire:

> It was a really exciting experience with the foreign partners . . . we learned new things about each other and about our cultures and it was very interesting to learn about Spain because it is very similar to our culture. (CUT 01)

A student from UV refers to the teamwork, negotiation and interpersonal skills developed through participation in the virtual exchange project, thus building on the participants' response in the post-questionnaire, where 65.5% of students expressed the view that the project had been "very helpful" in those respects:

> All this has given to me the opportunity to understand how difficult it is to reach an agreement between the different members of a team. However, the effort is completely worth it because what we've done all together is impossible to do separately, it is called synergy. Furthermore, I have learnt the importance of self-confidence and emotional intelligence which are fundamental specially working with people you have never met. (UV 02)

Another student from UV refers to some cultural knowledge acquired along with knowledge relevant to the academic curriculum and future professional career. As the main project task required the conceptual creation of a new product that would be able to sell in both cultural contexts involved in this exchange, the students had to inform each other about the local markets, consumer trends, and standard of living, among others. In addition, the students had to come to an agreement in the problem-solving task as they were required to decide on viable solutions to the ill-structured problems presented in the scenarios.

> First of all, I can say I have learned lots of things about Cyprus, some of them pretty curious (Did you know that men needed to go to the army by two years since they finished highschool? That sounds really [rare] WEIRD, doesn't it?) But I have also learned some business issues that might be important for my future and for my academic training in my degree (how to deal with foreigners, speak with them and getting a final agreement seems to be easier from the outside, but, I can tell you, it is not.) (UV 03)

Two students from CUT mention how learning about another culture led to the appreciation of other cultures in different countries and the elimination of prejudice:

> By taking part to this project, I learned about other cultures especially for the University of Valencia. Now I can see and appreciate the cultures of other countries. (CUT 03)

> This Telecollaboration project helps me to get rid of any prejudices that I had for people in foreign countries and cultures. (CUT 06)

A student from the UV refers to the knowledge of another culture that was unknown before the virtual exchange project and mentions the drive to discover this new culture through images and information:

> I have always been interested in other countries and cultures and this is one of the reasons why I chose this degree, so for me this project has been an opportunity to know more from this country. In fact, even I am so interested in other countries I didn't know anything about Cyprus and now I feel like I know much more. This project has created in me more interest and I have looked for photos and some information of Cyprus too. (UV 011)

These comments and many others noted in the focus groups interviews and reflection papers[4] indicate that the BEGIN project was an enriching experience that helped students develop their intercultural communicative competence through their exposure to and interaction with a new, and in many cases, unknown culture. Furthermore, in some cases, the students' interactions even changed their views about other cultures in general. This was manifested in an attitude of openness and curiosity for exploring foreign cultures and developing an understanding of local practices. In addition, the students' development of intercultural communicative competence is reflected in their enhancement of skills in negotiating different cultural perspectives during their collaborative task engagement. The collaborative activities of the virtual exchange implied a discussion of their ideas and identification of solutions, explaining and negotiating perspectives and finally establishing an agreement within their international groups. This process contributed to the students' acknowledgement of the importance of self-confidence and emotional intelligence in a spirit of respect for different opinions. Finally, in some cases, the project seems to have contributed to the reduction of prejudice towards other cultures and a general appreciation of other ethnic backgrounds.

## 6.2 Discipline-specific knowledge

Content-based knowledge related to the students' academic domains seems to have developed through the BEGIN virtual exchange project. According to the qualitative data collected, the project was perceived as being useful in terms of communication, internationalisation, and knowledge about Business Management and International Business. In addition, the project was beneficial for the student's future academic and professional training as it entailed cross-cultural encounters and the establishment of an agreement with people of diverse origins. The benefits

---

4 A sample of the Reflective Essay directions and guidelines can be found at https://roderic.uv.es/handle/10550/78098

of the project, such as the development of openness to other cultures, seem to have been associated by learners with their current studies. Being able to interact and communicate with people from other countries who live abroad and who have different ideologies is critical in the particular degree and future profession. A student from CUT notes:

> Being more open is part of our major's themes as well. We deal with customers, with . . . the spectrum is very wide and I believe that this project has helped in . . . let's say in talking to people you don't know, who are not even living in your own country, who don't have the same ideologies as you, let's say. (CUT 02)

In addition, content knowledge related to the students' field of study seems to have developed through the specific project tasks. The video, which consisted in a 3 to 4-minute long digital story presenting the students' entrepreneurial ideas to address a gap in the market and be appealing to the consumers of both the context of the Cypriot culture and the Spanish culture, seems to have built on students' critical thinking and evaluation abilities as they had to think about the content and the audience to which this was addressed:

> I believe that the tasks helped us a lot, and the video we did. That was our first time, and it helped us with our degree, because we had created it ourselves, we had thought about it, we did everything on our own. (CUT 025)

The perception of the digital story as being a driving force in the project was confirmed by students' quantitative responses in the post-questionnaire, as 56.4% of respondents considered this part of the project was "very motivating". Similarly, the students seem to have acknowledged the benefits of the task sequence and topics towards the enhancement of discipline-specific knowledge in the field of business. In the following comment, a student from UV highlights the relevance of both the digital story and the scenario problem-solving tasks they were asked to complete collaboratively:

> I think that the activities we have carried out have been related with our degree, so at the time we were practicing English we were also treating business fields. For example, with the video it was a good way to practice marketing and how to sell the product, and when we did the Scenarios Problem Solving we were dealing with possible business problems that we might have in the future. Apart of the telecollaboration, what has really helped us it's been that we have done a lot of activities in class. Another thing that I have improved thanks to the presentations is talking in public and speaking more confidently. (UV 014)

In the following quote, a UV student indicates that the virtual exchange project was beneficial as it included situations similar to international life, especially in the field of business. Through the project, the students received information from different perspectives through the collaborative tasks which involved active cooperation and positive interdependence within their international groups. In order to complete the problem-solving scenarios and the digital story, the students were required to engage in a process of discussing ideas, agreeing, disagreeing, explaining, clarifying, negotiating perspectives, and finally reaching an agreement. That is something they will be called upon to do in their future career in business. This aspect of the project was valued by some students. In the case of the comment below, by a student from the "International Business" degree, he/she pointed out how the project had helped them develop different skills connected to this degree. This coincides with some of the goals of the International Business degree, as highlighted in the UV webpage:[5] one of the main goals of this degree is to answer the needs of local companies and bodies who work in an international context. In a more and more globalised economy, public companies and institutions need specialists who will support the process of internationalisation. Therefore, the International Business degree intends to provide students with the knowledge and tools required to make economic and financial, business and marketing decisions, while enabling them to consider the determining factors and the international repercussions. As a result, the degree fosters the development of skills connected to managing the international development of a company, as well as skills to work in the international institutions involved in transactions and international cooperation. Therefore, the main foci of the degree are, on the one hand, the analysis of the international economy and, on the other hand, learning languages, especially English:

> Probably, the most important aspects to talk about are the knowledge and skills related to my degree. It is clear that the improvement of my acquaintanceship is what made me feel worried at the beginning because, nowadays, my degree is one of the most important things in my life. Working with this project has been the best idea that teachers could ever have due to the meaning of my objective with International Business. As the name of the degree shows, we have to take information from different countries to get a general view of the international life, especially about businesses, which is the topic that we have worked as a whole. (UV 01)

Moreover, students seem to have learned vocabulary related to their field of study. This acquisition of new knowledge was acquired in a hands-on way (through project work) as students used the concepts and vocabulary in the tasks they were engaged in. The project's tasks implied the use of discipline-specific lexis both at the stage of negotiation within their English as a Lingua Franca interaction with foreign partners, as well as during the stage of collaborative

---

5 Available at: https://www.uv.es/uvweb/college/en/undergraduate-studies/undergraduate-studies-/degree-programmes-offered/degree-international-business-1285846094474/Titulacio.html?id=1285847460674

elaboration of business-related documents (business plan, investor's report), and the production of the digital story and business pitch which demonstrated an entrepreneurial idea. These tasks were supported by the two institutions' academic curricula and materials, such as lecture notes, articles and readings pertaining to entrepreneurship and innovation:

> Besides this, I have been able to improve my English skills and I have learnt new vocabulary that [it] will be helpful in the future, I'm sure of that. (UV 015)

Finally, students seem to have adopted an entrepreneurial mindset and got engaged in business activities, such as the elaboration of reports and the development of a product:

> This telecollaboration project has been useful to improve my knowledge and skills related to International Business, as I have had the chance to think like a businesswoman and do some reports about developing a product, which will certainly be helpful in the next years of university. Also, as my degree is oriented towards internationalization, this project has helped me improve my communication skills, not only with my partners from my degree but also with other students from Cyprus. (UV 022)

Overall, the BEGIN virtual exchange project seems to have been meaningful and useful for the students in terms of their field of study and future careers in business. The results of the project indicate that the aim of employing a content-based approach in virtual exchange has been fulfilled "in support of efforts for internationalisation of the curriculum through the incorporation of international, intercultural and/or global dimension into the content of the curriculum as well as the learning outcomes, assessment tasks, teaching methods and support services of a program of study" (Leask 2015: 9).

# 7 Conclusion

Given the limited literature on the instances of implementation of virtual exchange projects in university ESP courses, this project's aim was to address the need for technology-mediated projects that may develop students' cultural awareness through content-based task-design. The BEGIN project was carefully embedded in the students' academic courses and created a synergy between intercultural and ESP learning. The two instructors and researchers collected and analysed vast amounts of data, both quantitative and qualitative, which point to positive perceptions both in intercultural and discipline-specific learning. Overall, the BEGIN virtual exchange project seems to have been a valuable learning experience in many respects. These include, on the one hand, the development of aspects of intercultural communicative competence, such as an openness and curiosity for other cultures, the reduction of prejudice, and the negotiation of multiple perspectives. This is manifested in the rise of students' cultural awareness in the 13 Likert-scale items, as well as in their quotes during the focus groups and in their written reflections. On the other hand, the BEGIN project seems to have contributed to the students' enhancement of discipline-specific knowledge through the establishment of communication and internationalisation skills, as well as the acquisition of relevant ESP concepts and lexis. The researchers' efforts centred in the reformulation and refinement of a previous version of the project within an ecological framework whereby several contextual elements, such as the alignment of academic curricula, the close matching of the students' levels of English and academic performance, and the choice of topics and tasks which were relevant to the students' academic and future professional needs, were taken into consideration. This appears to have contributed to making this online exchange a dynamic environment, rich in affordances and supportive of intercultural learning within content-based language instruction. The limitation of the study lies in the absence of criticality and agency which can be engineered through social-oriented tasks, such as a social entrepreneurship project which amalgamates an innovative and profitable business idea and a human-oriented initiative in a spirit of active citizenship. The researchers acknowledged this limitation and in the subsequent iteration the tasks were reformulated towards this direction (see Sevilla-Pavón and Nicolaou 2020; Nicolaou 2020). As this study aimed at contributing to the limited implementation of virtual exchange projects embedded in content-based instruction, future research should be directed towards the design of projects situated in different areas of content-based ESP learning, beyond the field of business and economics which seem to have been more prevalent in the studies reviewed.

# References

Aguilar Pérez, Marta. 2018. Integrating intercultural competence in ESP and EMI: From theory to practice. *ESP today* 6 (1). 25–43. https://doi.org/10.18485/esptoday.2018.6.1.2

Anderson, Terry & Julie Shattuck. 2012. Design-based research: A decade of progress in education research? *Educational researcher* 41 (1). 16–25. DOI: 10.3102/0013189X11428813

Beelen, Jos & Elspeth Jones. 2015. Redefining internationalization at home. In: Adrian Curaj, Liviu Matei, Remus Pricopie, Jamil Salmi & Peter Scott (eds.), *The European higher education area*, 59–72. Springer, Cham. https://doi.org/10.1007/978-3-319-20877-0_5 (accessed 9 December 2020).

Bennett, Janet. 2011. Developing intercultural competence. In 2011 Association of international education administrators conference workshop, San Francisco, CA. https://www.mes

siah.edu/download/downloads/id/923/developing_intercultural_competencefor_international_education_faculty_and_staff.pdf (accessed 12 January 2021).

Blyth, Carl. 2009. From textbook to online materials: The changing ecology of foreign language publishing in the era of ICT. In Michael J. Evans (ed.), *Foreign language learning with digital technology*, 174–202. London: Bloomsbury Academic. http://dx.doi.org/10.5040/9781474212052.ch-008

Brinton, Donna. 2012. Content-based instruction in English for Specific Purposes. *The encyclopedia of applied linguistics*. Hoboken, New Jersey: Wiley Blackwell. http://dx.doi.org/10.1002/9781405198431.wbeal0191

Brinton, Donna, Marguerite Ann Snow & Marjorie Bingham Wesche. 2003. *Content-based second language instruction*. Michigan: University of Michigan Press.

Brown, Ann. 1992. Design experiments: Theoretical and methodological challenges in complex interventions in classroom settings. *The Journal of the Learning Sciences* 2(2). 141–178. http://dx.doi.org/10.1207/s15327809jls0202_2

Byram, Michael. 1997. *Teaching and assessing intercultural communicative competence*. Clevedon, UK: Multilingual Matters.

Byram, Michael, Bella Gribkova & Hugh Starkey. 2002. Developing the intercultural dimension in language teaching: A practical introduction for teachers. *Language Policy Division, Directorate of School, Out-of-School and Higher Education*, Council of Europe. http://www.tandfonline.com/doi/abs/10.1207/s15327809jls0202_2 (accessed 17 November 2020).

Byram, Michael, Prue Holmes & Nicola Savvides. 2013. Intercultural communicative competence in foreign language education: Questions of theory, practice and research. *The Language Learning Journal* 41 (3). 251–253.

Candel-Mora, Miguel Angel. 2015. Attitudes towards intercultural communicative competence of English for Specific Purposes students. *Procedia-Social and Behavioral Sciences* 178. 26–31. DOI: 10.1016/j.sbspro.2015.03.141

Cheikhrouhou, Nadia & Małgorzata Marchewka. 2020. Exploring foreign entrepreneurial ecosystems through virtual exchange. In Francesca Helm & Ana Beaven (eds). *Designing and implementing virtual exchange– a collection of case studies*, 81–91. Dublin: Research publishing.net. https://doi.org/10.14705/rpnet.2020.45.1117

Chun, Dorothy. 2015. Language and culture learning in higher education via telecollaboration. *Pedagogies: An International Journal* 10 (1). 5–21.

Clarke, Victoria & Virginia Braun. 2017. Thematic analysis. *The Journal of Positive Psychology* 12 (3). 297–298, DOI: 10.1080/17439760.2016.1262613.

Collins, Allan. 1992. Toward a design science of education. In Eileen Scanlon & Tim O'Shea (eds). *New directions in educational technology*, 15–22. Springer, Berlin, Heidelberg: Nato ASI Series. https://doi.org/10.1007/978-3-642-77750-9_2

Council of Europe. Council for Cultural Co-operation. Education Committee. Modern Languages Division. 2001. Common European Framework of Reference for Languages: learning, teaching, assessment. Cambridge University Press.

Council of Europe 2018. Common European Framework of Reference for Languages: Learning, Teaching, Assessment. Companion Volume with New Descriptors. Strasbourg: Council of Europe Publishing.

Cunningham, Darren Joseph & Nina Vyatkina. 2012. Telecollaboration for professional purposes: Towards developing a formal register in the foreign language classroom. *Canadian Modern Language Review* 68 (4). 422–450.

Deardorff, Darla. 2006. Theory reflections: Intercultural competence framework/model. *Journal of Studies in International Education* 10. 1–6.
Dey-Plissonneau, Aparajita & Françoise Blin. 2016. Emerging affordances in telecollaborative multimodal interactions. In Sake Jager, Malgorzata Kurek & Breffni O'Rourke (eds), *New directions in telecollaborative research and practice: selected papers from the second conference on telecollaboration in higher education*, 297-304). Dublin: Research-publishing.net. https://doi.org/10.14705/rpnet.2016.telecollab2016.521
Fantini, E. Alvino & Jack C. Richards. 1997. *New ways of teaching culture*. Alexandria: TESOL.
Ferreira-Lopes, Luana & Ingrid Van Rompay-Bartels. 2020. Preparing future business professionals for a globalized workplace through intercultural virtual collaboration. *Development and Learning in Organizations* 34 (2) 21–24. https://doi.org/10.1108/DLO-08-2019-0194
Gibson, James J. 2014. The theory of affordances. 1979. In Jen Jack Gieseking, William Mangold, Cindi Katz, Setha Low & Susan Saegert (eds.), *The People, Place, and Space Reader*, 90–94. Abingdon, UK: Routledge.
Godwin-Jones, Robert. 2019. Telecollaboration as an approach to developing intercultural communication competence. *Language Learning & Technology* 23 (3). 8–28.
Guariento, Bill, Nazmi Al-Masri & Anna Rolinska. 2016. Investigating EAST: A Scotland- Gaza English for Academic Study telecollaboration between SET Students. *ASEE's* (American Society for Engineering Education) 123rd Annual Conference & Exposition, New Orleans, Louisiana, USA.https://doi.org/0.18260/p.2547
Guth, Sarah & Francesca Helm (eds.). 2010. *Telecollaboration 2.0: Language, literacies and intercultural learning in the 21st century (Vol. 1)*. Bern: Peter Lang.
Háhn, Judit & Katarzyna Radke. 2020. Combining expertise from linguistics and tourism: a tale of two cities. In Francesca Helm & Ana Beaven (eds.), *Designing and implementing virtual exchange – a collection of case studies*, 11–22. Dublin: Research-publishing.net. https://doi.org/10.14705/rpnet.2020.45.1111
Helm, Francesca. 2013. A dialogic model for telecollaboration. *Bellaterra Journal of Teaching & Learning Language & Literature* 6 (2). 28–48.
Hoskins, Laüra & Alexandra Reynolds 2020. Implementing E+VE at the University of Bordeaux within English for specific purposes courses. In Francesca Helm & Ana Beaven (eds.), *Designing and implementing virtual exchange – a collection of case studies*, 179–190. Dublin: Research-publishing.net. https://doi.org/10.14705/rpnet.2020.45.1125
Hoven, Debra & Agnieszka Palalas. 2011. (Re) conceptualizing design approaches for mobile language learning. *CALICO Journal* 28 (3). 699–720.
Jooste, Nico & Savo Heleta. 2017. Global citizenship versus globally competent graduates: A critical view from the South. *Journal of Studies in International Education* 21 (1). 39–51.
Koris, Rita & Jean-François Vuylsteke. 2020. Mission (im)possible: developing students' international online business communication skills through virtual teamwork. In Francesca Helm & Ana Beaven (eds.), *Designing and implementing virtual exchange – a collection of case studies*, 69–79. Dublin: Research-publishing.net. https://doi.org/10.14705/rpnet.2020.45.1116
Kovačić, Andreja, Goran Bubaš & Tihomir Orehovački. 2012. Integrating culture into a Business English course: Students' perspective on a collaborative online writing project. 23rd Central European Conference on Information and Intelligent Systems.
Kramsch, Claire. 1995. The cultural component of language teaching. *Language, culture and curriculum* 8 (2). 83–92.

Leask, Betty. 2015. *Internationalizing the curriculum*. Abingdon, UK: Routledge.
Lee, Lina & Alfred Markey. 2014. A study of learners' perceptions of online intercultural exchange through Web 2.0 technologies. *ReCALL* 26 (3). 281–297. https://doi.org/10.1017/S0958344014000111
Levy Mike. 2007. Culture, culture learning and new technologies: Towards a pedagogical framework. Language Learning & Technology 11 (2). 104–127.
Lindner, Rachel. 2016. Developing communicative competence in global virtual teams: A multiliteracies approach to telecollaboration for students of business and economics. *CASALC Review* 1. 144–156.
McCloskey, Erin. 2012. Global teachers: a conceptual model for building teachers' intercultural competence online. *Comunicar. Media Education Research Journal* 20 (1). https://www.revistacomunicar.com/index.php?contenido=detalles&numero=38&articulo=38-2012-06 (accessed 12 September 2020).
Nicolaou, Anna. 2020. *The affordances of virtual exchange for developing global competence and active citizenship in content-based language learning*. Unpublished doctoral thesis, Trinity College Dublin, the University of Dublin.
Nicolaou, Anna & Ana Sevilla-Pavón. 2016. Exploring telecollaboration through the lens of university students. In Sake Jager, Malgorzata Kurek & Breffni O'Rourke (eds.), *New directions in telecollaborative research and practice: Selected papers from the second conference on telecollaboration in higher education*, 113–120. Dublin: Research-publishing.net. doi:10.14705/rpnet.2016.telecollab2016.497
Nicolaou, Anna & Ana Sevilla-Pavón. 2017. Redesigning a telecollaboration project towards an ecological constructivist approach. In Colpaert, Ann Aerts, Rick Kern & Mark Kaiser (eds.), *CALL in CONTEXT: Proceedings of XVIIIth International CALL Conference: CALL in Context*, 589–597. Antwerp: University of Antwerp.
Ngan, Nguyen Thi Chau. 2011. Content-based instruction in the teaching of English for Accounting at Vietnamese College of Finance and Customs. *English Language Teaching* 4 (3). 90–100.
O'Dowd, Robert. 2011. Online foreign language interaction: Moving from the periphery to the core of foreign language education? *Language Teaching* 44 (3). 368–380. http://dx.doi.org/10.1017/S0261444810000194
O'Dowd, Robert. 2016. 17. Learning from the Past and Looking to the Future of Online Intercultural Exchange. In Robert O'Dowd & Tim Lewis (eds.), *Online Intercultural Exchange: Policy, Pedagogy, Practice*, 273. Routledge: London.
O'Dowd, Robert. 2018. From telecollaboration to virtual exchange: state-of-the-art and the role of UNICollaboration in moving forward. *Journal of Virtual Exchange* 1. 1–23.
Orr, Thomas. 2002. *English for specific purposes*. Alexandria, VA.: Teachers of English to Speakers of Other Languages.
Risager, Karen. 2005. Languaculture as a key concept in language and culture teaching. In Bent Preisler, Anne Fabricius, Hartmut Haberland, Susanne Kjærbeck & Karen Risager (eds.), *The consequences of mobility: Linguistic and sociocultural contact zones*, 185–196. Roskilde, Denmark: Roskilde Universitet.
Salmon, Gilly. 2013. *E-tivities: The key to active online learning*. Abingdon, UK: Routledge.
Sapir, Edward. 2004. *Language: An introduction to the study of speech*. North Chelmsford, MA:Courier Corporation.
Scarantino, Andrea. 2003. Affordances explained. *Philosophy of Science* 70 (5). 949–961.

Sevilla-Pavón, Ana & Anna Nicolaou. 2017. Online intercultural exchanges through digital storytelling. *International Journal of Computer-Assisted Language Learning and Teaching (IJCALLT)* 7 (4). 44–58. http://call2017.language.berkeley.edu/wpcontent/uploads/2017/07/CALL2017_proceedings.pdfISBN:9789057285509.

Sevilla-Pavón, Ana & Anna Nicolaou. 2019. *Business English 3.0: Hands-on online and virtual collaboration tasks*. Granada: Editorial Comares.

Sevilla-Pavón, Ana & Anna Nicolaou. 2020. Artefact co-construction in virtual exchange: 'Youth Entrepreneurship for Society'. *Computer Assisted Language Learning* 1–26. DOI: 10.1080/09588221.2020.1825096

Stoller, Fredricka L. 2008. Content-based instruction. In Nancy H. Hornberger (ed.), *Encyclopedia of Language and Education*, 59–70. Boston, MA.: Springer. https://doi.org/10.1007/978-0-387-30424-3_89

van Lier, Leo. 2004. *The semiotics and ecology of language learning*. Utbildning & Demokrati 13 (3). 79–103.

van Lier, Leo. 2010. The ecology of language learning: Practice to theory, theory to practice. *Procedia-Social and Behavioral Sciences* 3, 2–6.

Walker, Ute Gerda & Christina vom Brocke. 2009. Integrating content-based language learning and intercultural learning online: An international eGroups collaboration. In A. Brown (ed.), *Proceedings of CLESOL 2008*, 218–235. http://hdl.handle.net/10179/7647

Wesche, Marjorie Bingham. 2010. Content-based second language instruction. In Robert B. Kaplan (ed.), *The Oxford Handbook of Applied Linguistics (2 ed)*. Oxford University Press. https://doi.org/10.1093/oxfordhb/9780195384253.013.0019

White, Cynthia. 2007. Focus on the language learner in an era of globalization: tensions, positions and practices in technology-mediated language teaching. *Language Teaching* 40 (4), 321–326.

Yuan, Pinghua & Liming Yu. 2008. An empirical study on content-based instruction in the Chinese college English context. *Foreign Language Teaching and Research* 1, 59–64.

Martin Parsons, Mikel Garant, Elizaveta Shikhova
# Chapter 7
# Video exchange telecollaboration: Towards developing interculturality in EFL environments

## 1 Introduction

Most EFL learners at the university level in Japan, China, and Russia will have studied English for several years, but have had little opportunity to use English in any meaningful way in daily life outside the classroom. Many find themselves in teacher-centered learning environments which tend to focus on rote memorization of English with a primary goal of passing tests and examinations for entry into higher levels of education (Andreeva, 2019; Kikuchi and Sakai 2009; Yeung 2017). This rarely allows for the kinds of communication opportunities thatwould assist in discussing or learning more about their own or other cultural contexts. Although it is by no means unique, it remains a fact that in EFL contexts such as Japan, China or Russia most learners will need to create situations or reasons to use English outside structured academic contexts.

In Japan, this has been further exacerbated by a trend among younger Japanese to avoid moving abroad for study or work (Haslett 2018; Sanno 2017). In recognition, the Japanese Ministry of Education, Culture, Sport, Science and Technology (MEXT) has been eager to develop more technologically capable, internationally minded students, calling for educational approaches which promote information and communications technology approaches such as blended learning, flipped-classes, and approaches that will develop a knowledge-based society and global human resources (2008, 2010, 2013).

The Chinese Ministry of Education (MOE) has also made efforts to create a culture of learning that emphasizes an outward view. Together with the Chinese government's Belt and Road Initiative, Ministry of Education initiatives aim to develop in Chinese students the ability to discuss Chinese culture in English (MOE 2019a). New educational approaches have also been advocated in China stressing the use of critical thinking (MOE 2018). And while the MOE has reported that some

---

**Martin Parsons,** Hannan University, Japan, E-mail: mp@hannan-u.ac.jp
**Mikel Garant,** Beijing Institute of Technology, Zhuhai, China, E-mail: mikel.garant@cgt.bitzh.edu.cn
**Elizaveta Shikhova,** ITMO University, Russia, E-mail: e.shikhova@itmo.ru

https://doi.org/10.1515/9783110727364-008

662,100 students were studying abroad in 2018 (MOE 2019b), this is little more than a drop in the ocean of the total number of Chinese students, most of whom still have little or no opportunity to interact directly with foreigners.

Within the Russian context, the Russian Ministry of Education underlines the importance of "the cultural capital" of every student, i.e. richness in a form of basic cultural values; intellectual, moral and social characteristics, that form the professional competence of a modern student (Lapteva et al. 2012). The Russian Ministry of Education also clearly states that one of the goals of EFL education is to equip students with advanced, practical language skills for further self-education and solving social and communicative problems in everyday life and in professional situations (Samoylova et al. 2014). Unfortunately, those high ideals do not correspond with reality, most evidently in the lack of contact hours in the bachelor level curriculum essential to achieving such goals. The number of contact hours for EFL decreases sharply in the master level curriculum, although it is at this level of education that future graduates are expected to actively engage in the process of mastering professional norms and values.

The historical and cultural relations between Japan and China encompass more than 1,000 years of interaction, involving a vast and diverse range of cultural exchange, particularly in terms of cultural borrowing by Japan from China, from orthography to art, religion and ethics, cuisine and more. However, in recent times relations between the two countries have been strained over events in the latter years of the 19$^{th}$ century and the first half of the 20$^{th}$ century. Residual concerns from these events continue to create friction in political, cultural and popular spheres. Suzuki (2007: 38) notes that for the Chinese, the history of Japanese aggression still matters. It has transcended generations and is not limited to people who personally experienced World War II. Nor is this a one-sided phenomenon. A survey conducted by the Pew Research Center (2020) found that 85% of Japanese people have an unfavorable view of China.

Relations between Japan and Russia and the former Soviet Union have not covered such a long period or been as closely interwoven. However, there have been flashpoints along the way, including a brief war in 1904–5 and frosty relations since the end of WWII. Two bones of contention on the Japanese side relate to the final days of the war and its aftermath. Russia entered the war against Japan shortly before WWII ended and claimed territory north of Hokkaido, known as the Kuril Islands in the West and the Northern Territories in Japan, leading to a dispute over ownership that has yet to be settled. Japan was also angered by the forced evacuation from Chinese territory of thousands of Japanese after WWII, many of whom ended up in Russian prison camps. According to Hook et al. (2012: 371), opportunities to create closer political ties with Russia after the collapse of the Soviet Union were "constrained . . . by domestic public opinion opposed to developing closer relations whilst the Northern Territories dispute continued unresolved." Research by the Pew Research Center (2020) suggests that 69% of Japanese have an unfavorable view of Russia.

Political relationsbetween Russia and China have been relatively good since the dissolution of the Soviet Union in 1989, but this has not always been the case. In fact, they have experienced a centuries-old history of international relations, which have had their ups and downs (Sevalnev and Cherepanova 2020). The first diplomatic contacts between Imperial Russia and the Qing Dynasty can be traced to the 17$^{th}$ century. This period of collaboration can be characterized by the discovery of long-rooted differences between the two cultures. Ambassadors played the role of mediators (Myasnikov 1980) and in 1689, the first treaty between Russia and China was signed. It consolidated a trade agreement between the two countries and contributed to the development of peaceful bilateral relations.

However, in the mid-1800s the previous peaceful relations came to an end as China was forced to sign a series of Unequal Treaties with various countries (Imperial Russia and Japan being among them), seen in China as the beginning of the Century of Humiliation that ended on October 1, 1949 with the foundation of the People's Republic of China (Lo 2010). Scholars from both countries consider the participation of Imperial Russia in the suppression of the Boxer Rebellion in China one of the key causal factors for the period of alienation in Sino-Russian relations, which lasted until the first quarter of the 20$^{th}$ century. In 1924, diplomatic relations blossomed briefly between the newly founded Soviet Union and China only to be broken again in 1927 and the two countries remained estranged throughout the 1950s. After the fall of the Soviet Union in 1991, China was one of the first states to recognize the new government of the Russian Federation leading to better, though imperfect, relations.

In recent years, international trends appear to indicate increasing political polarization in many parts of the world so that even small issues between countries can become exacerbated. To avoid and resolve such issues, better understanding of the cultural mores of other societies is required, something in which education has a role to play. During a time of global pandemic, where travel restrictions make international and inter-cultural collaborations more difficult than usual, devising methods of praxis which take advantage of the affordances of the internet becomes essential. This chapter describes a supra-national, collaborative project, in which students from universities in Japan, China, and Russia used video podcasting technology and peer-feedback via the internet to attempt to promote intercultural understanding by planning, writing, recording and editing video podcasts in English, based on cultural and historical events from their own country.

## 2 Interculturality in the language classroom

The notion of culture is fluid, encompassing many different viewpoints which may evolve differently in place and over time. A universally accepted definition is difficult to formulate, though in broad-brush terms, culture can be thought of as the values, practices and beliefs of a particular group of people. Therefore, as Moeller and Nugent (2014) note, any definition of interculturality comes with a large degree of ambiguity. Even the terminology surrounding the notion is ambiguous, with terms such as intercultural understanding, intercultural awareness, intercultural communication, and intercultural competence being commonly "used to refer to the same concept and . . . the use of terminology is often inconsistent and confusing" (Schauer 2016). Deardorff (2006) defines intercultural competence, a widely used term, as the "ability to communicate effectively and appropriately in intercultural situations," and suggests that there are several different components to this, such as knowledge, skills, attitudes and awareness, which center around ideas of respect, curiosity, openness, and willingness to engage in learning about other cultures and norms (Deardorff 2004).

"Intercultural situations" are now commonplace and foreign language education can assist learners in developing their abilities to interact appropriately with others from different backgrounds (Byram and Wagner 2018; Danovitz and Tuitt 2011; Kramsch and Aden 2012). Developing interculturality in an EFL setting is not, however, a straight-forward proposition. L2 speakers of English might nowadays realistically expect to interact with mother-tongue speakers and/or ESL/EFL speakers of English from almost anywhere on the globe, many of whom may have conflicting notions of culture and profoundly different attitudes to what constitutes appropriate forms of communication. Any cohort of students, including those in the study described here are not monolithic or necessarily representative of wider society. Yet, as Nikitina and Furuoka (2019) point out, all people do have mental images of others and the language classroom can be of help in revising these images in a positive way. Consequently, bespoke approaches which are relevant to the cultural context(s) involved may be required. This project was designed as a preliminary, exploratory step in beginning a process of engendering intercultural situations for students who may not otherwise have that opportunity.

## 3 Telecollaboration in the classroom

The logistics of cross-border collaborations are not always easy to negotiate. Time zone differences, class scheduling, technical limitations and financial concerns can make meetings, even online, problematic. In lieu of personal interaction, some form of digital interaction which takes advantage of the affordances provided by the internet for telecollaboration presents as a viable alternative. The technology involved is now robust and relatively simple to utilize, making it a potentially useful tool for learners and educators alike. Research in various L2 settings suggests podcasts can be of use in developing foreign language skills, promoting deeper engagement with materials, and raising motivation among learners (e.g. Fouz-González 2019; Hasan and Hoon 2013; Phillips, 2017). It is therefore reasonable to ask whether they may also prove of benefit in helping students to develop or improve their intercultural awareness and competency. Further, one potentially powerful resource that may at this point be being underutilized is the students themselves. Having students actively participate in the production and review of digital resources to be shared with students in the other country may promote deeper engagement with both their own culture, and that of the other country, and possibly give rise to a greater appreciation of the point of view of the other.

Telecollaboration in language classes has become a reasonably common practice in recent years (O'Dowd 2016), proving potential for universities to enhance their internationalization strategies (Helm 2015). Various synchronous, asynchronous, and other models have been attempted, using a wide variety of tools, such as e-mail, audio-visual conferencing, and blogs. Most projects focus on some form of task aiming to help learners improve language, communicative competence (Jauregi and Bañados 2010), and pragmatic skills (Hilliker et al. 2020). The positive possibilities of telecollaboration for developing intercultural communication has also been noted in research (Chun 2011; O'Dowd 2012).

# 4 The study

The trilateral study reported here, which took an information exchange approach to telecollaboration (O'Dowd and Ware 2009), involved undergraduate students in Russia, Japan, and China in EFL courses taught by the authors of this chapter. All students had an A2 to B2 level of proficiency in English.

In Japan, the 26 students that participated were predominately second year students at a national university majoring in a variety of subjects. In China, the 74 participants were second and third-year students studying in an English immersion program in a private university, majoring in various business-related fields and computer science. In Russia, the project was advertised among the students of the ITMO University and 35 volunteers, from the 1st and 2nd-year of studies, joined it. These students' majors were related to Information Technology or Computer Programming.

As the study was undertaken during the COVID-19 pandemic, all classes were conducted remotely. In fact, due to sudden travel restrictions, one instructor was based in Finland during the entire course of the project, dealing with students who were scattered all over China. Additionally, because of different time zones, different semester starting and finishing dates in each country, and the fact that the beginning of the Japanese semester was postponed for one month, it was decided that a fully asynchronous approach to the project was necessary.

The basic procedure was as follows:
1. Students chose a topic of historical significance related to their own country's culture, art, poetry, or popular culture that they felt may be of interest to a person in a foreign country. They then wrote a short script in English on the topic, which was lightly edited by their English teachers for general issues relating to intelligibility.
2. Students then either took or acquired photographs and images to create a visual representation of their written script, while attempting to avoid copyright infringement.
3. Next, students recorded their script and created a draft video podcast describing their chosen topic, which may have incorporated video clips, photographs and other images, an audio recording of the script they had written, and background music or sound effects.
4. Feedback from teachers was provided on factors such as English pronunciation and grammar, quality control in video editing and relevance of images to the story.
5. The podcasts were then uploaded to Padlet, an online collaborative platform (see Figure 7.1), for exchange with international peers.
6. Students were able to watch all the video podcasts produced and give feedback by adding comments expressing their impressions, which all students were able to view. Each student was required to comment on a minimum of one video from each of the other two countries. It was ensured that all videos received comments from students in both other countries.

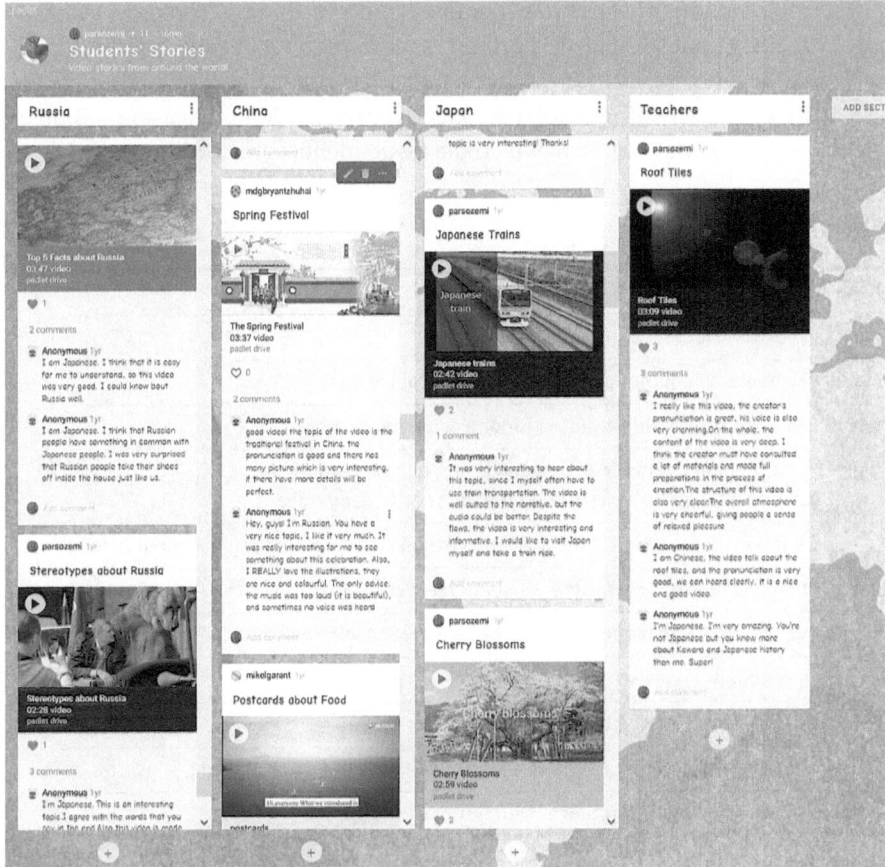

**Figure 7.1:** Screen shot of the website used to share video podcasts.

# 5 Research question

This project set out to examine the accuracy of a simple question:

> If Japanese, Chinese, and Russian students had an opportunity to interact with one another, even via an online scenario as has been outlined above, would their attitudes towards the other countries involved improve?

A series of 12 statements were designed by the authors to discern changes in the attitudes of the learners toward the other two nations (see Table 7.1). The words "my country" and "other country" would be replaced with names of the three countries in the study, according to which students took the survey. These questions were administered in pre-project and post-project surveys. A further question, "After completing this project, how do you feel towards [other country]?" was included in the post-project survey. The statements and question were administered via an online survey application, Survey Monkey, using a 5-point Likert scale to test the degree to which the respondents agreed with them.

**Table 7.1:** Survey questions.

| |
|---|
| I have a positive attitude towards [other country] people. |
| I would like to visit [other country] as a tourist. |
| I would like to study in [other country] for a short course. |
| I would like to study in [other country] for one semester or more. |
| I believe that relations between [my country] and [other country] are: normal and peaceful; good and neighbourly; amicable; dangerous |
| If I found a job in [other country] that paid more than one in [my country], I would take it. |
| It would be fine with me if my brother or sister married a person from the [other country]. |
| I would like to live in [other country] for a while if given the opportunity. |
| In 2020, [my country] – [other country] relations are good. |
| [My country] – [other country] relations are better than they were 30 years ago. |
| I believe [my country] – [other country] relations will be better in the future. |
| Personally, I don't have any problems with [other country]. |

# 6 Results

The survey items which most clearly indicate students' attitudes to the other countries are: "I have a positive attitude towards [other country] people", which was asked in both the pre-project survey and the post-project survey; and "After completing this project, how do you feel towards [other country]?", which was asked in the post-project survey. The results from these items are represented in Figures 7.2, 7.3 and 7.4 below. Black represents the attitudes of Chinese students, grey the attitudes of Japanese students, and black and white stripes the attitudes of Russian students.

Figure 7.2 shows the results of Chinese and Russian students' attitude towards Japan and Japanese people.

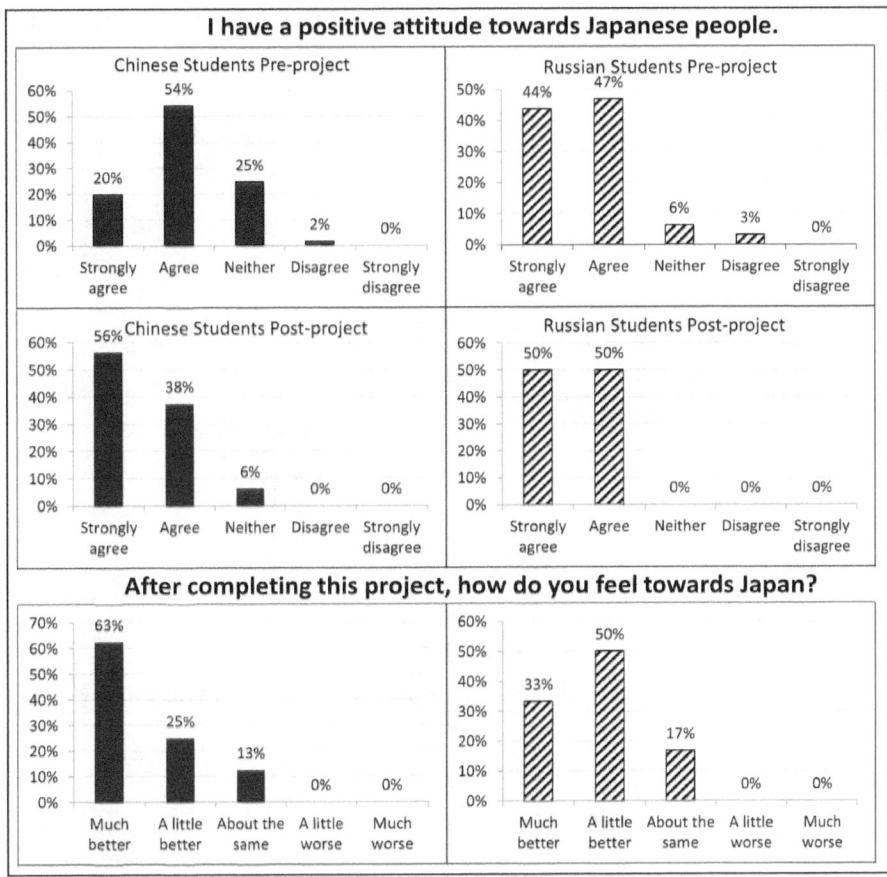

**Figure 7.2:** Attitudes towards Japan and Japanese people.

Prior to the project beginning, most Chinese and Russian students had a relatively positive attitude towards Japanese people, although a small percentage of students in both countries disagreed with this proposition, and in the case of China a quarter of students claimed to be ambivalent. As can be seen, after completing the project attitudes towards Japanese people had improved. 94% of Chinese students and fully 100% of Russian students now claimed to have a positive attitude towards Japanese people, with no students disagreeing with the statement.

In response to the question about feelings towards Japan after completing the project, 88% of Chinese students and 83% of Russian students considered their feelings to be better or much better. This reveals a clear positive shift in attitudes towards Japan and Japanese people over the course of the project.

Figure 7.3 shows the results of Japanese and Russian students' attitude towards China and Chinese people.

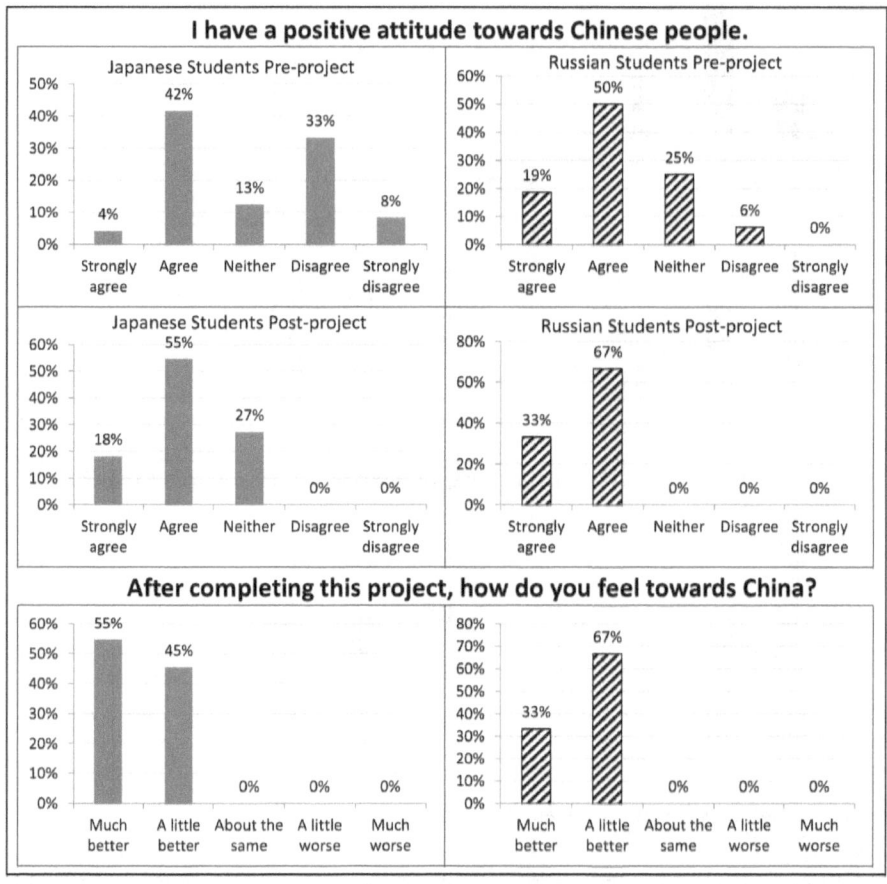

**Figure 7.3:** Attitudes towards China and Chinese people.

Prior to the project beginning, a majority of Russian students had a positive attitude towards Chinese people, although 25% neither agreed or disagreed and 6% disagreed with the statement. The situation with Japanese students was not as positive. Although 46% of Japanese students had a positive attitude, 41% of Japanese students disagreed or strongly disagreed. After completing the project, 100% of Russian students and 73% of Japanese students had a positive attitude towards China. No Japanese students disagreed.

Regarding the question about feelings towards China after completing the project, 100% of both Russian and Japanese students considered their feelings to be better or much better. In the case of the Japanese students more than half, 55%, said they feel much better towards China, again revealing a clear positive shift in attitudes towards China and Chinese people over the course of the project.

Figure 7.4 shows the results of Japanese and Chinese students' attitude towards Russia and the Russian people.

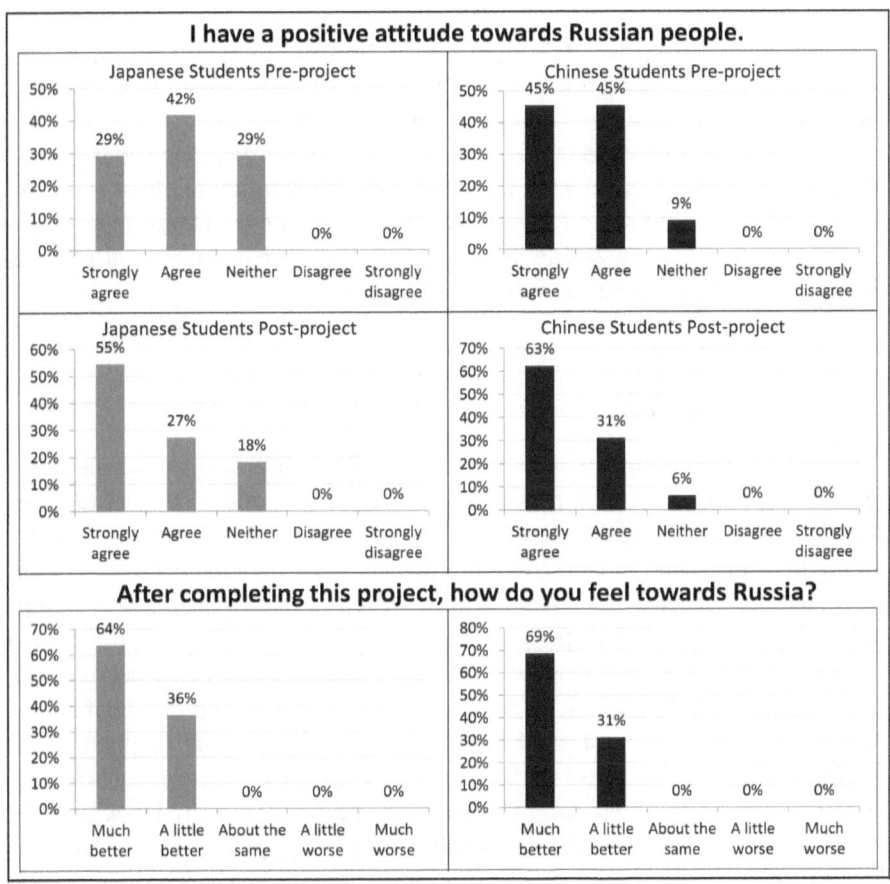

**Figure 7.4:** Attitudes towards Russia and Russian people.

Before the project began, most Japanese and Chinese students had a positive attitude towards Russian people. No students disagreed with the statement, although more than a quarter of Japanese students and 9% of Russian students neither agreed nor disagreed. After completing the project, the percentage of Japanese students strongly agreeing to positive attitudes towards Russian people had almost doubled. Over 90% of Chinese students either strongly agreed or agreed with the statement.

Feelings towards Russia after completing the project are similar in both groups. Approximately 2/3 of students considered that they felt much better towards Russia, and the remaining 1/3 felt better towards Russia, once again expressing a strong positive shift in attitudes towards Russia and Russian people over the course of the project.

These results suggest that if Japanese, Chinese, and Russian students have an opportunity to interact with one another, their attitudes toward each other will improve has indeed proven to be correct.

The results of responses to other statements in the surveys also tend to bear this out. For example, a series of three statements regarding bilateral relations were posed in both the pre- and post-project surveys. These statements are more objective in that they are asking about relations between countries, rather than about the individual's personal attitudes and feelings:

> In 2020, bilateral relations are good.
> Bilateral relations are better than they were 30 years ago.
> I believe bilateral relations will be better in the future.

Although not universal, the general trend of the results was towards a more positive response in the post-project surveys. Russian students tended to show more favorable responses in the post-project survey regarding bilateral relations, but the responses from Japanese and Chinese students were more varied. For example, the percentage of Chinese students who agreed that bilateral relations with Japan were good in 2020 fell after completing the project. However, the percentage rose for bilateral relations being better than 30 years ago and being better in the future. In contrast, the percentage of Japanese students agreeing that bilateral relations with Russia are good in 2020 rose, and those disagreeing dropped. Additionally, the percentage agreeing that relations were better 30 years ago and will be better in the future also rose. However, the percentage of students strongly agreeing that relations with Russia were better 30 years ago and will be better in the future dropped.

# 7 Discussion and conclusions

In reflecting on this study, some points should be kept in mind. A telecollaboration project of this sort can only be undertaken through the affordances of the internet. However, in China internet use can be problematic. A simple example is that some sites, such as Google or YouTube, are not available in China. Other sites could only be accessed through certain browsers or VPN routing, meaning that projects need to be planned carefully in order to see them through. A project of this kind requires careful planning to undertake successfully, including providing guidance for students in certain areas (e.g. issues surrounding copyright, in selecting appropriate topics, in prosody and pronunciation, and technical complexities in video editing). As in any educational endeavour, one aim of this project was to provide students with the resources and assistance they need to grow, to be able to realize or actualize their potential, without encroaching upon their autonomy.

This is particularly germane because of the occurrence of the COVID-19 pandemic, during which this project was undertaken meaning that all contact with students was online. Not meeting with students face-to-face created a different "classroom" dynamic, which could plausibly have had an effect on students' impressions of the project and of the intercultural exchanges they engaged in. An unexpected level of complexity was introduced to the project, which also meant that all participants were forced to adapt to using a variety of telecollaboration tools. It is also unknown what effect the fact that the initial outbreak of COVID-19 occurred in China may have had on the attitudes of Japanese and Russian students towards China.

However, survey results indicate that this supra-national, collaborative project based on the exchange of videos on historical and cultural topics gave students a unique opportunity to have contact with students from another culture that would otherwise be unavailable to them, and that their personal attitudes towards the other two countries improved as a result.

Future research should attempt to understand why the results of some students' thoughts about bilateral relations between their countries in the past, present and future were inconclusive. Attempts should also be made to understand if students' socio-cultural backgrounds, areas of study and other factors have any effect on the likelihood of attitudes changing in this kind of project.

# References

Andreeva, Nataliya Dmitrievna, Aranova Svetlana Vladimirovna, Lazukova Nataliya Nikolaevna, Pisareva Svetlana Anatolievna, Podhodova Nataliya Semenovna, Primchuk Nadezhda Viktorovna, Trubitsina Olga Ivanovna Trubitsina & Tryapitsina Alla Prokophievna. 2019. *Pedagogical strategies for ensuring the continuity of methodological learning systems in a modern school.* St. Petersburg: Asterion.

Byram, Michael & Manuela Wagner. 2018. Making a difference: Language teaching for intercultural and international dialogue. *Foreign Language Annals 51 (1).* 140–151.

Chun, Dorothy M. 2011. Developing intercultural communicative competence through online exchanges. *Calico Journal, 28 (2)*. 392–419.

Danowitz, Mary Ann & Frank Tuitt. 2011. Enacting inclusivity through engaged pedagogy: A higher education perspective. *Equity and Excellence in Education, 44 (1)*. 40–56.

Deardorff, Darla K. 2004. Internationalization: In search of intercultural competence. *International Educator, 13 (2)*. 1–15.

Deardorff, Darla K. 2006. The identification and assessment of intercultural competence as a student outcome of internationalization at institutions of higher education in the United States. *Journal of Studies in International Education, 10 (3)*. 241–166.

Fouz-González, Jonás. 2019. Podcast-based pronunciation training: Enhancing FL learners' perception and production of fossilised segmental features. *ReCALL, 31 (2)*. 150–169.

Helm, Francesca & Sarah Guth. 2010. The multifarious goals of telecollaboration 2.0: Theoretical and practical implications. In Francesca Helm & Sarah Guth (eds.). *Telecollaboration 2.0: Language literacies and intercultural learning in the 21st century*, 69–106. Bern: Peter Lang.

Hasan, Md. Masudul & Bee Hoon Tan. 2013. Podcast Applications in Language Learning: A Review of Recent Studies. *English Language Teaching, 6 (2)*. 128–135.

Haslett, Michael. 2018. *Why don't more Japanese study abroad? The cost and the hassle, survey shows.* The Japan Times. https://www.japantimes.co.jp/community/2018/01/24/issues/dont-japanese-study-abroad-cost-hassle-survey-shows/#.XbC9yOgzY2w (accessed February 24, 2021).

Helm, Francesca. 2015. The practices and challenges of telecollaboration in higher education in Europe. *Language Learning and Technology, 19 (2)*. 197–217.

Hilliker, Shannon M., Chelsea Ann Lenkaitis & Yahya Bouhafa. 2020. The role of intercultural virtual exchanges in developing pragmatic awareness. In Ching-Ching Lin & M. Cristina Zaccarini (eds.). *Internationalization in Action: Leveraging diversity and inclusion in globalized classrooms*, 95–109. New York: Peter Lang.

Hook, Glenn, Julie Gilson, Christopher Hughes & Hugo Dobson. 2012. *Japan's International Relations: Politics, economics and security.* Oxon: Routledge.

Jauregi, Kristi & Emerita Bañados. 2010. An Intercontinental Video-Web Communication Project between Chile and The Netherlands. In Francesca Helm & Sarah Guth (eds.). *Telecollaboration 2.0: Language literacies and intercultural learning in the 21st century*, 427–452. Bern: Peter Lang.

Kikuchi, Keita & Sakai, Hideki. 2009. Japanese learners' demotivation to study English: A survey study. *JALT Journal*, 31 (2), 183–204.

Kramsch, Claire & Joëlle Aden, J. 2012. ELT and intercultural/transcultural learning. In Joëlle Aden, Françoise Haramboure, C. Hoybel & Anne-Marie Voise (eds.). *Approche culturelle en didactique des langues: hommage à Albane Cain*. 39–59. Paris: Le Manuscrit Université.

Lapteva Irina Valerievna & Pakhmutova Elena Danilovna. 2012. *Formirovanie kul'turnogo kapitala specialistov Respubliki Mordovija posredstvom distancionnogo obuchenija* [Growing Cultural Capital of Mordovia Republic workforce through distance learning]. Vestnik NIIGN pri Pravitel'stve Respubliki Mordovija [NIIGN Bulletin under the Government of Mordovia Republic]. no. 4, pp. 227–233.

Lo, Bobo. 2010. *How the Chinese See Russia.* (Russie Nei Visions, No. 6.). Russia/NIS Center. https://www.ifri.org/sites/default/files/atoms/files/rnr6chinaloengdec2010.pdf

MEXT. 2008. *Basic Plan for the Promotion of Education*. http://www.mext.go.jp/en/policy/education/lawandplan/title01/detail01/1373797.htm (accessed February 24, 2021).
MEXT. 2010. *The Concept of Global Human Resource Development Focusing on the East Asian Region*. http://www.mext.go.jp/en/policy/education/highered/title02/detail02/sdetail02/1373900.htm (accessed February 24, 2021).
MEXT. 2013. *Measures based on the Four Basic Policy Directions*. Retrieved from: www.mext.go.jp/en/policy/education/lawandplan/title01/detail01/sdetail01/1373805.htm (accessed February 24, 2021).
Ministry of Education. 2018. *Release of China's first oversight report on quality of compulsory education*. http://en.moe.gov.cn/News/Top_News/201808/t20180801_344002.html (accessed February 24, 2021).
Ministry of Education. 2019a. *National Education Informatization Conference held in Kunming*. http://en.moe.gov.cn/news/press_releases/201904/t20190415_377948.html (accessed February 24, 2021).
Ministry of Education. 2019b. *More Chinese study abroad in 2018*. http://en.moe.gov.cn/news/media_highlights/201904/t20190401_376249.html (accessed February 24, 2021).
Moeller, Aleidine Kramer & Kristen Nugent. 2014. Building intercultural competence in the language classroom. In Stephanie Dhonau (ed.). *2014 Report of the Central States Conference on the Teaching of Foreign Languages*, 1–18. Richmond: Robert M. Terry.
Myasnikov, Vladimir Stepanovich. 1980. *Imperiya Tsin i Russkoye gosudarstvo v XVII veke [Qing Empire and the Russian State in the XVII Century]*. Moscow: Nauka.
Nikitina, Larisa & Fumitaka Furuoka. 2019. Language learners' mental images of Korea: insights for the teaching of culture in the language classroom. *Journal of Multilingual and Multicultural Development*, 40 (9). 774–786.
O'Dowd, Robert. 2012. Intercultural communicative competence through telecollaboration. In Jane Jackson (ed.). *The Routledge handbook of language and intercultural communication*, 340–356. Oxon: Routledge.
O'Dowd, Robert. 2016. Emerging Trends and New Directions in Telecollaborative Learning. *Calico Journal*, 33 (3). 291–310.
O'Dowd, Robert & Paige Ware. 2009. Critical issues in telecollaborative task design. *Computer Assisted Language Learning*, 22 (2). 173–188.
Pew Research Center. n.d. *Global Indicators Database. 2020*. https://www.pewresearch.org/global/database/indicator/ (accessed February 24, 2021).
Phillips, Brigit. 2017. Student-Produced Podcasts in Language Learning – Exploring Student Perceptions of Podcast Activities. *IAFOR Journal of Education*, 5 (3). 157–171.
Samoylova, Elena Vladimirovna, Olesya Vladimirovna Nazarova & Natalia Sergeevna Korniletskaya. 2014. Aktual'nye problemy i perspektivy prepodavanija inostrannogo jazyka studentam nejazykovyh special'nostej vuzov v ramkah integrirovannogo podhoda [Relevant issues and prospects for teaching a foreign language to non-linguistic adult students in the context of integrated approach]. *Integracija obrazovanija [Integration of Education]*. No. 2 (75). 117–123.
Sanno Institute of Management. 2017. *Shinnin shain no gurobaru ishiki chosa [Survey of the Global Consciousness of New Company Employees]*. Sangyo-noritsu University. https://www.sanno.ac.jp/admin/research/global2017.html (accessed February 24, 2021).
Schauer, Gila. 2016. Assessing intercultural competence. In Dina Tsagari & Jayanti Banerjee (eds.). *Handbook of second language assessment*, 181–202. Berlin, Boston: de Gruyter.

Sevalnev, Vyacheslav Viktorovich & Ekaterina Viktorovna Cherepanova. 2020. Kitayskiy vektor v sovremennoy vneshney politike Rossii: politiko-pravovoy aspekt [The Chinese Vector in the Modern Foreign Policy of Russia: Political and Legal Aspect]. *Comparative Politics Russia, No. 1.* 32–43.

Suzuki, Shogo. 2007. *The importance of 'othering' in China's national identity: Sino-Japanese relations as a stage of identity conflicts.* Pacific Review. https://doi.org/10.1080/09512740601133195 (accessed February 24, 2021).

Yeung, Phillip. 2017. *Why can't Chinese graduates speak good English? Blame the teaching methods.* South China Morning Post. https://www.scmp.com/comment/insight-opinion/article/2110113/why-cant-chinese-graduates-speak-good-english-blame-teaching (accessed February 24, 2021).

Eduardo Viana da Silva, Ana Cristina Biondo Salomão
# Chapter 8
# Taking action in a virtual exchange with Brazilian and U.S. students

## 1 Introduction

Since the beginning of the teletandem (Telles & Vassallo 2006) exchange between Brazilian students from São Paulo State University (UNESP, Araraquara) and U.S. students from the University of Washington (UW Seattle) in 2015, a range of sociopolitical events have marked many of the interactions. Among some of the most significant events were the presidential transitions both in Brazil and in the United States. The impeachment of the leftist President Dilma Rousself in Brazil in 2016, the election of the right-wing President Jair Bolsonaro in 2018, the election of Donald Trump in 2016, and of Joe Biden in 2020 were among some of the significant political changes in both countries. In addition, social activism also brought more awareness to important issues, such as women's rights (Me too Movement in 2017 in the U.S.; *Deixa Ela Trabalhar#* Let her work in Brazil) and antiracism (Black Lives Matter in 2020 in the U.S.; *Vidas Pretas Importam* in Brazil in the same year). As the synchronous sessions would take place, instructors and moderators would overhear the name of social issues and presidents being mentioned on a regular basis among students.

For the past five years, teletandem sessions consisted of 50-minute online exchanges, between 4 and 5 times per academic quarter (Autumn and Spring quarters). In these sessions, students spoke in pairs or groups of three for 25 minutes in Portuguese and for 25 minutes in English. Although socio-political discussions were certainly taking place, students did not have a framework to guide their conversations. Instead, participants navigated through topics based on their own willingness and pace, which the teletandem organizers also thought to be an advantage since it provided students with the freedom to choose what to talk about and when to talk about a certain topic. Nonetheless, there was a lack of guidance on how students could elaborate their thoughts, compare their opinions, investigate issues, and hopefully take action as global citizens in matters that were relevant to them. Given this educational scenario, in the Spring quarter of 2019, the Global Competence Matrix was incorporated in the planning of specific

**Eduardo Viana da Silva,** University of Washington, e-mail: evsilva@uw.edu
**Ana Cristina Biondo Salomão,** São Paulo State University, e-mail: ana.salomao@unesp.br

https://doi.org/10.1515/9783110727364-009

tasks to guide students in the discussion of social issues. The Global Competence Matrix was created in 2011 by the U.S. Global Competence Task Force and it proposes categories to analyze issues of global relevance.

The Global Competence Matrix is divided into four categories as follows:
- Investigate the world: Students Investigate the world beyond their immediate environment;
- Recognize perspectives: Students recognize their own and other's perspectives;
- Communicate ideas: Students communicate ideas effectively with diverse audiences;
- Take action: Students translate ideas and findings into appropriate actions to improve conditions. (Global Competence Matrix 2011)

Salomão and Viana da Silva (2020) investigated the use of the Global Competence Matrix with a series of activities fostering the development of global competence among Brazilian and U.S. students in a teletandem exchange in the Spring of 2019. Students watched short videos on the issues of women's rights and education and looked at the items of the Global Competence Matrix as a guideline to facilitate their conversations. The study concluded that the Global Competence Matrix was indeed a valuable pedagogical tool and it facilitated the discussion of sensitive and complex topics. The 2019 study also showed that more attention to the "take action" item from the Matrix was necessary in order to possibly engage students in the exercise of their global citizenship. The current exploratory research presented in this chapter was stemmed from this need and it looks at the possible applications of the "take action" item in a teletandem exchange with 48 university Brazilian students and 44 university U.S. students. The main topic chosen for this study was the protection of forests and natural resources and the role of indigenous peoples, particularly in the Amazon Forest in Brazil and in Alaska, United States. We hope that this chapter will contribute to a larger dialogue about the meaning of forming global competent citizens in the language classroom. The next section will present some studies on global competence. Nonetheless, to the best of our knowledge, there are no other research projects focusing on global competence in virtual exchanges in the Lusophone world (Portuguese-speaking countries).

## 2 Review of literature

Research on global competence followed the creation of the Global Competence Matrix in 2011 by the EdSteps Global Competence Task Force (Boix Mansilla & Jackson 2011). Many of the studies on global competence have been developed by Project Zero from Harvard University. In addition, there are studies focusing on the use of critical global competence as a framework for social studies educators to prepare informed, responsible students as agents to participate in complex and unequal world systems (Harshman 2016). However, there is a scarcity of research focusing on the matrix and its potential for language teaching. The only study that we are aware of including students from Brazil and the U.S. and using the Global Competence Matrix is the one conducted by us (Salomão & Viana da Silva 2020).

The results of the EdSteps Global Competence Task Force, which was funded by the Bill and Melinda Gates Foundation, were published in a book manual format in 2011: *Educating for Global Competence: Preparing our youth to engage the world* (Boix Mansilla & Jackson 2011). This action research counted with the participation of several educators from K-12 and colleges in the U.S., and Governmental and Federal agencies, culminating in the creation of the Global Competence Matrix. Global competence is described as: "the capacity and disposition to understand and act on issues of global significance" (Boix Mansilla & Jackson 2011: xiii). One of the main arguments in favor of global competence presented by the 2011 EdSteps Global Competence Task Force is the need of global citizens who can deal with a flattened global economy, an unprecedented global migration, and climate instability and environmental stewardship. These elements have been widened nowadays to include the challenges imposed worldwide by the COVID-19. In this context, global competent students are able to: (1) investigate the world beyond their immediate environment; (2) recognize perspectives, others' and their own; (3) communicate ideas effectively with diverse audiences; and (4) take action to improve conditions. In addition to the general Global Competence Matrix, there is a series of subject-specific matrices, integrating the four competences into several areas of knowledge, namely: languages, mathematics, science, social studies, and the arts. An important aspect of becoming a global competent student is agency:

> Students engage in deep learning when they find internal motivation to do schoolwork – when they come to "own" the questions that guide their investigation of the world through core educational concepts. They set out to learn not merely to pass the next quiz, but because they experience the excitement and fulfilment of coming to understand the world and their role in it. (Boix Mansilla & Jackson 2011: 18)

Agency and engagement in issues of global significance are key elements when discussing the role of a global citizen. In other words, a student is not only a spectator in a lecturer hall, but the one who also decides which questions s/he wants to answer and how to investigate and engage with them. Following this line of research applied to language pedagogy, Project Zero (PZ) from the Graduate School of Education at Harvard is one of the pioneers in the development of creative ways to engage students with learning through the arts. Project Zero's mission is: "to understand and enhance learning, thinking and creativity for individuals and groups in the arts and other disciplines" (Project Zero website, PZ's mission, last access Dec. 8, 2020). PZ started conducting research on the development of learning processes in children, adults, and organizations in 1967. The project's commitment with learning is also in alignment with the principles of Global Competence. Among its 27 research projects for the 2018/2019 academic year are: The Global Children Project, Educating Global Citizens through a US and China Lens, and Idea into Action. Table 8.1 below presents a synopsis of the PZ's research mentioned here, showing its relevance for the teaching of global competence.

**Table 8.1:** Samples of Harvard Project Zero's Research 2018/2019 Available at the URL: https://pz.harvard.edu/resources/project-zero-annual-report-2018-2019.

| Projects | Description |
| --- | --- |
| The Global Children Project | Connects teachers in the US and Japan to nurture global competence in early childhood pz.harvard.edu/projects/global-children |
| Educating Global Citizens through a US and China Lens | Enhances students' understanding of the world and natures global thinking dispositions. pz.harvard.edu/projects/educating-global-citizens-through-a-us-and-china-lens |
| Idea into Action | A quest to translate ideas (principles, plans, good intentions, etc.) into action on the ground. pz.harvard.edu/projects/idea-into-action |

One common denominator among the Global Competence Matrix and the research above mentioned from Harvard Project Zero is the agency component; students are expected to engage actively with issues of significance to them. The list of research publications from Project Zero collaborators for 2018/2019 academic year include 78 books, chapters, articles, and blogs (2018–2019 Annual Report). Among them, many focus on the pedagogical practices that motivate students' participation and engagement (Boix Mansilla 2019; Chen, Wang, Grottzer & Dede 2018; Clapp & Hanson 2019; Hogan et al. 2018; Kamarainen et al. 2018; Mardell 2019; Ross & Clapp 2018; Sheya 2018a; Winner 2018).

In regard to the Global Competence Matrix, Orozco-Domoe (2015) discusses its potential uses in foreign language teaching at the university level, arguing that universities must foster global competence throughout the curriculum, by internationalization, language requirements, and study abroad opportunities. In doing so, universities affect students' "values, ideas and ideals about people in the world" and change the way that "individuals interact with one another on a personal level" (Orozco-Domoe 2015: 68). The author suggests that teaching "must boldly address some of the most pressing issues of our time" and that students should have experiences outside the classroom to realize "how their studied language connects them to people and global concerns in a different way than their native language(s) do" (82). The work with teletandem presented in this chapter builds on the possibility of creating such opportunities for students to experience dialogic interactions in which they can be empowered to look at themselves and one another by exploring their (inter)subjectivity as participants in diversity. In this way, we argue for teletandem as a possibility for participants to experience "the emergence of culture, viewed as dynamic, in the interaction with the Other" (Salomão, 2015: 362).

Moreover, some have argued in favor of incorporating global competence in the teaching of foreign languages, focusing on its importance in the job market. Abdel-Kader (2020) has defended that employability skills are enhanced by proficiency in a language other than English and by global competence. He defines common traits of "Globally Competent Students" as demonstrated in the table 8.2 below:

**Table 8.2:** Common Traits of Globally Competent Students by Abdel-Kader (2020).

| COMMON TRAITS OF GLOBALLY COMPETENT STUDENTS | They are attuned to their local economy and understand how it is affected by global economic forces. |
|---|---|
| They are able to communicate effectively across language and culture barriers. | They are attuned to the differences as well as the similarities of cultures. |
| They understand that the world is a system, in which their actions, as well the actions of nations, have consequences across the globe. | They see history as an ongoing story with many threads, rather than a series of unconnected events. |
| They see the interconnectedness of humans with the landscape and environment; they understand why people settle and live where they do. | They are aware of the big questions that doctors, scientists, and policymakers are trying to answer and recognize the forces that impede or accelerate progress. |

As significant as the items on the table above are, Abdel-Kader (2020) do not emphasize the importance of agency (take action) as one of the traits of a global competent citizen. He focuses, however, on the other elements presented in the

Global Competence Matrix: investigate the world, recognize other perspectives, and communicate ideas. The element of action is just presented without intentionality: "their actions [of students], as well the actions of nations, have consequences across the globe" (28). Nonetheless, we defend the position that the "take action" is an important and arguably the most impactful aspect of being globally competent.

Along the lines of the pedagogical need for teaching global competence, the article by Wu-Pope (2020) focuses on the impact of global competence in classroom instruction through Singapore's Character and Citizenship Education (CCE) Program. The CCE is offered to students in Singapore from the age of 6 to 19 years old. It comprises weekly classes that address social-emotional learning, character development, higher education, and career guidance. It seems that just as in the approach suggested by Abdel-Kader (2020) one of the main focus of being a global competence citizen in Wu-Pope (2020) concerns the development of employability skills, devoting attention to the following:
- Values-clarification approach through narratives: using the stories from the target culture (real and fiction) to develop cultural perspectives,
- Experiential approach: focusing on employability skills, students participate in co-curricular activities to put into practice what they learn,
- Ipsative assessment approach: a space for reflection on what is being learned.

Most of the studies on global competence focus on K-12 students and there is a gap of studies on the agency element of the Global Competence Matrix (take action), especially when applied to university students of world languages. We expect the research presented in this chapter contributes to lessening this gap.

The current study is exploratory in nature. We aimed at looking at the possible applications of the Global Competence Matrix in a virtual exchange with a group of university students in Brazil and in the United States. While the study focuses on the application of the 'take action' item of the Global Competence Matrix, there are not pre-determined assumptions about the outcomes of this project. The only premise is that students should be free to decide whether or not to take action by engaging on social activism on the issues discussed with their colleagues. We believe that global competent students decide by themselves if and when to engage with issues of relevance to them.

In the next section, we will describe the methodology used in this exploratory research. In order to facilitate the reading of this chapter and given the number of tasks and the complexity of the issues discussed, the methodology section is followed by the presentation of the results by tasks. The results are divided in the parts: pre-tasks survey, collaborative tasks, and the post-task surveys. We then discuss the results in a later section of the chapter.

## 3 Methodology

This is a mixed-method research, combining qualitative data through the analysis of pre-task surveys, collaborative tasks, and quantitative data through a post-program survey using a Likert scale. The participants were 48 university Brazilian students from São Paulo State University (UNESP, Araraquara campus) and 44 U.S. university students from the University of Washington (UW, Seattle campus), with a total of 92 participants. The Brazilian students were participating as volunteers in the teletandem project to improve their English and their cultural understanding of the United States. They were mostly undergraduate students majoring in several areas of knowledge. The U.S. students were enrolled in first- and second-year Portuguese classes at the UW and they participated in the exchange during their class time. The UW students were also majoring in different fields. From the 44 U.S. students, 16 of them were enrolled in a second year intermediate Portuguese class while the remaining 28 students came from two first-year Portuguese classes and had been taking Portuguese for 7 weeks by the time that the teletandem exchange started.

Students met in four online interactions that lasted 50 minutes each. They conversed for 25 minutes in Portuguese and 25 minutes in English. In the first interaction, students had time to get to know each other and there was no task involved. In the second, third, and fourth interactions, students completed a pre-task survey prior to the interaction and during the teletandem exchange they discussed short videos about climate change, focusing on the Amazon Forest and Alaska and the role of the Indigenous populations. In the last interaction, students talked about a short video on the importance of forests for the planet and they also strategized ways of engaging with the issue of climate change. They brainstormed ways to contribute with social activism to protect forests and its Indigenous populations in Brazil and in the U.S.

## 4 Procedures

The videos were shared with students through a Google form in the pre-task surveys, in which they answered short questions about their previous knowledge on the subject, then watched the video and wrote a short paragraph about the new information acquired. This session of the research corresponded to the "Investigate the World" category. The selection of videos was done by the researchers as they took into consideration the quality of the resources and the reputation of the News companies.

During the sessions, students had a shared Google Doc, 'Collaborative Tasks' with questions for discussion and spaces to collaboratively write their conclusions. The tasks were planned to incorporate the "Recognize Perspectives" and "Communicate Ideas" categories of the Matrix. The last task, based on the "Take Action" category attempted to encourage students to brainstorm on possible actions they could take together or individually during or after the teletandem session. After the fourth interaction, students answered the post-program survey using a Likert scale, in which they analyzed the outcomes of their participation in the teletandem interactions according to statements based on the Global Competence Matrix.

Students were encouraged to answer all surveys in their native language. During the collaborative tasks, they had the option to work with either Portuguese and/or English. The U.S. students taking first-year Portuguese classes were encouraged to conduct the collaborative tasks in English, given their limited language proficiency in Portuguese.

Content analysis was used with the data of the pre-task surveys and the collaborative tasks in order to find recurrent themes in students' individual and collaborative work. The post-program survey was analyzed quantitatively in the items of the Likert Scale and through content analysis in the open questions.

# 5 Results

The results are divided into 3 categories. The first is the "pre-task surveys" conducted before the teletandem interactions. These surveys had questions about the students' previous knowledge on the topic of the future interaction, followed by a short video(s) on the topic, and questions about the video. The second category of results is the "collaborative tasks", which were completed either in pairs or in groups of 3, including students from Brazil and the U.S in each group. The collaborative tasks were an opportunity for students to listen to each others' perspectives and communicate their understanding on the issue at hand as a group. Finally, the third category of results is the "post-survey" given to students after the four teletandem interactions were completed to find out their perspectives on the competences that the experience had helped them build.

Given the exploratory nature of this research, as previously mentioned, the questions in the pre-task survey are open-ended, having the goal of helping students to investigate the world. The pre-task surveys are presented in Table 8.3 as they guide the discussion of our results in this section. For the purposes of this chapter, we will limit the presentation and discussion of results to the pre-tasks and tasks 2 and 3, which will then guide students to the 'take action' portion of this project. Pre-task and task 1 were introductory as they presented basic information about the Amazon Forest in Brazil and how it was exploited and protected from 1960's to 2019.

**Table 8.3:** Pre-task Surveys distributed on Google Forms.

| |
|---|
| **Pre-Task Survey 1**<br>The Amazon Forest (*N*=86, 44 Brazilian students and 42 U.S. students)<br>Question 1: What do you know about the Amazon?<br>Question 2: What do you think about the preservation of the Amazon?<br>Video: The Destruction of the Amazon Explained, Vox, Nov 21, 2019. – 11:44 min.<br>https://www.youtube.com/watch?v=SAZAKPUQMw0<br>Question 3: What are your reactions to the information presented in the video. |
| **Pre-Task Survey 2**<br>Indigenous populations in Brazil and the U.S. – Amazon and Alaska (*N*=78, 35 Brazilian students and 43 U.S. students)<br>Question 1: What do you know about indigenous peoples of your country?<br>Question 2: What do you know about indigenous peoples of your teletandem partner's country?<br>Vídeo 1 (BR): How Indigenous Tribes Are Threatened by the Amazon Rainforest Fires – Now This News, Nov 11, 2019, – 5:10 min.<br>https://www.youtube.com/watch?v=4-IJieq5NOw<br>Vídeo 2 (US): This Is The Story Of Alaska Natives' Fight For Their Land<br>Our Fight To Survive, Pt. 1. Al Jzeera, Nov.19, 2017–10:43 min.<br>https://www.youtube.com/watch?v=50_kse-Uh-g<br>Question 3: What are your reactions to the information presented in the videos? |
| **Pre-Task Survey 3**<br>The preservation of forests (*N*=84, 40 Brazilian students and 44 U.S. students)<br>Question 1: Have you ever engaged in an activist movement in defense of the Amazon Forest and/or Alaska and/or the indigenous populations? Explain.<br>Video: Our Planet, how to save our forests. WWF, Nov. 21, 2019. 7:35 min.<br>https://youtu.be/umGCKs0BhAQ<br>Question 2: In what ways do you think you can engage and contribute to a better world? |

## Pre-Task Survey 2: Indigenous populations in Brazil and the U.S. – Amazon and Alaska (*N*=78, 35 Brazilian students and 43 U.S. students)

In the second pre-task survey about Indigenous populations in Brazil and in the United States, many students recognized the struggles of Indigenous populations in their countries and the genocide and silence associated with the history of colonization. Out of the 78 students who answered the survey, around half of them (*n*=42, 54%) demonstrated a good knowledge about the role and challenges of Indigenous peoples in their countries. The answers varied from descriptions focusing on the role of the Brazilian and U.S. Government in forcing the migration of Indigenous peoples to some specific examples of how Indigenous peoples have been exploited. One example of it is the case of cultural appropriation with the inaccurate portrayal of Pocahontas by Disney and also in the whitewashed version of history textbooks, including the celebration of Christopher Columbus and of the history of the Pilgrims associated to Thanksgiving. There were mentions of how the COVID-19 pandemic has affected Indigenous peoples disproportionately (*n*=5); the number of missing Indigenous women in the U.S. (*n*=2, U.S. students); and the presence of boarding schools for Indigenous children, also in the U.S. (*n*=3, U.S. students). In addition, a few students have taken classes at the university about Indigenous peoples (*n*=5 U.S. students; *n*=1 Brazilian student). One U.S. student explained that he was learning about the Indigenous population in the U.S. by reading the *Braiding Sweetgrass* (2015) by the Indigenous women writer Robin Wall Kimmerer.

Some of the students from the sample above mentioned the word genocide or massacre of the Indigenous peoples when describing that the colonizers invaded their lands and killed their people (*n*=14). One student from the U.S. referred to the Indigenous peoples as "first nations," which is a terminology used more commonly in Canada; other 3 U.S. students self-identified as Indigenous and 4 students mentioned that they live in Indigenous lands in the United States. One of them said that even though the Pacific Northwest of the U.S. does recognize its Indigenous peoples and their lands nowadays, much has to be done in the rest of the country. Only 3 students mentioned the significance of Indigenous peoples from Central America and Mexico in the United States.

If on one side, about half of the students seemed to have a good understanding of the role and struggles faced by Indigenous peoples in their countries; on the other side, half of the students was less knowledgeable (*n*=36, out of 78 participants, 46%). Some wrote that they did not know much about the history and cultures of Indigenous peoples in their country (*n*=12); one stated that his/her understanding was probably based on stereotypes (*n*=1, Brazilian student), while the rest presented superficial and/or vague/simplified descriptions of the role of Indigenous peoples in historical and cultural terms (*n*=24).

As for the second question of the pre-task survey 2, referring to the students' previous knowledge about Indigenous peoples in the country of their teletandem partner (either Brazil or the United States), many of the participants stated: "I don't know anything" or "I don't know much" (*n*=51 out of 78 participants, 65%). Others mentioned the devastation of the Amazon Forest in Brazil and the role and struggles of the Brazilian Indigenous peoples in its protection (*n*=11). The topic of genocide appeared in some of the responses as well (*n*=6) and a few students (*n*=4) mentioned the similarities between the situation in Brazil and in the U.S. concerning some of the challenges faced by the Indigenous populations. One U.S. student mentioned that her grandmother is from the Xucuru tribe in Brazil and for that reason she is more familiarized with the history of Indigenous peoples in Brazil. The comment below from a Brazilian student summarizes some of other students' comments who were more aware about the lives of Indigenous peoples in the other country; it also highlights the diversity within the Indigenous peoples:

> I believe that something very similar occurs when concerning the native Americans in the US, since the colonization worked upon the same basis of oppression and violence against the indigenous peoples, causing a series of damage to our relation with the country's identity and inequalities to those who have been neglected ever since. Although, I think – when it comes to a cultural and ethnicity – there is a huge diversity between North American and Brazilian indigenous natives. (Brazilian student)

The third question from survey 2 addressed the participants' reactions to the videos about the Indigenous peoples in the Amazon Forest being threatened by the deforestation through fires and a video about the history of Indigenous peoples in Alaska. Most students described how the Indigenous people were treated by the settlers as saddening, shocking, and appalling. Terms like discrimination, cultural genocide, and unequal treatment from the government were also used to describe how Indigenous peoples were/are treated in both Brazil and the U.S. A few students (*n*=2) described how close they feel to the issues as they are from Indigenous backgrounds and watching the video made them emotional. Others used the words 'anger, desperation, and guilty' to describe their reactions to the videos. The name of the Brazilian president Jair Bolsonaro was mentioned by a few students (*n*=3) as one of the persons responsible for the fires in the Amazon Forest. The comment below by a U.S. student summarizes some of the reactions from other participants in this survey and it highlights the similarities in the struggles of Indigenous peoples in Brazil and in the United States:

> It is remarkable how similar the two peoples are treated by their respective governments. Indigenous people in Alaska and Brazil are both being pushed off their land in order to advance economic growth. It is incredibly sad to see these people and their lands being abused for the purpose of economic development. It is also sad because these people knew and know how to sustainably manage their land but the governments and colonizers are taking it over to make money instead of respecting the people who live there. (U.S. student)

Many of the Brazilian students expressed surprise to the history of native peoples in Alaska, as much of the information was new to them. Some of the U.S. students were also surprised at the level of devastation in the Amazon Forest and the impact to the lives of Indigenous populations. Overall, students found that the Governments of Brazil and the United States and big corporations are responsible for the devastation of the forests and the crimes committed against Indigenous populations. The general feeling of the answers was of outrage.

## Pre-Task Survey 3: The preservation of forests (*N*=84, 40 Brazilian students and 44 U.S. students)

In the third pre-task survey about the preservation of the forests, only 24% of the students (*n*=20 out of 84 participants) claimed to have participated in activism related to the protection of the forests and/or Indigenous peoples in Brazil and/or the United States (see Figure 8.1 below). Among students who have engaged in social activism (*n*=20), about half of them (*n*=9) have participated through social media only: Instagram, Facebook, and the promotion of Infographics on climate change were some of the examples. Only two students from the 20 involved with activism have participated in rallies related to climate change (*n*=2, U.S. students). In both cases, they protested the construction of the Keystone Access Pipeline (one student participated in a rally in North Dakota and one in the Seattle area). Others engaged in issues related to climate change and protection of Indigenous populations through signing petitions (*n*=4) and making donations (*n*=5).

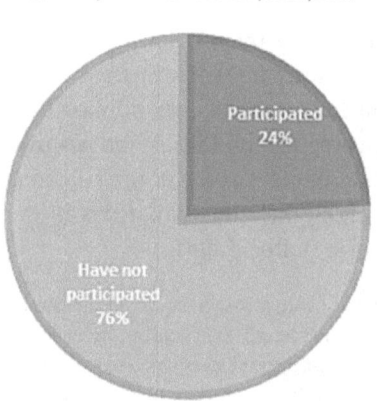

**Figure 8.1:** Number of students who participated in social activism on climate change and the protection of Indigenous people.

In addition, there was also a small group of students who have worked as volunteers with issues related to climate change (*n*=4, 1 Brazilian student and 3 U.S. students). This select group has worked with the following campaigns/

NGOs: Greenpeace in protection of the Amazon Forest; MMIW and #Stolenland, a social media grassroots campaign targeted at stopping oil drilling in the Arctic through an Environmental class; the development of a social media grassroots campaign for saving Alaska's Tongass National Forest and the Arctic National Wildlife Refuge, which is expected to open for drilling sales in January 2021; and the ecological restoration of Tarboo Creek through the S'klallam tribe.

Other forms of social engagement on climate change done by participants included: reduction of the consumption of goods, recycling and reusable items ($n=1$), collection of legislative letters to address climate change ($n=2$), and cold calls ($n=1$). One student from the Seattle area mentioned that s/he donates to the Duwamish tribe monthly in order to pay back for the privilege of living in the land that was originally stolen from the Duwamish people. Another student also stated that s/he donates to local Indigenous tribes to help support their causes. Some of the answers mentioned the Indigenous tribes by name: Gwich'in, Duwamish, and S'klallam.

The majority of students ($n=64$, out of 84), 76% of them, have not engaged in social activism related to climate change and/or the protection of Indigenous populations. Nonetheless, some of them have expressed an interest in participating in social activism related to these issues ($n=8$), while a few students ($n=3$) have participated in other social movements, such as Black Lives Matter and social activism in the political sphere in Brazil. Some students ($n=2$) explained that they had not received any kind of formal environmental education and/or history background about the struggles faced by Indigenous communities. The lack of knowledge on the subject was also mentioned by a few other students ($n=3$), in addition to the lack of opportunities to engage ($n=7$). Only one participant stated that these issues do not affect her/him directly, but after learning more s/he might engage in some activist movement in the future.

On the last question about ways to contribute to a better world, there was a range of recurrent suggestions, many focusing on reforestation/planting trees ($n=20$) as the documentary that accompanied this pre-task survey focused on the ancient forests of the world and their importance to the planet. The number one suggestion, however, was to take personal responsibility and change everyday habits in order to have less impact on the environment ($n=43$). Participants mentioned several factors, among them:
- buying second-hand clothes and avoiding fast fashion items
- consuming less plastic
- recycling more
- producing less littering
- saving water, spending less time in the shower

- saving electricity, turning off lights not being used
- purchasing environmentally sustainable products
- reducing consumption of goods and "the next new thing"
- reducing meat and dairy consumption
- having a plant-based diet
- having a home garden

Similarly to the personal responsibility stated above, some students ($n=14$) also argued for the reduction of the carbon footprint, condemning the careless use of flights and cars, also suggesting that more people should use public transportation and bicycles to limit the emissions of CO2. Another initiative mentioned repeatedly ($n=17$) was the importance of putting pressure on local and Federal Governments to support legislation to protect natural resources and to stand against the interests of big corporations. This same group defended the importance of voting and of political action. In addition, the need for self-education was emphasized by some ($n=13$), suggesting that one should read more about environmental issues, watch documentaries on the subject, and bring awareness to children, friends, and family. Finally, a large number of participants ($n=47$) concluded that active participation through activism is needed, including participation in rallies, charity events, social media, and volunteer work with local organizations and NGOs. A few students ($n=5$) mentioned donation to good causes as an alternative to protect the environment and sustainable farming appeared in the answers only twice.

## Collaborative tasks

The collaborative tasks were conducted mostly during part of the teletandem interaction, usually during the 25-minute session in English since most of the U.S. students were beginner speakers of Portuguese ($n=28$ out of 44 students) and did not possess the language skills to discuss these kinds of issues in the target language. On the other hand, most of the Brazilian students ($N=48$) spoke English at the intermediate level or higher. The attendance during the teletandem sessions was high, with most students attending every session. There were times, however, when a few students would not attend the interaction on each side, usually less than 6 students per time in total out of the 92 participants. In a large group of students, it is common for a few of them to miss classes because of sickness or other personal issues. There were also times when students attended sessions, but did not complete the collaborative tasks, either by choice or for having technical difficulties to access the Google doc. This last situation occurred rarely.

Questions a and b of the 'collaborative tasks' in Table 8.4 functioned mostly as a review of the pre-task surveys in which students could explain their own and recognize each other perspectives. The last question was a way to introduce the "take action" element of the Global Competence Matrix as the question focuses on what participants can do to advance the rights of Indigenous peoples and to protect the forests. For the sake of this chapter, we will focus on the "take action" element presented in the last questions and also on the conclusions of the collaborative tasks. As mentioned before, we will limit the presentation and discussion of the results to tasks 2 and 3. Task 1 was introductory and set the mood in a broad perspective to acquaint students with the topic.

**Table 8.4:** Collaborative tasks distributed on Google Docs.

---

**Collaborative Task 1 – The Amazon Forest**
Having in mind the video about the devastation of the Amazon, discuss the information presented with a colleague. You may use the following questions to guide the discussion.
a) What did you know previously about the topic?
b) Was there any new information?
c) How do you see the issue of the protection of the Amazon Forest? What can we do to preserve it?

Take notes about the discussion and write the conclusions about the topic collaboratively. You may write in the language of your choice (Portuguese or English)

---

**Collaborative Task 2 – Indigenous Populations** (*N*=27 groups)
Having in mind the video about indigenous peoples, discuss the information presented with a colleague, focusing on the interrelations that could be established. You may use the following questions to guide the discussion.
a) What did you know previously about the topic?
b) Was there any new information?
c) How do you see the issue of indigenous people's rights in both countries?
d) What can we do in relation to this issue?

Take notes about the discussion and write the conclusions about the topic collaboratively. You may write in the language of your choice (Portuguese or English).

---

**Table 8.4** (continued)

---

**Collaborative Task 3 – Contributing to a better world** (*N*=31 groups)
Having in mind the video about saving the forests, discuss ways you could engage and contribute to a better world.
a)  Do you know any NGOs? Have you participated in any activist movements?
b)  Reflect about concrete ways in which you could engage (sharing information with colleagues and friends, changing habits, using social media to act in some way, etc.)
c)  If you want, participate in a campaign for the protection of the forests and/or Indigenous communities with your teletandem partner during today's interaction and write below what you have done.

Take notes about the discussion and write the conclusions about the topic collaboratively, explaining what you have done together or what can be done in the future, in case you decide to take action. You may write in the language of your choice (Portuguese or English).

---

## Collaborative Task 2 – Indigenous populations (N=27 groups)

In task 2 (Indigenous populations), students discussed the content of the videos about the Amazon Forest being threatened by the deforestation through fires and the video about the history of Indigenous peoples in Alaska, then summarized their conclusions collaboratively. Twenty-seven groups completed task 2 (*n*=27).

Only one group suggested the creation of organizations to fight and advocate for the rights of Indigenous peoples, while others focused on putting pressure in the current governments to reform legislation and on elections (*n*=8) to advance the agenda of Indigenous rights and the preservation of the forests. Supporting existing organizations, such as NGOs (*n*=1), talking about the topic with friends, sharing information, and promoting education about the Indigenous populations was also mentioned as strategy (*n*=12). One suggestion was to support Indigenous businesses and arts and not buy products/produce that endanger Indigenous peoples (*n*=3). Another suggestion was to learn about the land and groups of Indigenous peoples in one's region (*n*=2). One group stated that the United States Government should be involved with the protection of the Amazon Forest.

In addition, getting rid of offensive mascots in professional football was mentioned (*n*=1). One group raised the point of taking pride in one's history and the role of Indigenous peoples (*n*=1) while another group mentioned the importance of retelling history from the perspective of Indigenous peoples as well (*n*=3). Finally, one group suggested that the governments should give more independence to small tribes (*n*=1). Some groups did not offer a suggestion to deal with the issues of deforestation and climate change facing Indigenous peoples (*n*=5). They either left their answers in blank or did not offer a "take action" alternative.

## Collaborative Task 3 – Contributing to a better world (N=31 groups)

In the third and final collaborative task, students were asked to consider their positionality with issues of relevance to them and also if they would consider taking action on the environmental issue for the protection of the Amazon Forest and Alaska, in addition to the protection of their Indigenous populations. This cohort of participants was divided in 31 groups formed by pairs and trios (n=31). The first question was about the students' knowledge of Non-Governmental Organizations (NGOs) and whether or not they have taken part in any social issue. The table 8.5 below offers the name of NGOs and social movements, some were mentioned repeatedly, as in the case of UNICEF, Black Lives Matter, and S.O.S. Mata Atlântica.

**Table 8.5:** List of NGOs and Social Movements mentioned by participants.

| AIESEC | Make a Wish foundation |
|---|---|
| Amnesty International | Movimento Sem Terra (MST) |
| Amigos da América | Native American Rights Fund |
| Amor e Proteção Animal (APA) | O Instituto Onça Pintada |
| Ampara Animal | Os doutores da alegria |
| APAE | PETA |
| Arbinq | S.O.S. Mata Atlântica |
| Associação de Assistência à Criança Deficiente (AACD) | St. Judes |
| Bill and Melinda Gates Foundation | TETO |
| Black Lives Matter (BLM) | UNICEF |
| Cultural Survival | United Nations |
| Doctors without Border | Viva Rio |
| Fundação Nacional do Índio (FUNAI) | WHO |
| Fridays For Future | Women's marches |
| Fruto Urbano | WWF |
| Gatos de Rua-Piracicaba | Sierra Club |
| Greenpeace | |

Only four groups reported that they do not know of any NGOs, but one of them mentioned that they would like to take part in a social movement ($n=4$ out of 31 groups). About one-third of participants have been part of a social movement ($n=9$ out of 31 groups), namely: Amigos da América, AIESEC, Cultural Survival, Black Lives Matter, Native American Rights Fund, S.O.S. Mata Atlântica, and Women's marches. In addition, a few students have donated to social causes ($n=4$), while others have participated as volunteers in NGOs ($n=4$). One comment that stood out was about the importance of taking the participation in protests as more than a "performative act" only: "protesting, working with marginalized communities; not being performative, not just virtue signaling" (U.S. Student).

On the question about ways to participate in social activism, approximately half of the groups mentioned the importance of taking personal responsibility to protect the environment ($n=15$ groups). The list of actions involved changing buying habits and reflected what was answered individually in the pre-task survey (see pre-task survey 3), including the reduction on the consumption of meat and plastic, the limitation of water usage and of products derived from animals, such as furs and leather, among others. In addition, some groups highlighted the importance of self-education on issues related to the preservation of the environment and the defense of Indigenous rights ($n=4$ groups). One U.S. engineering student pointed out the lack of awareness to environmental issues in her education:

> In my engineering program, it's all learning about theoretical problems, how stuff works, etc., but not what is going on in the world. We talk about how engineers can help in these issues with technology, but we never learn about any of these issues or hear from others who experienced these hardships, we have to learn on our own free time. (U.S. Student)

About one-third of the groups defended the importance of contributing to social causes through donations ($n=10$ groups), promotion of issues on social media ($n=9$); and conversations with friends and family to bring awareness ($n=10$). Others also highlighted the need of voting to governmental officials who have an environmental and Indigenous agenda ($n=9$).

Finally, on the questions about taking action as a group, a few of the participants were pro-active and took some time during the interaction to contribute to a social cause related to the environment and/or Indigenous rights ($n=4$ groups). They did the following:
- sent a twitter about the protection of the Amazon Forest,
- signed-up to a global petition to protect the Amazon Forest on change.org
- donated $5 to Sierra Club, an American NGO focused on protecting forests in the United States

– downloaded the app "Forest", which works in partnership with the NGO Trees for the Future. This app functions as a game that blocks the cell phone while the participant is studying. The longer one studies, the more coins one earns. When a person collects 2,500 coins from the game, the NGO plants a real tree.

Other groups reflected on the importance of keeping themselves engaged with causes related to environmental issues and the rights of Indigenous peoples, emphasizing the importance of keeping the conversation going and of bringing awareness to their friends and families (*n*=8 groups). There were also participants who mentioned that while they would like to participate in activism, the time of the last interaction was not enough for them to choose an organization or a way to engage with an issue of relevance to them (*n*=3). Similarly, a few other groups did not know how to engage with an NGO during the interaction (*n*=4), as was stated by one of the groups: "We don't know how to participate in a non-profit organization right now but we are going to search more about it in the future." In addition, about one-third of the groups did not answer the take-action question (*n*=9) and some stated the importance of the conversations about activism that they conducted during the teletandem interactions without providing a specific plan for taking-action, but mentioning their desire of being engaged (*n*=6).

**Post-Program Survey:** Sixty-seven students responded to the post-program survey (see results in Table 8.6 below). They had to mark how much they agreed or not that teletandem had helped to develop the competences presented in the statements (based on the Global Competence Matrix).

**Table 8.6:** The impact of pre-tasks and collaborative tasks in developing global competence.

| The activities done during the teletandem helped me: (N=67) | Completely Agree | Agree | Neither Agree nor Disagree | Disagree | Completely Disagree |
|---|---|---|---|---|---|
| 1) Develop an argument based on compelling evidence that considers multiple perspectives. | 43.9% | 47% | 7.6% | 1.5% | 0% |
| 2) Recognize your own and other's perspectives. | 77.6% | 20.9% | 1.5% | 0% | 0% |
| 3) Articulate how the consequences of differential access to knowledge, technology and resources affect the quality of life and influences perspectives. | 52.2% | 37.3% | 9% | 1.5% | 0% |

**Table 8.6** (continued)

| The activities done during the teletandem helped me: (N=67) | Completely Agree | Agree | Neither Agree nor Disagree | Disagree | Completely Disagree |
|---|---|---|---|---|---|
| 4) Recognize that diverse audiences may perceive different meanings from the same information. | 66.7% | 24.2% | 9.1% | 0% | 0% |
| 5) Explain how effective communication impacts understanding and collaboration in an interdependent world. | 62.7% | 29.9% | 7.5% | 0% | 0% |
| 6) Recognize my capacity to advocate for and contribute to improvement locally, regionally, or globally. | 59.7% | 34.3% | 4.5% | 0% | 0% |
| 7) Identify opportunities for personal and collaborative action to address situations, events, issues, or phenomena in ways which can make a difference. | 58.2% | 34.3% | 4.5% | 3% | 0% |
| 8) Assess options for action based on evidence and the potential for impact, taking into account varied perspectives and potential consequences for others. | 44.8% | 46.3% | 7.5% | 1.5% | 0% |
| 9) Act creatively and innovatively to contribute to improvement locally, regionally or globally both personally and collaboratively. | 43.3% | 44.8% | 10.4% | 1.5% | 0% |

There were also three open questions for students to have an opportunity to give their opinions on the experience (see Table 8.7 below).

The analysis revealed that participants were very positive about the competences built through the collaborative activities in teletandem. There was a high score of agree and completely agree in all the statements, representing 80% or more of the participants' choices, and no marks for the item completely disagree. It is also interesting to notice that the percentage of students who were not sure whether they agreed or disagree with the statement was usually below 10% and the rate of participants who disagreed with the statements was very low, which

**Table 8.7:** Open questions about the Virtual Exchange.

| |
|---|
| Question 1: What did you think of the activities proposed? |
| Question 2: Did you participate or intend to participate in any activist movement or in another initiative in defense of the Amazon Forest/Alaska and/or the indigenous populations? Explain. |
| Question 3: What do you suggest for future activities in the teletandem? |

shows that the experience was overall meaningful in terms of building the expected competences.

The answers to the open questions also showed that students were willing to get more informed and participate more actively in activist movements after the experience, as can be seen in the following excerpts:

> I intend to. I still know very few things in this regard, but the activities allowed me to realize how important and present these issues are to us today.

> I would love it! Getting involved in movements that collaborate to improve the world has become one of my goals, whether here in Brazil or elsewhere in the world. I believe that the meetings and conversations that took place made me "wake up" to look for more information and get out of my comfort zone.

> Yes, I intend to research more on this topic. The last video was essential for this decision.

The reasons for their willingness are related to "the activities", "the meetings and the conversations", and "the last video", which shows that the planning brought about elements for the development of awareness, as we will address in the discussion of the results. 6 Discussion of Results.

This exploratory study aimed at investigating the possible applications of the Global Competence Matrix in a virtual exchange with a group of university student in Brazil in the United States, especially in relation to the 'take action' component. The results show that the activities proposed have helped students to develop the traits of globally competent citizens (Abdel-Kader 2020), especially leading to understanding the world as a system, in which their actions, as well the actions of nations, have consequences across the globe. They also fine-tuned their perceptions to the differences as well as the similarities of cultures.

The pre-tasks surveys seem to have been fundamental in making students think about the issues prior to the discussion with their teletandem partners during the virtual exchange. They also provided students with an opportunity to learn more about environmental issues related to the Amazon Forest and Alaska, in addition to the rights and struggles of Indigenous peoples in Brazil and in the United States to protect their land.

In pre-task 2 and task 2, students discussed the lives of Indigenous peoples in the Amazon Forest in Brazil and in Alaska, in the United States. The pre-task surveys showed that about half of the students, 54% ($n=42$ out of 78 participants), had some good previous knowledge about the challenges of Indigenous peoples in their countries. The other about half of the students, 46% ($n=36$ out of 78 participants), did not demonstrate a deeper understanding of the lives of Indigenous peoples and the many challenges faced by them to protect their land and livelihood. For this latter group of students, the informative videos presented new information and helped construct a very basic-knowledge about the issue at hand. Given the exploratory nature of this research, the results of the surveys are unpredictable, especially considering the many variables involved, such as the participants' educational background, levels of racial and environmental literacy, and previous contact with Indigenous groups, among other aspects.

During collaborative task 2, students had an opportunity to discuss their points of views. Among the 27 groups who completed this task, 12 groups suggested that one should take responsibility by getting educated on the history and struggles of Indigenous populations, and also by sharing information with friends and family. Some mentioned the importance of passing legislation to protect Indigenous rights ($n=8$ groups). Activism was just mentioned by one group. It is important to note that the last question of the collaborative task 2 emphasized the action component "What can we do in relation to this issue?" Nonetheless, the question did not state if students had engaged with NGOs or activist groups, nor did it ask what students thought about the role of NGOs and activism. It is, however, in pre-task 3 and task 3 that students are asked specifically about these elements.

Pre-task 3 reveals that 24% of students surveyed ($n=20$ out 84 participants) have participated previously in some form of activism in regards to the protection of the Indigenous populations and/or the protection of the forests. Some of these students have participated in protests (N=2) and even participated as volunteers for NGOs ($n=4$). The remaining students (N=14) have either signed petitions, donated money, and/or engaged with activism on social media. Considering that most of the students surveyed are undergraduate students between the ages of 18 and 22, having 24% of them engaged in activism is indeed impressive. Nonetheless, 76% of students have not engaged in any kind of activism related to the issue discussed in pre-task 3. This is not to say that students do not value engagement with social issues of relevance to them. Among the 84 students surveyed, 56% of them ($n=47$ out of 84 participants) believe that their participation through activism is needed, including participation in rallies, charity events, social media, and volunteer work with local organizations and NGOs. In addition, 51% of students (*n*=43 out of 84 participants) also believe that taking personal responsibility and changing everyday habits are important in order to lessen the impact on the environment. In other words, there is a good level of understanding among students on the importance of being globally competent and on engaging with issues of global relevance.

It was in collaborative task 3 that students had a chance to brainstorm in groups the possibilities of taking action on environmental issues and on the protection of Indigenous rights. Given the complexity of issues related to the environment and Indigenous peoples, it is not surprising that students would need more time to discuss the possibility of engaging with such issues and how to choose the best venues for them. This collaborative task counted with the participation of 31 groups, from which they listed 33 NGOs and social movements, including: *Fundação Nacional do Índio* (FUNAI), Greenpeace, and Native American Rights Fund. Differently from task 2, where only one group mentioned the importance of activism, in task 3, 4 groups engaged in social activism during these virtual interactions, while other 10 groups mentioned the importance of participating with donations, and 6 groups mentioned the desire to engage in social activism in the near future. Approximately half of the groups, 48%, (*n*=15 out of 31 groups) emphasized the importance of taking personal responsibility in protecting the environment. This aspect reflects the answers obtained in pre-task 3, in which 51% of students also stated personal responsibility as an important aspect (*n*=43 out of 84 students). Collaborative task 3 also demonstrated the importance given by the groups to donations (*n*=10 groups), engagement in social media (*n*=9 groups), and raising awareness of issues to family and friends (*n*=10 groups). Civic engagement through the election of politicians with an environmental agenda was also emphasized by 9 groups.

While this study is not conclusive, we were able to conduct surveys with 92 university students and encouraged them to think and rethink their role as global citizens. By directly addressing some of the most pressing issues of our times, as proposed by Orozco-Domoe (2015), students experienced dialogic interactions in which they were led to look at themselves and one another and explore the emergence of culture and their own (inter)subjectivity as participants in diversity. For some, the information presented in the videos was completely new and it reinforced the need of pursuing self-education on the issues at hand. For others, the information was a reminder of the importance of engaging in social issues. The fact that many students are not actively engaged on social issues does not mean that they are not interested or do not give importance to such issues as one group highlighted: "We also discussed that while we are both inactive at the moment, we are interested in participating in a movement in the future" (U.S. and Brazilian students).

When comparing the students' experience in this study with previous teletandem interactions, in which there was not a selection of a topic, we noticed that students were indeed much more focused in the current study. There was an intentionality behind the interactions and, as a consequence, students seemed to engage with the issues more deeply. The information presented through the videos, as mentioned above, also contributed to their engagement, in addition to the fact that these are relevant issues to most of them. In future teletandem interactions, we plan to alternate the approaches, so participants will have both experiences. During some quarters we will provide a similar framework of activities, focusing on the 'take action' item, while in other quarters we will let students talk freely about topics of their choice, still providing them with the information from the Global Competence Matrix and the possibility of engaging on social activism if they decide to do it.

# 6 Research limitations

One of the limitations of this particular virtual exchange is the fact that participants have several levels of language proficiency, both in Portuguese and English, ranging from beginning to advanced. From the U.S. students ($n=44$), who participated in this study, only 16 of them had an intermediate level of proficiency in Portuguese, while the other 28 students had been taking Portuguese for only 6 weeks by the time that the teletandem exchange started. Given that most of the discussions took place in English, most Brazilian students ($n=48$ in total) had to defend their points of view and explain historical and complex information in their L2.

In addition to the language limitations, students also dealt with time constraints, as they participated in only 4 virtual interactions. Each interaction lasted 50 minutes, from which 25 minutes was in English and the other 25 minutes was in Portuguese. Despite of the limitations mentioned here, the comment from one of the U.S. students exemplifies the level of in-depth conversation that can take place in these types of virtual exchanges, especially if students are guided and supported with pedagogical tools, such as the informational videos, pre-task surveys, and collaborative tasks:

> Due to our similar academic major and personal interests, the class conversations on Alaska, the Amazon rainforest, and the indigenous communities of the United States and Brazil were both insightful and informative. More specifically, Leticia is quite politically

involved with Brazilian politics, and she was able to talk extensively about the *Ruralistas*, the negative effects their policies are having on the Amazon and indigenous communities that live there, and the role IBAMA has played in stopping deforestation. Moreover, she gave me an in-depth presentation about the different provinces of Brazil, highlighted the various social movements in each of them, and spoke about what it is like to be a student and live in the province of São Paulo. Here, I was able to learn about the Black Lives Matter movement in Brazil, which has recently impacted both Brazilian and American culture. Further, I had the possibility to hear about our cultural differences through her explanation of the Enem exam and elaboration on how university students live in Brazil.

(U.S. Student)

Even if not every student will have the same kind of in-depth conversation and have the chance to exchange ideas with a colleague who is knowledgeable about the issue at hand, the process of investigating about the world and the collaborative work on brainstorming solutions and possible actions on issues is valid indeed and we would argue that necessary if the goal of the virtual exchange is to go beyond the casual conversations about one's life. At the same time, we understand that bonding and forming friends in a virtual exchange is just as important and for that reason time for that should not be neglected either. We believe that more interactions would be needed in order to continue exploring the topics proposed in the exchange analyzed here. Nonetheless, because of different time schedules between institutions, this possibility is not always available. Above all, we believe that by connecting students and creating an inviting and thought-provoking environment, language instructors are able to promote global competence in their language classrooms and to engage students with social issues, motivating them in taking action on issues of global relevance to them.

# 7 Conclusion

By watching four short videos (between 5 to 11 minutes each) and interacting in the virtual exchange, participants were able to elaborate on their perspectives both individually and collaboratively through the tasks involved in this study. Moreover, this exploratory study raised the level of awareness among students on issues about deforestation, climate change, the history and challenges faced by Indigenous peoples in the Amazon Forest and Alaska. Participants demonstrated indignation to the lack of social justice with Indigenous peoples both in Brazil and in the United States, in addition to frustration and anger with the deforestation of the Amazon Forest and the degradation of natural resources in Alaska. These feelings might have motivated them to take action during the last interaction of the teletandem and potentially in the near future as well. The long-term ramifications of these teletandem interactions regarding the "take action" item of the Global Competence Matrix is unknown. A longitudinal study is needed in order to pinpoint the impact of this type of research project in motivating students to engage as global citizens in social activism while participating in a world language class.

The "take action" aspect is time demanding as students educate themselves on social-political issues of relevance to them and decide if they want to contribute and how. The four 50-minute interactions from the teletandem project described in this chapter are perhaps the beginning of the conversation for some participants that can bridge the lack of information among university students of how to collaborate on issues of significance to them, such as the preservation of forests and the protection of Indigenous peoples.

As a final remark, we chose not to decide for students which form of social activism they should select nor to require that students engage with social media platforms and/or with NGOs. Our premise was that global competent students decide by themselves whether or not to engage with issues of relevance to them and also how to engage. In future studies, we suggest, however, that a few options of NGOs or social engagements are offered as alternatives to students, to help guiding those who are less aware of ways to be involved with social activism. However, the decision of whether to participate in it or not, should be theirs and not ours.

We believe this study contributes to a larger conversation about the importance of forming globally competent citizens. The world language classroom presents an ideal opportunity to expose students to other cultures and further their understandings of the need to engage with local and global issues of relevance to them. Following this framework, student not only investigate the world, recognize other perspectives, and communicate ideas in their own language and in the additional language, but they also engage with issues by taking action.

# References

Abdel-Kader, Mohamed. 2020. Employability Skills Enhanced by Language and Intercultural Competence. *The Language Educator* 15 (2). 27–30.

Boix Mansilla, Veronica. 2019. Signature Pedagogies. *Global Education: Unveiling principles driving master practices*. Project Zero: Harvard Graduate School of Education. https://pz.harvard.edu/resources/project-zero-annual-report-2018-2019 (accessed 4 December 2021).

Boix Mansilla, Veronica & Anthony Jackson. 2011. Educating for global competence: preparing our youth to engage the world. *CCSSO and Asia Society*. New York: Asia Society. https://asiasociety.org/files/book-globalcompetence.pdf (accessed 6 March 2021).

Boix Mansilla, Veronica & Devon Wilson. 2020. What is global competence and what might it look like in Chinese schools? *Journal of Research in International Education* 19 (1). 3–22. https://doi.org/10.1177/1475240920914089 (accessed 6 March 2021).

Chen, Juanjuan, Minhong Wang, Tina A. Grotzer & Chris Dede. 2018. Using a three-dimensional thinking graph to support inquiry learning. *Journal for Research in Science Teaching* 55 (9). 1239–1263. https://doi.org/10.1002/tea.21450 (accessed 6 March 2021).

Clapp, Edward Peter & Michael Hanchett Hanson. 2019. Participatory creativity: Supporting dynamic roles and perspectives in the classroom. In Ronald Beghetto & Giovanni E. Corazza (eds.), *Dynamic perspectives on creativity*: New directions for theory, research, and practice in education, 27–46. Cham, Switzerland: Springer.

Gardner, Howard. 2011. Preface. In Veronica Boix & Anthony Jackson (eds.), *Educating for global competence:* preparing our youth to engage the world. CCSSO and Asia Society. New York: Asia Society. https://asiasociety.org/files/book-globalcompetence.pdf (accessed 6 March 2021).

Harshman, Jason. 2016. Critical Global Competence and the C3 in Social Studies Education. *The Social Studies* 107 (5). 160–164, https://doi.org/10.1080/00377996.2016.1190915

Hogan, Jillian, Kara Murdock, Morgan Hamill, Anastasia Lanzara & Ellen Winner. 2018. Looking at the process: Examining creative and artistic thinking in fashion designers on a reality television show. *Frontiers in Psychology*. https://www.frontiersin.org https://doi.org/10.3389/fpsyg.2018.02008 (accessed 6 March 2021).

Kamarainen, Amy, Joseph Reilly, Shari Metcalf, Tina A. Grotzer & Chris Dede. 2018. Using Mobile Location-Based Augmented Reality to Support Outdoor Learning in Undergraduate Ecology and Environmental Science Courses. *Bulletin of the Ecological Society of America* 99 (2) (April). 259–276. https://doi.org/10.1002/bes2.1396 (accessed 6 March 2021).

Mardell, Ben. 2019. Playful learning in early childhood classrooms: It's complicated. *Exchange* 41 (3). 53–56.

Orozco-Domoe, Jaclyn S. 2015. Journey to Global Competence: Learning Languages, Exploring Cultures, Transforming Lives. In: Moeller, A. J. (ed.). *Learn languages, Explore Cultures, Transform Lives. Report of the Central States Conference on the Teaching of Foreign Languages*. https://files.eric.ed.gov/fulltext/ED598272.pdf#page=77 (accessed 6 March 2021).

Ross, Jessica & Edward Peter Clapp. 2018. The Agency by Design inquiry cycle: Documenting inquiry and practice in the maker-centered classroom. *Agency by Design, Project Zero*: Harvard Graduate School of Education. www.agencybydesign.org (accessed 6 March 2021).

Salomão, Ana Cristina Biondo. 2015. The cultural component in language teaching: historical development and contemporary perspectives. *Trabalhos em Linguística Aplicada* 54 (2). 361–392. http://dx.doi.org/10.1590/0103-18134500150051 (accessed 11 December 2020).

Salomão, Ana Cristina Biondo. 2019. Teletandem and teacher's beliefs about culture and language. *International Journal of Computer-Assisted Language Learning and Teaching* 9. 1–18. https://www.igi-global.com/gateway/article/227373 (accessed 10 December 2020).

Salomão, Ana Cristina Biondo & Eduardo Viana da Silva. 2020. The application of the Global Competence Matrix in a virtual exchange program with US and Brazilian students. *Journal of Virtual Exchange* 3 (SI-IVEC 2019). 1–12. https://doi.org/10.21827/jve.3.35804 (accessed 10 December 2020).

Sheya, Sarah. 2018a. Elevating Youth Voice: The Power of Participatory Design. *Out of Eden Learn Blog*. https://walktolearn.outofedenwalk.com/2018/08/16/elevating-youth-voice-the-power-of-participatory-design/ (accessed 11 October 2020).

Sheya, Sarah. 2018b. Uncovering the Big Idea of Planetary Health. *Out of Eden Learn Blog*. https://walktolearn.outofedenwalk.com/2018/10/18/uncovering-the-big-idea-of-planetary-health/ (accessed 11 October 2020).

Telles, João Antonio & Maria Luisa Vassallo. 2006. Foreign language learning in-tandem: theoretical principles and research perspectives. *The ESPecialist* 27(1). 83–118.

Tully, James. 2014. On global citizenship. London: Bloomsbury. http://citeseerx.ist.psu.edu/viewdoc/download?doi=10.1.1.1025.2815&rep=rep1&type=pdf (accessed 10 November 2020)

Winner, Ellen. 2018. Valuing thinking in the arts. *Creative Teaching and Learning* 8 (4). 8–17.

Wu-Pope, Jeniffer. 2020. Singapore's Approach to Global Competence Development. *The Language Educator 15* (2). 41–44. https://www.thelanguageeducator.org/actfl/summer_2020/MobilePagedArticle.action?articleId=1616799 (accessed 15 December 2020).

Clara Bauler, Devin Thornburg, Óscar Ceballos, Carlos Pineda, Esther Kogan, Pirjo Sorri

# Chapter 9
# Tackling problems, finding solutions: Creativity and collaboration in cross-cultural virtual exchange during a pandemic

COVID-19 brought much uncertainty about our ability to travel or interact with communities across the globe. The many restrictions imposed by the pandemic directly affected the field of study abroad in higher education, closing down many programs and dreams of experimenting and engaging with diverse communities *in loco*. As educators whose primary concern is to value, promote and include cultural and linguistic diversity in our pedagogical practices, we immediately sought to procure ways we could continue to foster cross-cultural interactions and experiences in spite of the physical limitations of lockdowns and inability to travel. An increasingly important component to traditional study abroad experiences is virtual exchange among students who reside in geographically distant parts of the world (Hilliker 2020; O'Dowd & O'Rourke 2019). While there have been studies of telecollaboration over the past decade (e.g. Helm & Guth 2010), the most current form of virtual exchange usually entails telecollaboration via Zoom or other synchronous meeting platforms, such as Skype, Instagram Live, or Google Meets. Enhanced synchronous technology can afford possibilities for educators to reimagine cross-cultural encounters in a world that was completely shut down by a global health crisis.

Determined to provide authentic international experiences to our students, we, six educators at opposite sides of the Atlantic, came together to design and implement curriculum that would help a diverse group of high school students from a private multilingual school in Sevilla, Spain to develop proficiency in English while affording higher education freshman students in a private university

---

**Clara Bauler,** Adelphi University, e-mail: cbauler@adelphi.edu
**Devin Thornburg,** Adelphi University, e-mail: thornburg@adelphi.edu
**Óscar Ceballos,** CIEE, Sevilla, Spain, e-mail: oscarceballospina@gmail.com
**Carlos Pineda,** CIEE, Sevilla, Spain, e-mail: carlospinedagonzalez@gmail.com
**Esther Kogan,** Adelphi University, e-mail: kogan@adelphi.edu
**Pirjo Sorri,** Mission Laïque Française, Sevilla, Spain, e-mail: Pirjo.sorri@mlfmonde.org

in New York, United States, the opportunity to engage in cultural and linguistic exchange via weekly synchronous meetings. The focus of the conversations was on identity development, multilingualism, and multiculturalism via a series of projects designed to support these conversations, using both visual and written literacies. We examined our pedagogical practice and the application of the curriculum through an action research lens, which included qualitative data collection in four stages: planning, action, observation, and reflection (Richards and Farrell 2005). We documented and monitored what happened before, during, and after curriculum implementation via the collection of relevant artifacts, such as emails, conversation transcripts, classroom materials, and student work. The action research lens enabled us to engage in a critical dialogue about the consequences of our educational practices in order to transform our understandings, conduct, and conditions under which we implemented our curriculum (Kemmis, McTaggart & Nixon 2013). The ultimate goal of our action research was to collectively engage in dialogue to impact meaningful change for our students and for ourselves.

In the next sections, we outline our action research questions and goals following Richards and Farrell's (2005) cycle. The planning stage entailed asking questions and exploring ideas via collaborative discussion and relevant literature. The action stage included the design and implementation of the virtual exchange curriculum. The observation stage involved the identification of affordances and constraints of the curriculum, especially focusing on the use of synchronous platforms. During this stage, we collected artifacts such as student reflections, student work, e-mails, field notes as well as transcripts taken during synchronous remote learning classes to analyze student learning outcomes. Finally, at the reflection stage, we consider lessons learned and recommendations for future virtual exchange curriculum that aims at promoting cross-cultural dialogue.

# 1 Planning

## 1.1 Exploring relevant literature

The design and implementation of the virtual experience involved three higher education faculty from a private university in New York, United States, two higher education faculty from a public university in Spain and one high-school English as a foreign language teacher from a network of multilingual schools in Sevilla, Spain. From the beginning, we envisioned our pedagogical framework as a virtual cross-cultural collaborative experience that would address the needs of our two groups of students in the aftermath of the COVID-19 crisis. The most important premise was to foster authentic dialogue through activities that would generate genuine conversation and encounters via weekly synchronous meetings. Our choice for the synchronous media was motivated by two ideas. On one hand, synchronous weekly meetings had the potential to establish bonds between the participants by creating a platform to share and discuss ideas about culture, language, and self. On the other hand, the immediacy of the synchronous medium could provide an enhanced English learning experience as students would be in direct contact with peers who could act as tutors or more competent peers (Vygostsky 1978). This socio-cultural approach considers language and the Internet cultural tools that mediate human activity (Thorne 2003). The English language would become a shared communication tool for cross-cultural dialogue.

Studies on virtual exchange among linguistic, culturally, and geographically diverse students have demonstrated that learners gain linguistic knowledge (Hilliker 2020), engage in high levels of interaction (Fuchs 2019), develop an increased sense of global connectedness (Lehtomaki 2016), engage in sharing of stories and think critically about self and others (Masterson 2020) and achieve an enhanced ability to deal with on-the-spot communicative pressure, boosting in self-confidence (Kern 2014). Our virtual exchange curriculum followed a popular trend in the use of synchronous tools, such as Zoom, Instagram Live, WhatsApp, Skype, to connect students in Sevilla and New York.

In spite of the high praise and interest in synchronous media, research has also cautioned against the sole use of this tool in cross-cultural virtual exchange experiences. Kern (2014) asks educators to consider different types of media and technology to use according to different activities. There is a concern with how the medium can impact the quality of communication as there might be an imbalance of technological knowledge and cultural practices involving technology (Fuchs 2019). In addition, students' perceptions and attitudes on language, culture and identity will not be automatically transformed by the synchronous virtual dialogue only (O' Dowd 2019). There needs to be a change in stance (García 2020) in the course design and reflective activities to foster reflection and critical analysis of ideas, beliefs, and biases regarding linguistic and cultural diversity. In this sense, combination of synchronous and asynchronous learning is ideal with the exploration of all mediums to provide a more flexible and relational pedagogy (Cunningham & Akiyama 2018).

Research on intercultural competence and the use of English as a "Lingua Franca" in cross-cultural encounters has shed light on how students can develop both *nested interculturality* (Avineri 2019) and *contact zone competence* (Canagarajah 2014) through engagement in synchronous online courses. "Nested interculturality" is a collective of dispositions (enduring attitudes that guide behavior) and practices (behaviors and action that embody those dispositions) for ethical engagement in intercultural interactions (Avineri 2019); this model foregrounds the role of tensions at micro, meso, and macro levels. "Contact zone competence" reflects skills necessary for diverse individuals to negotiate time-and-place-bound spaces of mutual attention and mutual intention, transcending (perceived) boundaries between languages and groups (Canagarajah 2014). Platforms such as Zoom can foster critical empathy and other intercultural competence dispositions via screen sharing, allowing students to enter each other's home and familial spaces, and muting self and using virtual backgrounds, affording students the ability to listen and not show themselves or their homes if they do not feel safe (Avirneri, Guillen, and Sawin 2020). However, educators and students should not rely on synchronous meetings alone for meaningful cross-cultural interactions without enough support and pedagogical strategies. Guillén, Sawin, and Avineri (2020) suggest using Instagram, Twitter, and other social media posts to group discussions to tap into learners' linguistic and cultural questions in order to make learners "hungry" for content in synchronous classes. Following these suggestions, we also planned asynchronous interactions via Google Classroom and online discussions on Flipgrid.

## 1.2 Collaborating and discussing ideas

We met synchronously via Zoom weekly and exchanged ideas via email almost daily. Our virtual discussions were aimed at finding meaning and designing assignments. We tried to keep an open mind as we were getting to know each other's philosophies and pedagogies. We believed in the strength of collaboration to move this project forward. The first step was to overcome our first challenge; namely, integrating higher education freshman course content with high school foreign language learning objectives. The goals of the higher education freshman courses focused on critically examining and discussing key social and educational issues in the study of multilingualism, intercultural competence, and communication. We believed that engaging in cross-cultural dialogue through virtual exchange with multilingual students in Sevilla would help higher education freshman students in New York to question assumptions, concepts, and understandings of complex topics involving cultural, and linguistic diversity through an authentic experience. The objectives of the virtual exchange for high school students was to develop English proficiency through sharing and creating personal stories with a real audience of English speakers. The synchronous virtual exchange conversations would provide a platform for multilingual learners to express identity and creativity while practicing mutual understanding and empathy. We believed that for both groups of students the virtual exchange dialogue would provide a forum for learning about self and others by examining their own role as agents in a multilingual and multicultural society.

## 2 Action

### 2.1 Curriculum design

The virtual exchange weekly design involved pairs or trios formed of one freshman student from the private university in New York and one or two high school students from the multilingual secondary high school in Sevilla. The pairs or trios would meet synchronously weekly for 12 weeks. The high school student population included a total of 41 multilingual learners – 12th (7), 11th (11), 10th (10) and 9th (11) grades. The main language of instruction in the school was French. Selected content classes were offered in Spanish. English was offered as a foreign language class that met for 3 hours a week. The languages spoken by the high school students included French, Spanish, Arabic, English, and Russian.

The higher education freshman student population included 27 students who were taking one of the two freshman seminar courses on multilingualism (n=22) and multiculturalism (n=5). The higher education students were also linguistically, culturally and racially diverse, speaking English and many other languages. There were international students connecting from Pakistan, who spoke Urdu and/or Punjabi, Albania, who spoke Albanian, Brazil, who spoke Portuguese, Russia, who spoke Hebrew and Russian, Rwanda, who spoke French, Kinyarwanda, Burundi, and Kirundi as well as New York-based students who spoke or were exposed to multiple languages at home, such as Portuguese, Spanish, Italian, Cantonese, Jamaican Patois, Punjabi, Mayaylam, Gujarati, and Hindi. The higher education freshman students also reported having studied Spanish, Hebrew, Sign Language, Italian, Swahili, and German as foreign languages.

Students decided when to connect, including the day of the week, time of the day and synchronous platform to use (e.g., Zoom, Google Meets, WhatsApp, Instagram Live, etc.). We believed the freedom to choose a time to meet would allow for greater flexibility and comfort for the students as they would be able to connect from home and share their closest environment during their meetings. One of our colleagues in Sevilla was responsible for creating a spreadsheet with names, emails, age, cohort, class, language proficiency, and other notes for the purpose of organizing the pairs of students. He paired students by course and level of proficiency. If higher education students spoke French or Spanish, they would be paired with Lycée students whose English proficiency was emerging. He then introduced pairs or trios of students via email. Together we created a calendar of activities to organize and guide the weekly conversations displayed in Table 9.1:

**Table 9.1:** Calendar of Activities and Projects for the Virtual Exchange.

| Date | Activity | Main Projects |
| --- | --- | --- |
| SEPTEMBER 4–6 | Finalized students list, pairs matched, contacts shared by email | |
| SEPTEMBER 7–11 | First virtual meeting pairs; students would report to their professors that meetings took place; from them on, it was their responsibility to continue with their meetings once a week; professors on both sides would decide how to follow up with their students | |
| SEPTEMBER 7–11 | Professors in Sevilla, Spain, would join courses at university online and high school face to face, introducing themselves and the five projects students were to complete together (see below); deadlines for five projects announced; materials and activities for each of the projects shared via Flipgrid and Google Classroom | |
| SEPTEMBER 18 | Website of Collaborative Study Abroad active | |
| SEPTEMBER 25 | Final date for project 1 | Self-Portrait: Who am I? |
| OCTOBER 9 | Final date for project 2 | My community: What is my world? |
| OCTOBER 21 | Final date for project 3 | The others: Who is the most important person in my life? |
| NOVEMBER 13 | Final date for project 4 | The place where I come from: How did I become who I am? |
| DECEMBER 4 | Final date for project 5 | The place where I am going: What will be the best version of myself in the future? |
| DECEMBER 14–18 | Find date for joint celebration of all participants synchronously | |

The professors in Sevilla met two to three times with the high school students face to face to go over instructions for projects and to support the high school students in designing their work which would entail written narrative structure techniques, written profile composition, visual narration, video editing, and photographic portraiture. Models and specific scaffolds were provided to the high school students. The first two projects were to be created as visual projects (short videos and photographs), the next two were to be written narratives and the last, a combination project. A website was built for the multilingual class to archive and showcase the learners' stories described in the five projects. The faculty member for that course believed all stories deserved to be properly told and heard, broadening our knowledge about ourselves and about others in a world that needs sharing more than ever.

The faculty member for the multilingualism course also organized a Google Classroom for all students to share their work and post reflections weekly. The Google Classroom included Flipgrid discussions and reflections as well as written collaborative assignments using Google documents and discussion boards. These asynchronous activities would complement weekly synchronous meetings, providing scaffolds while fostering community building and sharing among the two groups of students. See Figures 9.1 and 9.2 for examples of asynchronous modules and activities.

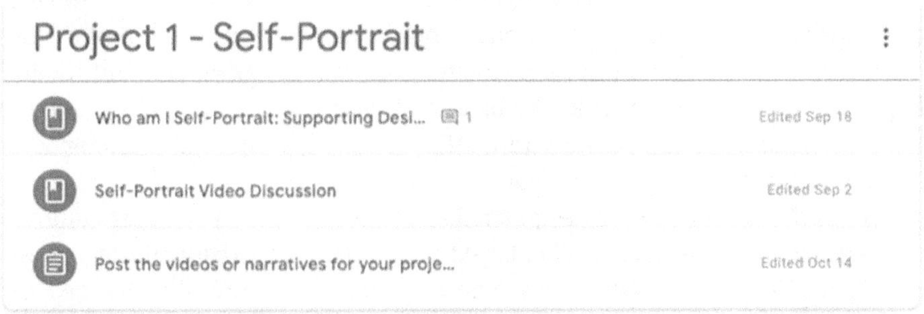

## Project 1 - Self-Portrait

- Who am I Self-Portrait: Supporting Desi... — Edited Sep 18
- Self-Portrait Video Discussion — Edited Sep 2
- Post the videos or narratives for your proje... — Edited Oct 14

**Figure 9.1:** Google Classroom Module 1 – Self-Portrait.

## 2.2 Curriculum implementation

Reality is always different from dreams. When it came to the implementation of the curriculum, we faced many unanticipated bumps in the road. We had to make quick changes to the curriculum to adapt to challenging circumstances. Due to COVID-19 school closures and uncertainties, high school students in

### Self-Portrait: Who am I?

0 responses · 0 views · 0 comments · 0 hours of engagement

Hello all! This week we will start to get to know each other as well as the international students we are working with. We will start by talking about ourselves through a "self-portrait video clip."

Post: Choose one or more of the topics below to share in a 90-second video:

*Who am I and who do others think I am in relation to...*
- My language(s)
- My Family
- My cultures
- Symbols of my country and community
- Different life contexts: home, school, street, social networks
- Other

You can use the sentence starters: *One important thing to know about me is... OR I love... OR This is what you need to know about me...*

Comment: Choose three peers and tell them what you would like to learn more about them. Ask questions using WHO, WHY, WHAT, WHERE, WHEN, HOW.

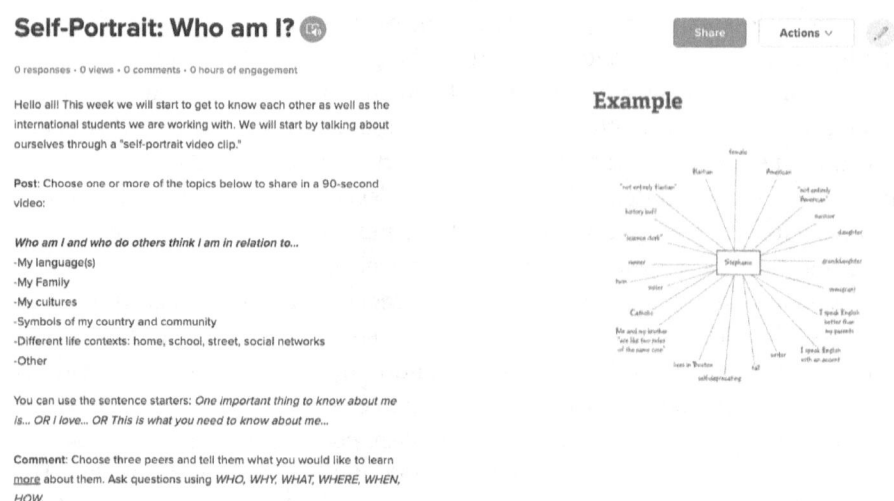

Example

**Figure 9.2:** Flipgrid Asynchronous Discussion – Who Am I?.

Sevilla started the semester later than the higher education freshman students which caused a change in the virtual exchange schedule we had originally created. In addition, the flexibility of having students choose at what times to meet and what platform to use generated confusion and frustration for some of the students who could not reach out to one another or could not find a common time to meet. To add up, the Google Classroom sharing community and Flipgrid asynchronous activities we had designed failed to be implemented due to security limitations of G-suite in adding email accounts that are outside of the host institution.

All of these sudden changes pushed us to quickly modify the curriculum to address needs and concerns. We started communicating frequently by emails, doing check-ins for students who were not communicating. We changed the schedule to accommodate for additional holidays and school closures and the late start of the curriculum implementation. We decreased the number of projects students would complete and made a few changes to roles and responsibilities. In the multilingual class, higher education freshman students did not complete the same projects with the high school students but assisted them in talking about the topics of their projects. The focus of the conversations became more centered on multilingualism. In the multiculturalism class, fewer higher education freshman students volunteered to be part of the virtual exchange, decreasing the actual number of students who participated. The multilingualism class involved integration of the projects into the class but, with 12 nations represented in the class and stranded by the pandemic in their own lands, the choice was offered of exchanging with students in Spain, New York City (in a public school only serving immigrant students), or other regions of the world of the students' choice. The students who volunteered still completed the same projects as the high school students. In the multilingualism class, the expectation was that all students would complete the same projects and share them with their cultural exchange partners, whether in Spain, New York City, or elsewhere. Finally, in both the multilingualism and multiculturalism class, the professors in New York started addressing issues and successes of their virtual exchange during synchronous Zoom classroom discussions. Classroom assignments were created to address the lack of sharing and communication via asynchronous platforms. Figures 9.3 and 9.4 demonstrate instances of synchronous Zoom classroom activities specially engaged to support or reflect on the virtual exchange dialogue and experience.

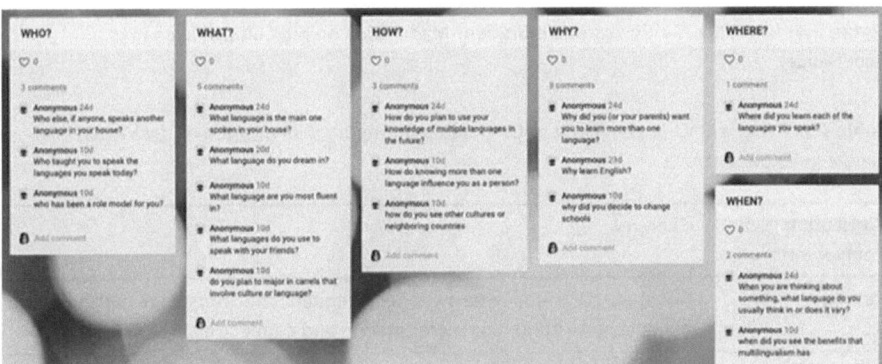

**Figure 9.3:** New York Multilingualism Freshman Students' Questions for their Partners in Sevilla.

The faculty member of the multilingualism course had the students who were to be engaged in a cultural exchange in New York City meet as a group with him present with the public school students from different language backgrounds from their own with a staff member offering translations into Spanish and Arabic. The students did not limit themselves to the topics selected, but initiated exchanges of other topics with the educators' input, including technology and music. Overall, the changes we made helped keep us afloat and move the curriculum forward. Our passion and collaboration were key in the actual implementation of the virtual exchange experience for both groups of students. Table 9.2 describes the components of the curriculum we had to change due to challenges in implementation.

## Cultural exchange partners: ▓▓▓▓▓▓

Communities: family, friends, school italian, Spanish, Sports team "A community is made from the people who you are around most often and the things you love doing"

Religion: Orthodox Christianity,

Familial terms: there is a sense of formality when talking with family but it depends who is being spoken to.

Education: Classes are taught in french other than history and geography which are done in Spanish and french, private schools are better because the class sizes are smaller which lets the teachers give more attention to each student.

Non-verbal gestures: When introduced to older person shake hands and kiss on both cheek

Festivals and celebrations: favorite holiday is is Halloween but second favorite is la cabalgata de los reyes magos

**Figure 9.4:** New York Multiculturalism Student-Made Slide on his Cultural Exchange Experience.

**Table 9.2:** Recurrent Changes Made to Curriculum during Implementation of the Virtual Exchange Experience.

| Curriculum Components | Changes |
|---|---|
| Pairing | Some partnerships were switched; frequent check-ins were carried out to make sure partnerships were thriving and connecting |
| Schedule | Holidays and other disruptions were taken into account; the schedule became more flexible and responsive to students' needs and pace of learning |
| Number of Projects | The number of projects decreased from 5 to 4; students on the higher education side had more freedom to complete or not the projects |
| Technology | Reliance on synchronous mode of instruction and communication; new classroom assignments were created to support and reflect on the virtual exchange experience during synchronous Zoom class meetings; introduction of asynchronous tasks by each instructor to support or augment the synchronous communication |

## 3 Observation

### 3.1 Data collection

In order to assess affordances and constraints of the virtual exchange experience, we collected varied sources of data, such as our own notes, anecdotal information coming from higher education freshman students and high school students, e-mails we shared almost daily, and higher education student work. These artifacts shed light on issues as well as successes we were having with the curriculum implementation, helping us reflect about what aspects would enhance or hinder student participation. Unfortunately, we could not gather data on the actual recordings of the conversations students had during their synchronous virtual meetings. Table 9.3 illustrates each phase of the action research stage (Richards and Farell 2005) in relation to the goals and data we collected. We want to be clear that this table does not imply a linear process to the action research work, which was much more dynamic and recursive, jumping from observation and collaborative reflection to action on several occasions.

**Table 9.3:** Data Collection in the Virtual Exchange Action Research.

| Action Research Stage | Goals | Data Source |
| --- | --- | --- |
| Planning | Ask questions and explore ideas | Faculty e-mails<br>Faculty meeting notes<br>Curriculum materials |
| Action | Design and implement new pedagogy | Faculty and Student e-mails<br>Faculty meeting notes<br>Spreadsheets<br>Higher education student work<br>Zoom transcript of class discussions |
| Observation | Collect and analyze data on student learning | Faculty and Student e-mails<br>Higher education student video reflections<br>Higher education student reflection<br>Anecdotal information |
| Reflection | Consider implications of the new pedagogy adopted | Curriculum presentations<br>Faculty meeting notes<br>Faculty and student e-mails<br>Faculty reflection notes |

## 3.2 Data analysis

Through e-mails and our notes, we discovered right from the start that some partners would work well with each other while other partnerships would fall apart due to many constraints including time difference, scheduling conflicts, and technology. The trios seemed to have afforded a more relaxed and productive structure for synchronous conversations; however, due to the fact that the study was a pilot, we could not systematically analyze the impact of different groupings or age on the quality of the virtual exchange conversations. Most frequently, the most cited problem for all groups of students was the time difference which created scheduling conflicts. A few partnerships had difficulties connecting every week as illustrated in Higher Education Student A's reflection: "Meeting my partner from Seville was not an easy work. It was so difficult. Scheduling a time with him for a meeting and we missed a few meetings due to the confusing time difference. Finally we met." Given these challenges, many students started using asynchronous modes of communication to interact. Students started texting or messaging their partners constantly, establishing connections and sharing ideas this way. This incidental use of WhatsApp, Instagram and other messaging tools was a resourceful way students found to circumvent two apparent road blocks: time difference and busy schedules.

One other obstacle was the length of the meeting associated with the lack of specific guidelines for what to say during the conversations. Many students struggled to keep the conversations going either due to not being confident with the English language yet or due to personality as Higher Education Student B reports:

> One thing I learned about having a conversation with my partner was definitely that you can make somebody who was definitely shy turn into very like friendly and outgoing. I know for me and her, we had different personalities. I'm very outgoing, friendly, and she's very shy, closed off, didn't know what to say and this was definitely not going well. Obviously it's a problem because with two different personalities it's hard to make conversation, but I notice as time goes on, we've been getting more and more close where we found a bond. I feel like she's even my friend now.

To tackle perceived communication problems in English, students used all creative sorts of mediation tools to facilitate the conversation. As many higher education students and high school students were multilinguals, they engaged in translanguaging strategies and practices (García, Johnson & Seltzer 2017), tapping into all of their linguistic repertoires to make meaning and express themselves about complex topics involving family, self, religion, education, and community. Others utilized Google translate and other technological tools to help them convey their messages, ideas and thoughts. Higher Education Student C's response illustrate the translanguaging practices she and her high school partners engaged in:

> It's a very fun experience because for my group, they speak English, but they have some struggles with some words. It's okay with me because I speak French and I understand a bit of Spanish, so sometimes they'll start a sentence in English and then end it completely in French which is really fun because I thought I was the only person who did that. But it is really fun because we get to talk about a bunch of different things and I think that at this point they're very comfortable with me, so that they're able to open up and they're able to ask questions and I'm able to also ask questions that make them think a little bit more. And you know we've covered a lot recently um we've covered a lot about family and the differences.

These were creative solutions students utilized to develop their multilingual identities in an environment that was flexible and accepting of their translingual practices. In other words, the synchronous virtual exchange was supportive of all the students' multilingualism, not suppressing students' voices and resources.

In spite of the challenges, most partnerships were successful in establishing bonds and conversations through the weekly synchronous virtual meetings. Students reported enthusiasm about the meetings and ongoing interactions with their partners. In particular, students reported the importance of having a human connection at times of isolation. The majority of students were excited about the similarities they shared with their peers. Others mentioned how the interactions helped them consider or develop new perspectives. Higher Education Student D's reflection is an example of how finding shared goals and interests helped her and her partner keep the dialogue going:

> I was really excited to learn that my partner and I had very similar lives. We were both going through schooling during COVID and because of that we were able to relate to each other. We laughed about needing to wear masks and discuss the ways that we have been to our lives have been affected by Corona. Something else that I thought was really cool is that our schooling systems are very similar. We both need to go to high school for four years and then take an exam as the SAT. I don't remember what his was called, but based off that test you get accepted into universities. And College is something else that was very important was that we discussed the areas that we lived in. He showed me outside of his house. The streets were all built of stone and he told me that he lives in the old city of Seville. I told him that it reminded me of the old city of Jerusalem because they both have the same kinds of stone.

High School Student A and High School Student B had a similar experience: "We have also chatted about daily routines here. What we do in a day here versus what he's doing in a day over there. We have also talked about stuff that has been going on lately, like pandemic, Coronavirus, Black Lives Matter and a tiny bit of politics." Higher Education Student E's response, in turn, sheds light on the importance of cross-cultural dialogue to help him develop new perspectives and empathy: "I think it was something that just made me learn to be more comprehensive and like try to be a better person with the others like never judge anyone and I think I've got more mature than I was with these cultural exchanges and like getting to know more people better." Overall, the virtual experience yielded positive learning outcomes, empowering students to find solutions to perceived problems that may arise during cross-cultural dialogue. Table 9.4 outlines the perceived problems students had and the creative solutions they used to solve them.

**Table 9.4:** Student Problems and Solutions during the Virtual Exchange Experience.

| Perceived Problems | Solutions |
|---|---|
| Scheduling and time conflicts | The use of both synchronous and asynchronous modes of communication |
| Developing English proficiency | Translanguaging and the use of translation tools |
| Finding topics for conversation | Sharing common goals and interests |

# 4 Reflection

## 4.1 Lessons learned

We learned two important lessons during our 12-week virtual exchange experience. The first lesson was the importance of faculty collaboration. Through our passion, commitment and, above all, teamwork, we were able to tackle implementation problems that were completely unanticipated during the design phase of the curriculum. The pandemic heightened issues of connectivity and communication. In specific, during planning, we had intentionally designed multiple media for both synchronous and asynchronous interactions without foreseeing that technological tools demand familiarity and favorable conditions to work on both sides of the virtual partnership (Fuchs 2019). Nevertheless, we were able to respond to students' needs and difficulties by working together through dialogue (Kemmis, McTaggart & Nixon 2013). We met constantly and we e-mailed frequently. Consistent communication led us to act fast with concerted goals to make necessary changes. Our strong collaboration helped us overcome adversity, reflect on what was just for our students while affording an improved virtual exchange experience for all.

The second lesson was the incredible resourcefulness of our students' creativity. Because we did not plan or want to monitor the actual encounters and conversations partners were having, students were left to their own devices when issues occurred. On one hand, we perceived this extreme freedom as reflecting our lack of support for sustaining dialogue. On the other hand, the freedom and flexibility of the synchronous weekly meetings allowed students to become more autonomous, devising on-spot solutions to problems that could hinder or damage cross-cultural dialogue (Kern 2014). Translanguaging via the use of the multilingual students' full repertoires or translation tools emerged as an extremely effective way to keep the conversations going while fostering and valuing multilingualism and pluralism of a very diverse group of students (García, Johnson & Seltzer 2017). Finding something in common allowed both groups of students to learn about self and others. The initial struggles both groups of students faced to communicate led them to critically examine and discuss key social and educational issues in the study of multilingualism, intercultural competence and communication via a genuine and authentic dialogue. In doing so, higher education freshman students accomplished the goals of the two university courses. We should never underestimate the power of student-led learning.

## 4.2 Recommendations

Given the two lessons learned, we recommend the following practical strategies to enhance virtual cross-cultural dialogue among geographically, culturally and linguistically diverse students:
- **Scaffold**: Use student pictures, shared activities, such a list of topics or interview questions, and conversation starters and models to provide language supports for students who are still emerging in their language learning proficiency in English. These supports will help both groups of students in expanding and stretching language while having a synchronous virtual conversation.
- **Combine different media**: Both synchronous and asynchronous modes of communication should be intentionally integrated in the course. A survey of what media students engage with the most on both sides can help choose the most preferable online platforms (Guillén, Sawin, and Avineri 2020). This way, informal or formal asynchronous learning can complement synchronous virtual meetings by providing a forum for students to share and build community. Students that are emerging in communicating their ideas in English might also appreciate having multiple ways to express themselves via asynchronous interaction by posting a video, writing a text message or participating in social media exchanges. The combination of synchronous and asynchronous tools

can offer a myriad of possibilities for educators to reimagine cross-cultural encounters in a world that has been completely transformed by a pandemic.
- **Support use of students' content and skill expertise in the development of the exchange**: While students might need support to build communication in virtual exchanges, it is clear that they also provide one another some rich and valuable knowledge with regard to their disciplinary expertise. Support in sharing that knowledge and skill can be provided with faculty direction and encouragement via brainstorming sessions and surveys that collect information about students' expertise.
- **Tap and utilize all students' linguistic repertoires**: Strategic and intentional use of translanguaging practices and pedagogies demands a change of attitude regarding the role of English learning; that is, "actions of bilingual students that go beyond those legitimated in schools are then perceived as virtuous, complex, fluid, creative and critical, and not simply as deficient. Teachers with a translanguaging stance trust that their bilingual students have the potential to make meaning for themselves" (García 2020).

In cross-cultural encounters, teachers should focus on developing the "how," negotiating and strategizing translanguaging practices and technological tools with students in order to support and boost dialogue (Canagarajah 2014). Honoring, affirming and using all multilingual students' linguistic repertoires while tapping into digitally mediated practices they take part in can enhance the cross-cultural experience, leading students to think broadly, deeply and more critically about the world we live in. Virtual Exchange curriculum design and implementation can be an opportunity for teachers and students to transform language education by following García's (2020) powerful call for action – using students' rich linguistic, racial, cultural and technological funds of knowledge to think, collaborate, reflect, empathize, create and engage in new ideas and social practices.

# References

Avineri, Netta. 2019. "Nested interculturality": Dispositions and practices for navigating tensions in immersion experiences. In *Redefining teaching competence through immersive programs*, 37–64. United Kingdom: Palgrave Macmillan. https://doi.org/10.1007/978-3-030-24788-1_2

Avineri, Netta., Gabriel Guillen & Thor Sawin. 2020. How Can We Foster a Mobile Mindset While Sheltering in Place?. https://iccglobal.org/2020/09/30/how-can-we-foster-a-mobile-mindset-while-sheltering-in-place/ (accessed March 18 2021).

Canagarajah, Suresh. 2014. In search of a new paradigm for teaching English as an international language. *TESOL Journal* 5 (4). 767–785. https://doi.org/10.1002/tesj.166

Chun, Dorothy, Richard Kern & Brian Smith. 2016. Technology in language use, language teaching, and language learning. *The Modern Language Journal 100* (S1). 64–80. https://doi.org/10.1111/modl.12302

Cunningham, Joseph D. & Yuka Akiyama. 2018. Synthesizing the practice of SCMC-based telecollaboration: A scoping review. *Calico Journal* 35 (1). 49–76. https://doi.org/10.1558/cj.33156

Fuchs, Carolyn. 2019. Critical incidents and cultures-of-use in a Hong Kong–Germany telecollaboration. *Language* Learning & Technology *23* (3). 74–97. http://hdl.handle.net/10125/44697

García, Ofelia. 2020. Singularity, complexities and contradictions: A commentary about translanguaging, social justice and education 11–20. Switzerland: Springer. https://link.springer.com/chapter/10.1007/978-3-658-28128-1_2 (accessed March 18 2021).

García, Ofelia, Suzanna Ibarra Johnson & Kate Seltzer. 2017. *The translanguaging classroom: Leveraging student bilingualism for learning*. Philadelphia, PA: Caslon.

Guillén, Gabriel, Thor Sawin & Netta Avineri. 2020. Zooming out of the crisis: Language and human collaboration. *Foreign Language Annals 53* (2). 320–328. https://doi.org/10.1111/flan.12459

Hare Landa, Melissa, Jocelyn Odòna-Holm & Lijuan Shi. (2017). Education abroad and domestic cultural immersion: A comparative study of cultural competence among teacher candidates. *The Teacher Educator 52* (3). 250–267. https://doi.org/10.1080/08878730.2017.1313922

Guth, Sarah & Francesca Helm, eds. 2010. *Telecollaboration 2.0: Language, literacies and intercultural learning in the 21st century*. Vol. 1. Bern, Switzerland: Peter Lang.

Hilliker, Shannon. 2020. Virtual Exchange as a study abroad alternative to foster language and culture exchange in TESOL teacher education. *TESL-EJ 23* (4). 1–13. http://www.tesl-ej.org/wordpress/issues/volume23/ej92/ej92a7/ (accessed March 18 2021).

Kemmis, Stephen, Robin McTaggart & Rhonda Nixon. 2013. *The action research planner: Doing critical participatory action research*. Switzerland: Springer Science & Business Media.

Kern, Richard. 2014. Technology as Pharmakon: The promise and perils of the internet for foreign language education. *The Modern Language Journal 98* (1). 340–357. https://doi.org/10.1111/j.1540-4781.2014.12065.x

Lehtomäki, Elina, Josephine Moate & Hanna Posti-Ahokas. 2016. Global connectedness in higher education: student voices on the value of cross-cultural learning dialogue. *Studies in Higher Education, 41* (11). 2011–2027. https://doi.org/10.1080/03075079.2015.1007943

Masterson, M. 2020. An Exploration of the Potential Role of Digital Technologies for Promoting Learning in Foreign Language Classrooms: Lessons for a Pandemic. *International Journal of Emerging Technologies in Learning 15* (14). 83–96. https://online-journals.org/index.php/i-jet/article/view/13297

Morley, Alyssa, Alisha MB Braun, Lodi Rohrer & David Lamb. 2019. Study Abroad for Preservice Teachers. *Global Education Review 6* (3). 4–29. https://ger.mercy.edu/index.php/ger/article/view/521

O'Dowd, Richard. 2018. From telecollaboration to virtual exchange: State-of-the-art and the role of UNICollaboration in moving forward. *Research-publishing.net 1*. 1-23. https://doi.org/10.14705/rpnet.2018.jve.1

O'Dowd, Richard. 2019. A transnational model of virtual exchange for global citizenship education. *Language Teaching 1* (14). doi:10.1017/S0261444819000077

O'Dowd, Richard & Breffni O'Rourke. 2019. New developments in virtual exchange in foreign language education. *Language Learning & Technology 23* (3). 1–7. http://hdl.handle.net/10125/44690

Richards, Jack C. & Thomas Sylvester Charles Farrell. (2005). Professional development for language teachers: Strategies for teacher learning. Germany: Ernst Klett Sprachen.

Siergiejczyk, G. 2020. Virtual International Exchange as a High-Impact Learning Tool for More Inclusive, Equitable and Diverse Classrooms. *European Journal of Open, Distance and E-learning 23* (1). https://doi.org/10.2478/eurodl-2020-0001

Thorne, Steven. 2003. Artifacts and cultures-of-use in intercultural communication. *Language Learning & Technology 7* (2). 38–67. DOI 10125/25200/

Vygotsky, Lev. 1978. Interaction between learning and development. *Readings on the development of children 23* (3). 34–41.

**Teacher education and virtual exchange**

Chesla Ann Lenkaitis
# Chapter 10
# Integrating the United Nations' Sustainable Development Goals into a teacher preparation program: Developing content for virtual exchanges

## 1 Introduction

Technology provides opportunities for people to communicate through computer-mediated activities. These activities can be either asynchronous (non-real-time) or synchronous (real-time). Regardless of the type of communication, how people communicate has changed significantly with technology (Kern 2006). Through the virtual exchange (VE), one of the recent communication tools, teacher candidates can connect with learners of their content area (Lenkaitis 2020b) in geographically different locations by using technological tools (Dooly 2017). Recent VEs have used synchronous computer-mediated communication (SCMC) tools like Skype (Terhune 2016) and Zoom (Lenkaitis 2020a). In VEs utilizing this type of SCMC, various opportunities exist (Lewis, Cappellini, and Rivens Mompean 2017), where learners create a virtual co-presence (de Fornel 1996) that mimics the face-to-face traditional class setting and gives students a platform to collaborate in real-time (Lenkaitis 2020a).

Research exists utilizing VEs for teacher preparation programs (Dooly and Sadler 2013; Fuchs, Hauck, and Müller-Hartmann 2012), but the research is still growing regarding the integration of the United Nations' Sustainable Development Goals (SDGs) into VE (Bruun 2018; Lenkaitis 2021). In this VE study that partnered the second language (L2) teacher candidates in the United States with the L2 teacher candidates in Colombia and Poland, the SDGs were used as a lens that would develop teacher candidates' pedagogy.

---

Chesla Ann Lenkaitis, *East Stroudsburg* Area High School South,
e-mail: chesla-lenkaitis@esasd.net

https://doi.org/10.1515/9783110727364-011

## 2 Literature review

### 2.1 Virtual exchange (VE)

In VE, teacher candidates can connect with learners of their content area (Lenkaitis 2020b) in geographically different locations by using technological tools (Dooly 2017). Although research exists regarding the value of telecollaborative projects in English language learning (Austin, Hampel, and Kukulska-Hulme 2017; Sevilla-Pavón 2016), the body of research on utilizing telecollaboration for teacher preparation programs (e.g., Dooly and Sadler 2013; Fuchs et al. 2012; The EVALUATE Group 2019; Zhang et al. 2016) is still growing as much as the research focuses on the development of educational technology strategies. Distinct from its counterparts, this study focuses on professional development through reflection (Lenkaitis 2020b; Körkkö, Kyrö-Ämmälä, and Turunen 2016) of the SDGs.

In a two-year telecollaborative study, Dooly and Sadler (2013) investigated student language teacher participants from both the USA and Spain who worked together to co-produce teaching materials. In order to educate participants about the innovative, technological resources that exist for teaching and the ways how to use these resources for the second language (L2) learning and teaching, both synchronous and asynchronous resources were used in the VE. Upon analyzing the results, participants realized not only the importance of using technology to be successful in their L2 classrooms but also the benefit of collaborating with other teachers to co-construct even better lessons.

Fuchs et al. (2012) focused on language candidates, including Teaching English to the Speakers of Other Languages (TESOL), from Germany, Poland, the United Kingdom, and the United States. In this study, participants were able to learn about L2 learning and teaching technological resources and raise their metacognitive awareness and autonomous skills (Holec 1985) through task completion. By utilizing less-structured technological resources, learners needed to develop their own strategies to navigate the technological unknown or the "digital wilds" (Thorne, Sauro, and Smith. 2015: 215).

The EVALUATE Group (2019) has been to date the largest study that showcases the partnering of teacher candidates in VEs to complete tasks that included developing curriculum and educational materials. In this exchange, 1,000 teacher candidates from over thirty countries made twenty-five partnerships. Both qualitative and quantitative results revealed that teacher candidates developed competencies such as digital-pedagogical, linguistic, and intercultural as a result of the collaboration.

Zhang et al. (2016) investigated some teacher candidates for both K-12 and adult education from Hong Kong and Canada that were partnered in a community of practice that allowed participants to reflect on learning and teaching in relation to technology. In order to answer questions on various topics, such as cultural diversity, social networking, and multimedia, students were asked to interact with their partners and discuss topics on an online forum. Through the analysis of online interactions and survey data, Zhang et. al (2016). found that participation in the forum contributed to candidates' raising awareness and developing knowledge about technologies and diversity in education.

Apart from the above studies that focused on educational technology, Lenkaitis (2020b) examined the reflections of fifteen TESOL teacher candidate participants, who taught English learners with beginner and intermediate proficiency levels during a 4-week VE (videoconferencing) program. The TESOL teacher candidates examined language produced by their partners as they considered their educational course content. They also reflected on their experiences by watching their video-recorded sessions. The analyses revealed that reflecting on a VE allowed participants to bridge theory into practice.

## 2.2 Sustainable Development Goals (SDGs)

Adopted by its Member States in 2015, the United Nations' SDGs are part of the 2030 Agenda for Sustainable Development. This agenda "has provided a blueprint for shared prosperity in a sustainable world – a world where all people can live productive, vibrant, and peaceful lives on a healthy planet" (United Nations 2019: 2). In order to improve world conditions, the SDGS are the objectives to be met by all countries "in a global partnership" (United Nations 2019). Due to the current global pandemic, these "goals provide a critical framework for COVID-19 recovery" (United Nations 2020a: para. 1).

There are seventeen SDGs as proposed by the United Nations. They include: 1) No poverty 2) Zero hunger, 3) Good health and well-being, 4) Quality education, 5) Gender equality, 6) Clean water and sanitation, 7) Affordable and clean energy, 8) Decent work and economic growth, 9) Industry, innovation, and infrastructure, 10) Reduced inequalities, 11) Sustainable cities and communities, 12) Responsible consumption and production, 13) Climate action, 14) Life below water, 15) Life on land, 16) Peace, justice and institutions, and 17) Partnership for the goals (United Nations 2020b). SDGs have been the focus of higher education (Albareda-Tiana, Vidal-Raméntol, and Fernández-Morilla 2018). However, there is limited research on the integration of the United Nations' Sustainable Development Goals (SDGs) into VE (Bruun 2018; Fors and Lennerfors 2020; Forward et al. 2020; Garcia-Esteban 2020; Lenkaitis 2021).

In Bruun's (2018) study, one class in Tanzania worked with a class in Sweden for seven weeks to complete a project where participants focused on SDG #14 and discussed and proposed solutions for how to reduce the amount of plastic pollution. Garcia-Esteban (2020) worked with SDGs in teacher trainee VE while Forward et al. (2020) created partnerships that connected participants with non-governmental organizations (NGOs) in order to take SDG-related actions. Echoing Fors and Lennerfors (2020), who discussed the importance to focus on global issues, and Lenkaitis (in press, 2021), who suggested that integrating SDG content into VE can support the United Nations' 2030 Agenda, these studies have shown the usefulness of integrating SDGs into VE.

# 3 Research question

There is a growing body of research for the teacher candidate VE; however, the research lacks utilizing the SDGs in VE, more specifically in teacher candidate VE. This study focuses on four teacher candidates and the ways how they were able to develop their pedagogy in an SDG-focused VE. The following research question is answered:
- In what ways did an SDG-focused VE allow L2 teacher candidates to develop their pedagogy, more specifically their teaching methods?

# 4 Methods

## 4.1 Participants

The study focuses on four L2 teacher candidates that participated in a VE program. In order to illuminate the developing and changing pedagogies of these four participants, this study utilized Merriam (1998) and Ayres, Kavanaugh, and Knafl's (2003) case study methodology. The average age of the four teacher candidates was 20.5 years old (SD = 2.38). The following are details of each participant in the case study:
1) Barbara[1] was a graduate student in a Master of Arts in Teaching in Spanish Adolescence Education program in the United States. She was 22 years old.

---

[1] Psedonyms are used for participants' names.

2) Charlotte was an undergraduate student from Colombia studying modern languages and cultures. She was 19 years old and preparing to be an English teacher.
3) Stanley was an 18-year-old undergraduate student from Colombia. He was studying modern languages and cultures and preparing to be an English teacher.
4) Anna was a graduate student from a Polish university, where she studied English philology and is preparing to be an English teacher. She was 23 years old.

## 4.2 Procedures

Participants were guided through weekly instructions to video conference through Zoom (https://zoom.us) with their partner(s) for at least 15 minutes for six weeks (Week 1–6).

**Week 1.** In addition to introductions, during this first session, participants decided as a group which top four SDGs from the list of 17 they would focus on.

**Weeks 2–5.** Each of the top four SDGs was the weekly topic for these four weeks. During each of these synchronous sessions, using Google slides, the group needed to summarize their discussion of the week's SDG and to come up with a list of at least four pedagogical actions that they could take to reach this goal.

**Week 6.** The group completed a final activity on Google slides. In this activity, they discussed the importance of the SDGs, more specifically, the top four SDGs they chose. The group also detailed some short- and long-term actionable items that they could implement in education to reach the SDGs. Participants also had the opportunity to comment on and summarize their VE experience.

# 5 Results

The results are presented by the weeks of the VE. Throughout the exchange, the four teacher candidates of the case study had over an hour and 20 minutes of synchronous meetings to discuss SDGs.

## Week 1

During this week, participants spent a total of 12 minutes, 31 seconds on Zoom. After introducing themselves, the group decided that the following four SDGs were its top 4:
1) Goal 4 – Quality education
2) Goal 5 – Gender equality
3) Goal 12 – Responsible consumption and production
4) Goal 14 – Life below water

Figure 10.1 shows the Google slide that the participants created during Week 1.

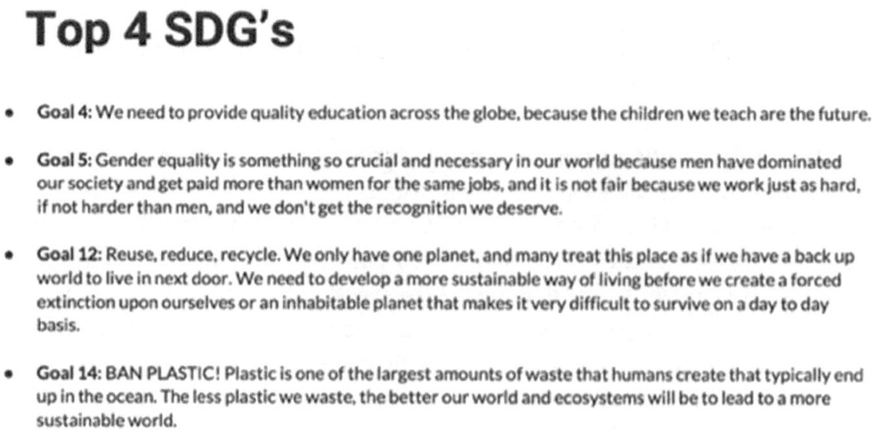

## Top 4 SDG's

- **Goal 4:** We need to provide quality education across the globe, because the children we teach are the future.

- **Goal 5:** Gender equality is something so crucial and necessary in our world because men have dominated our society and get paid more than women for the same jobs, and it is not fair because we work just as hard, if not harder than men, and we don't get the recognition we deserve.

- **Goal 12:** Reuse, reduce, recycle. We only have one planet, and many treat this place as if we have a back up world to live in next door. We need to develop a more sustainable way of living before we create a forced extinction upon ourselves or an inhabitable planet that makes it very difficult to survive on a day to day basis.

- **Goal 14:** BAN PLASTIC! Plastic is one of the largest amounts of waste that humans create that typically end up in the ocean. The less plastic we waste, the better our world and ecosystems will be to lead to a more sustainable world.

**Figure 10.1:** Participants' Google slide noting their top four SDGs.

## Weeks 2–5

During their discussions, which totaled over an hour, the group needed to come up with a list of at least four actionable things that it could do in education to reach the four SDGs that it identified as the top four. Table 10.1 details the time spent on Zoom for each of these weeks, while Table 10.2 lists examples of actionable things that the group summarized for each week's discussion.

# Chapter 10 Integrating the United Nations' Sustainable Development Goals — 215

**Table 10.1:** Time spent on Zoom during Weeks 2–5.

| Week | Time spent (hours: seconds) |
|---|---|
| 2 | 18:19 |
| 3 | 16:49 |
| 4 | 18:23 |
| 5 | 17:46 |

**Table 10.2:** Key points of discussions during Weeks 2–5*.

| Week | SDG focus | Examples of actionable things that were discussed |
|---|---|---|
| 2 | Quality education | Some issues that stem from poor quality education are underfunding. Other countries suffer from poor health care and unclean water, which prevents children from attending schools. |
| | | Something that we can implement is mentors. If children have mentors to help support them in their lives. If we can help other countries in regards to providing resources and support, we can hopefully break cycles of poor education. Because if children have access to clean drinking water and the doctor, they will be in school longer. |
| | | Another thing is funding. Schools should be funded equally across countries. Proper qualification for teachers in regards to children with special needs. |
| 3 | Gender equality | Women are going to experience different challenges than men will experience in life. Women and girls suffer from discrimination and violence. Women are 50% of the population, and they should have equal access to all things. Women should have increased political positions. This will give women and girls more rights and opportunities. It will empower them. |
| | | Destroying gender stereotypes within the home and then expanding it beyond and into the neighborhood. However, some people can stay closed-minded. At the same time, young people are not set in close-minded ways. We can also avoid making assumptions about gender roles. |

**Table 10.2** (continued)

| Week | SDG focus | Examples of actionable things that were discussed |
|---|---|---|
| 4 | Responsible consumption and production | While we desire to include the whole planet on board with becoming more sustainable, starting out on an individual scale is also just as important. Some things we could do is bring our own bags to the grocery store and not take plastic bags. We can reduce our energy consumption. If people own homes, they can also use solar panels. We can also more thoughtful when it comes to preparing foods ourselves. We can avoid going out to dinner. Rather, prepare food at home and use all the parts of the food and not throw them away. We can change our lifestyles. |
| | | Another thing we can also emphasize is how being more eco friendly will actually save people money. So using a reusable water bottle will be more cost-worthy than buying a 30 pack every week. |
| 5 | Life below water | We live in a circle of life, and we have to be conscious of our waste. Plastic waste, for example, is one of the biggest contributors to waste in the ocean. Animals are getting caught on them and they are also eating them. All of this is not good because plastic should not even be in the oceans in the first place! Not all countries think of investing in our world, in the sense of making things more environmentally friendly. |
| | | If there is not water, then there is not life. We cannot exist without water. Trying to reduce plastic and use fewer plastic products is crucial. |

*All examples, including any errors, have been taken verbatim from the participants' activities.

# Week 6

In the final week of the exchange, the group met on Zoom for 30 minutes, 15 seconds. In addition to discussing the importance of each of its top four SDGs in education, the group also discussed short- and long-term actionable items that they could do in education to reach the goals. Table 10.3 details the importance of each goal as given by the group, whereas Table 10.4 illustrates how the participants will take action.

**Table 10.3:** Importance of SDGs*.

| Week | SDG focus | Some topics that were discussed |
|---|---|---|
| 2 | Quality education | Providing quality education is so crucial. The children that we are teaching are going to be the next generation that is going to change the world. They are the future, and if we do not provide them quality education, they will have fewer opportunities to succeed and thrive in life. |
| 3 | Gender equality | Equality among men and women is something so crucial and something so overdue. Women should be valued just as equally as men are. However, that is not the truth within the society in which we live. Men have dominated society; getting better jobs, higher paying jobs, more privilege within society. Unfortunately, women have been considered inferior to men and, today, still suffer the consequences of that. This also affects education because boys have priority over education than women. |
| 4 | Responsible consumption and production | Responsible Consumption – We only have one planet, and most people treat this world as if we have a back up one next door. Mankind, as people in society, we need to be more conscious and aware of the choices we make and how that affects us, others, the environment, as well as the long-term effects it will have on the world. If you don't have a planet, then kids can't go to school! |
| 5 | Life below water | Plastic is contaminating our world. It is polluting our oceans and killing wildlife. If society comes together in an effort to ban plastic, the less plastic we waste that we create, the better our world and ecosystems will be, which will lead to a more sustainable world. If you don't have a planet, then kids can't go to school! |

*All examples, including any errors, have been taken verbatim from the participants' activities.

Also, in this week, three of the four participants (Stanley did not) noted their experiences during the SDG-focused VE. Figure 10.2 shows the Google slide where participants noted their experience. All names used are pseudonyms.

**Table 10.4:** Short- and long-term actionable items for each SDG*.

| Week | SDG focus | Short-term actions | Long-term actions |
|---|---|---|---|
| 2 | Quality education | Tutors, mentors, good teachers/ qualified teachers, unions, work | Law and policies, increase funding, develop education in developing countries with limited access to education, supporting foundations |
| 3 | Gender equality | breaking the stereotypes when someone says something incorrect, voting for women in political positions, encourage and empower girls to challenge themselves | We as women can show how we are not the weaker sex, we can fight for our gender, avoid making assumption about gender roles |
| 4 | Responsible consumption and production | Conscious consumption, daily choices, emphasize how to be more eco-friendly (being more green saves you money!!!), support recycling, second hand clothes/donating them | Changing the law, making restrictions, limit on waste, protesting against issues, fight for new laws, usage of solar panels to reduce energy consumption |
| 5 | Life below water | reducing plastic bag waste and using reusable bags, starting on a small scale within the neighborhood, reduce littering/ picking up garbage off the ground | banning plastic bags by law to reduce the waste. Laws and policies to have these take effect. Support teams and organizations to clean the ocean |

*All examples, including any errors, have been taken verbatim from the participants' final activity.

**Experience of collaborating across countries:**

Barbara: I truly found this experience very interesting and enlightening. It was fun to collaborate with others from around the world and discuss the issues that exist globally. Hearing all the different points of views and perspectives truly gave very interesting and insightful points of views on how each country deals with these issues and how it affects its citizens.

Annna: For me taking part in collaboration with people from other countries was really developing. It broadens my horizons when it comes to looking at the same problem from various perspectives. Sharing our opinions and ideas with other people not only from our homeland is really valuable and can give us solutions for different situations which we could never find on our own.

Charlotte: I feel it was a really interesting experience, hear all the different ideas and points of views of each person, gave me another perspective about some issues that are actually happening around the world and not only in my country. I learned the importance of being informed about everything and discuss about this, giving my opinion and receiving the opinion of others to reach a conclusion.

Stanley:

**Figure 10.2:** Participants' Google slide about their VE experience.

## 6 Discussion

Analysis of the weekly group discussions and the final activity provides an answer to the study's research question: In what ways did the SDG focus allow L2 teacher candidates to develop their pedagogy, more specifically their teaching methods?

It was no surprise that being teacher candidates, the group's top SDG was Quality education. During the synchronous sessions (weeks 2–5), participants focused on this and the other three chosen SDGs. Although directions were given to detail actionable items of what could be done for each SDG in education, no specifics were given in these weeks. Instead, the participants focused on what society as a whole needed to do to attain each of these goals, which suggested that participants realized education was only part of the SDGs. The group saw the SDGs as topics that were important to all of humanity and that everyone should be part of realizing these goals. Although this group's ideas were well-thought-out, the participants could have written actionable items in light of how society needed to be educated.

Even though participants did not focus on the SDGs and their connection to education in the weeks leading up to Week 6, during the final activity participants did make strong associations to the field. The participants commented:

> Providing quality education is so crucial. The children that we are teaching are going to be the next generation that is going to change the world. They are the future, and if we do not provide them quality education, they will have fewer opportunities to succeed and thrive in life.

Participants recognized the importance of their profession. They emphasized that their role of educators was vital now and in years to come.

Participants also developed their teaching methods as they bridged theory into practice (Lenkaitis 2020b) as they were able to focus on professional development through reflection (Lenkaitis 2020b; Körkkö et al. 2016) of the SDGs. By creating lists of short- and long-term actionable items, participants were able to focus on what they would do professionally by taking into account what could be done to create an educational community "where all people can live productive, vibrant, and peaceful lives" (United Nations 2019: 2). Not only did participants focus on things that could be done in their individual classrooms, such as "breaking the stereotypes when someone says something incorrect," but they also noted actions that could be done in the entire school and district like "starting on a small scale within the neighborhood." Although some of the actional items may not have coincided with content-specific pedagogy, all topics discussed were ones that could be addressed in the classroom with their students.

In addition, participants were able to gain perspective on the SDGs by collaborating with their international partners. This new-found perspective allowed each participant to deepen their teaching strategies even more. For example, Anna in Week 6 noted, "Sharing our opinions and ideas with other people not only from our homeland is really valuable and can give us solutions for different situations which we could never find on our own." It also made participants realize that they are all in this together, and every person plays a vital role in our society, which was exemplified by Charlotte in Week 6:

> I feel it was a really interesting experience, hear all the different ideas and points of views of each person, gave me another perspective about some issues that are actually happening around the world and not only in my country. I learned the importance of being informed about everything and discuss this, giving my opinion and receiving the opinion of others to reach a conclusion.

Echoing Lenkaitis (2020b), this VE demonstrated that teacher preparation programs must be re-envisioned to include VEs. More specifically, this case study showed that VE should have an SDG focus. Just as these participants noted in one of their Google slides, it is crucial that all teacher candidates realize that "Mankind, as people in society, we need to be more conscious and aware of the choices we make and how that affects us, others, the environment, as well as the long-term effects it will have on the world." With this realization and by "collaborate[ing] with others from around the world and discuss[ing] the issues that exist globally (Barbara, Week 6)" teacher candidates will be able to reflect on their duty and how it can be affected by the SDGs.

# 7 Study limitations & future directions

Implementing a VE consisting of more than six weeks of synchronous sessions would be helpful so that participants have more time to discuss additional SDGs or talk about SDGs more in-depth. Since the participants of this case study did not always make explicit connections to education, having additional instruments besides the Google slides would be beneficial to collect data that focuses directly on participants' content areas.

# 8 Conclusion

In this VE study, the SDGs were used as a lens through which L2 teacher candidates were able to look through their content area and subsequently develop their pedagogy. By having the opportunity to create "a global partnership" (United Nations 2019) with teacher candidates from other countries via an SDG-focused VE, participants had the opportunity to discuss ways to make the planet a better place and transform the world. Because of this, VE in teacher preparation programs with an SDG focus needs to be implemented not only to raise awareness about the SDGs so that teacher candidates can use a culturally sensitive critical lens to impact their classrooms, but also to internationalize the higher education curriculum.

# References

Albareda-Tiana, Silvia, Salvador Vidal-Raméntol & Mónica Fernández-Morilla. 2018. Implementing the Sustainable Development Goals at university level. *International Journal of Sustainability in Higher Education* 19 (3). 473–497. http://dx.doi.org/10.1108/IJSHE-05-2017-0069

Austin, Nick, Regine Hampel & Agnes Kukulska-Hulme. 2017. Video conferencing and multimodal expression of voice: Children's conversations using Skype for second language development in a telecollaborative setting. *SYSTEM* 64. 87–103. https://doi.org/10.1016/j.system.2016.12.003

Ayres, Lioness, Karen Kavanaugh & Kathleen A. Knafl. 2003. Within-case and across-case approaches to qualitative data analysis. *Qualitative Health Research* 13 (6). 871–883. https://doi.org/10.1177/1049732303013006008

Bruun, Sara. 2018. Global goals: A virtual project with students from Sweden and Tanzania. In Melinda Dooly & Robert O'Dowd (eds.), *In this together: Teachers' experiences with transnational, telecollaborative language learning projects*, 199–213). Bern: Peter Lang.

de Fornel, Michel. 1996. The interactional frame of videophonic exchange. (L. Libbrecht, Trans.). *Réseaux* 4 (1). 47–72. https://doi.org/10.3406/reso.1996.3305

Dooly, Melinda. (2017) Telecollaboration. In Carol A. Chapelle & Shannon Sauro (eds.), *The handbook of technology and second language teaching and learning*, 169–183. Oxford: John Wiley & Sons, Inc.

Dooly, Melinda & Randall Sadler. 2013. Filling in the gaps: Linking theory and practice through telecollaboration in teacher education. *ReCALL* 25 (1). 4–29. https://doi.org/10.1017/S0958344012000237

Fors, Per & Thomas Taro Lennerfors. 2020. Virtual exchange in education for sustainable development. *2020 IEEE Frontiers in Education Conference (FIE) Proceedings*, 1–5. https://doi.org/10.1109/FIE44824.2020.9273897

Forward, Mary Lou, Keiko Ikeda & Barbara LeSavoy. 2020, Sept. 14–16. *The global goals: Integrating the UN Sustainable Development Goals in COIL collaboration*s [Pre-recorded conference session]. International Virtual Exchange Conference, online.

Fuchs, Carolin, Mirjam Hauck & Andreas Müller-Hartmann. 2012. Promoting learner autonomy through multiliteracy skills development in cross-institutional exchanges. *Language Learning & Technology* 16 (3). 82–102. https://doi.org/10125/44301

Garcia-Esteban, Soraya. 2020. Telecollaboration for civic competence and SDG development in FL teacher education. *European Journal of Education 3*(3), 51–61. http://journals.euser.org/index.php/ejed/article/view/4878

Holec, Henri. 1985. On autonomy: some elementary concepts. In Philip Riley (ed.), *Discourse and learning*, 173–190. London: Longman.

Kern, Richard. 2006. Perspectives on technology in learning and teaching languages. *TESOL Quarterly* 40 (1). 183–210. https://doi.org/10.2307/40264516

Körkkö, Minna, Outi Kyrö-Ämmälä & Tuija Turunen. (2016). Professional development through reflection in teacher education. *Teaching and Teacher Education* 55. 198–206. http://dx.doi.org/10.1016/j.tate.2016.01.014

Lenkaitis, Chesla Ann. in press, 2021. Integrating the United Nations' Sustainable Development Goals: Developing content for virtual exchanges. *Language Learning & Technology*. Special Issue on 25 years of emerging technology in CALL.

Lenkaitis, Chesla Ann. 2020a. Technology as a mediating tool: Videoconferencing, L2 learning, and learner autonomy. *Computer Assisted Language Learning* 33 (5–6). 483–509. https://doi.org/10.1080/09588221.2019.1572018

Lenkaitis, Chesla Ann. 2020b. Teacher candidate reflection: Benefits of using a synchronous computer-mediated communication-based virtual exchange. *Teaching and Teacher Education* 92. https://doi.org/10.1016/j.tate.2020.103041

Lenkaitis, Chesla Ann & Benjamin English. 2017. Technology and telenovelas: Incorporating culture and group work in the L2 classroom. *MEXTESOL Journal* 41 (3). 1–20. http://mextesol.net/journal/

Lewis, Tim, Marco Cappellini & Annick Rivens Mompean. 2017. Introduction. In Marco Cappellini, Tim Lewis & Annick Rivens Mompean (eds.), *Learner autonomy and Web 2.0*, 1–11. Sheffield: UK: Equinox.

Merriam, Sharan B. 1998. *Qualitative research and case study applications in education*. San Francisco, CA: Jossey-Bass.

Sevilla-Pavón, Ana. 2016. Affordances of telecollaboration tools for English for Specific Purposes online learning. *World Journal on Educational Technology* 8(3),218–223. www.wj-et.eu

Terhune, N.M. (2016). Language learning going global: linking teachers and learners via commercial Skype-based CMC. *Computer Assisted Language Learning* 29 (6). 1071–1089. https://doi.org/10.1080/09588221.2015.1061020

The EVALUATE Group. (2019). *Evaluating the impact of virtual exchange on initial teacher education: A European policy experiment*. Research-publishing.net. https://doi.org/10.14705/rpnet.2019.29.9782490057337

Thorne, Steven L., Shannon Sauro & Bryan Smith. 2015. Technologies, identities, and expressive activity. *Annual Review of Applied Linguistics* 35. 215–233. https://doi.org/10.1017/S0267190514000257

United Nations. 2019. *The sustainable development goals report*. https://unstats.un.org/sdgs/report/2019/The-Sustainable-Development-Goals-Report-2019.pdf

United Nations. 2020a. *Sustainable development goals home*. https://www.un.org/sustainabledevelopment/

United Nations. 2020b. *Sustainable development goals knowledge platform*. https://sustainabledevelopment.un.org/sdgs

Zhang, Zheng, Jia Li, Feifei Liu & Zhuang Miao. Hong Kong and Canadian students experiences a new participatory culture: A teacher professional training project undergirded by new media literacies. *Teaching and Teacher Education* 59. 146–158. http://dx.doi.org/10.1016/j.tate.2016.05.017

Shannon M. Hilliker, Devindi Samarakkody
# Chapter 11
# Enhancing ELLs' understanding through the use of examples, questions, and native language connections during virtual exchange

## 1 Introduction

Virtual exchange connects individuals or groups who are geographically distant through online tools to communicate and interact with each other (Chun 2011). Today, it is integrated in education to achieve diverse learning outcomes (O'Dowd 2018). In English language learning, virtual exchange contributes toward language development of English Language Learners (ELLs) by connecting them with native/ near native speakers of English to increase their exposure to the language (Aristizábal and Welch 2017). Connecting teachers with ELLs is beneficial for both teachers (Hilliker 2020) and English Language Learners (Lenkaitis 2019b; Lenkaitis, Loranc-Paszylk, and Hilliker 2019), however, few studies have been conducted partnering ELLs with English teachers (Hilliker 2020; Dooly and Sadler 2013; Lenkaitis 2019). Therefore, this study focuses on how participants taking a linguistics for teachers course in the USA and ELLs at a Colombian university majoring in International Business co-construct knowledge using examples, questions, and making native language connections. Examples were used by native/ near native speakers of English to further explain the strategies suggested for ELLs to make an effective business pitch. Questions were posed by native/ near native speakers of English to check the understanding of ELLs and provide them with the necessary support. ELLs also asked native/ near native speakers of English questions to get the help they need to make a good business pitch. Lastly, native/ near native speakers made connections with Spanish which is ELLs' native language to clarify information ELLs struggled to understand in English. All these strategies helped these virtual exchange partners to co-construct knowledge during meetings. This article will highlight the benefits ELLs received in advancing their language skills and the teacher candidates' clinical experience assisting ELLs. The findings of the

---

**Shannon M. Hilliker,** Binghamton University, e-mail: hilliker@binghamton.edu
**Devindi Samarakkody,** Binghamton University, e-mail: dsamara1@binghamton.edu

https://doi.org/10.1515/9783110727364-012

study contribute to the expanding body of literature on virtual exchange in language teacher education and English for Specific Purposes (ESP).

## 2 Literature review

### 2.1 Virtual exchange

Positive impacts of virtual exchange on language learning have been researched in terms of enhancing linguistic and cultural experiences (Lenkaitis, Loranc-Paszylk, and Hilliker 2019; Chun 2016), raising students' intercultural awareness (Martí and Fernández 2016), and promoting learner autonomy (Austin & Kukulska-Hulme 2016). However, according to O'Dowd (2018), virtual exchange is not confined to language learning but in recent years its usage has progressed and been adapted in diverse settings and disciplines of education, achieving different learning objectives.

### 2.2 Virtual exchange and language L2 learning

Virtual exchange is one of the major tools of computer assisted language learning used by foreign language educators (Guth and Helm 2010). Virtual exchange in language learning is also referred to as 'online intercultural exchange,' and is implemented in learning both second languages (SL) and foreign languages (FL). This can be done through internet-based resources such as email, video conferencing tools such as Skype and Zoom, online discussion forums, and social networking sites (Chun 2015). Connecting students with native speakers (Aristizábal and Welch 2017) provides students with diverse linguistic as well as cultural experiences (Chun 2015). Sociocultural theory affirms that language acquisition is facilitated by meaningful communicative incidents (Aristizábal and Welch 2017). Hence, virtual exchange minimizes the challenges of providing language learners with communicative opportunities (Akiyama and Saito 2016) which contributes to the development of second language acquisition (Aristizábal and Welch 2017). Most importantly, appropriate scaffolding can lead to potential benefits of virtual exchange even in classes with low proficiency students (Aristizábal and Welch 2017).

Virtual exchange helps educators achieve several things that are difficult to achieve inside a classroom. For instance, online intercultural exchange promotes learner autonomy due to the limited role played by teachers, which transfers the responsibility to students to connect with their partners (Austin and Kukulska-

Hulme 2016). Furthermore, in classrooms, students' exposure to the target language is limited. Therefore, virtual exchange partnerships help educators provide students with more opportunities to practice the target language. More exposure to the target language increases not only students' confidence in their SL/ FL competence, but also their ability to self-monitor target language usage. Additionally, virtual exchange in language learning assigns different identity roles to students, which is difficult to achieve in the classroom. In an exchange between learners in Japan and the USA, students act as both learners when learning the target language and teachers when providing feedback on the usage of their native language by the other group (Akiyama 2017).

Another positive impact of virtual exchange is the opportunity for students to acquire elements of the target language that are culture specific. As recognized by students in an intercultural exchange between college students in Portugal and the USA, the opportunity to learn informal registers and slang was another advantage of virtual exchange, which is hard to learn in the classroom (Aristizábal and Welch 2017). In a study of novice and native Japanese speakers, Hirotani and Fuji (2019) explored the successful acquisition of proverbs that are culturally specific. A study carried out by Rafieyan (2016), unveils how virtual exchange contributes toward facilitating better understanding of the culture of the target language. This experience between students in an Iranian university with native speakers of English in the US improved the quality of translation of culturally embedded texts.

Virtual exchange in language learning supports the fundamental development of different aspects in language learning. Akiyama and Saito (2016) report the improvement of comprehensibility of the target language as a result of increased input and interaction during virtual exchange partnerships. Virtual exchange also has a positive impact on the selection of appropriate words, speech rate, and grammatical accuracy, which also lead to the comprehensibility of speech (Akiyama and Saito 2016). An online virtual exchange implemented using the videoconferencing tool Skype shows the advantages of online intercultural exchange as improving listening comprehension of students (Levak and Son 2017), motivation (Jauregi et al. 2012; Szedmina and Pinter 2010), and oral proficiency (Terhune 2016). Furthermore, virtual exchange prepares students for face to face interactions by creating possibilities for natural exchanges between students (Ware and Kramsch 2015). As Welch (2017) points out, virtual exchange creates "more organic and authentic" (p. 235) language among students. Also, Austin et al. (2016) confide the development of semiotic ways of communication such as gesture, intonation, and eye gaze, which underlines the efficiency of language learning via virtual partnerships.

Furthermore, virtual exchanges create opportunities for students to learn new information about other cultures that enhance their knowledge about the world

(Lenkaitis, Loranc-Paszylk and Hilliker 2019). In this virtual exchange students could discuss topics such as sports and patriotism, advertising, crime, and natural disasters. These discussions enriched global awareness, global identity (Lenkaitis, Loranc-Paszylk and Hilliker 2019) of foreign language learners, due to its networking of students representing different cultures.

## 2.3 Virtual exchange in language teacher education

Virtual exchange also plays a vital role in teacher education by connecting teacher candidates who represent different cultures (Hilliker, Loranc-Paszylk, and Lenkaitis 2020; Uzum et al. 2019). More specifically, via virtual exchange, teacher trainees in Poland and Germany created and assessed tasks for prospective learners, and this study disclosed how these teacher trainees enriched their opinions of technology-based learning tasks, as well as the interconnectedness between technology and instructional decisions (Kurek and Müller-Hartmann 2017). Researchers Tanghe and Park (2016) encourage more opportunities for virtual exchanges in teacher education as they contribute largely towards training teachers who need to cope with the diversity of student populations.

There is a growing body of research that is being conducted that partners teachers with language learners (Dooly and Sadler 2013). A virtual exchange between teacher candidates of Teaching English to speakers of other languages (TESOL) in the USA and foreign language learners in Colombia, shows potential benefits of connecting teachers and language learners (Lenkaitis 2019a). This virtual exchange of six weeks promoted student autonomy by allowing students to watch their recorded Zoom sessions and assess their language development. As acknowledged by students, the advantages of connecting them with teachers are practicing what they learn in class without being judged, receiving feedback to improve their language skills, and improving fluency in English (Lenkaitis, 2019). Another virtual partnership was carried out using both synchronous and asynchronous tools connecting trainee Spanish teachers in Chile and Spanish learners in the Netherlands. This was an authentic learning experience for Spanish learners to practice the target language and motivated students to improve their proficiency in Spanish (Jauregi and Bañados, 2008).

Most importantly, partnering English language learners with teachers/ teacher candidates not only benefits language learners but also enhances the teaching experience of teachers/ teacher candidates. For example, a study carried out by Hilliker (2020), shows how a virtual exchange partnership served the purpose of a study abroad program for undergraduates majoring in linguistics and TESOL teacher candidates by connecting them with ELLs in a Mexican university. This virtual exchange was a clinical experience as it provided them with the opportunity to analyze authentic language of ELLs in terms of linguistic aspects or simply to test what they had studied in class.

## 2.4 The use of examples

In this virtual exchange, the use of examples is a strategy used by partners in co-constructing knowledge, but studies have been found neither in the English as a Foreign Language learning field nor in the synchronous online exchange literature addressing this topic. However, positive impacts of the use of examples as a strategy in teaching have been investigated in other disciplinary subjects. Research by Schewe (1980) shows that the use of real-world examples has positive impacts on showing students the applications of behavioral science theories and concepts. Shewe's study (1980) found how the use of examples promoted in-depth learning in the classroom by enhancing students' knowledge of theories taught in class and also increased earning by showing the connection to the real world with concepts being presented in the class. In addition, Mvududu & Kanyongo (2011) outlined the potential benefits of using real life examples in teaching statistics. The use of examples promoted the students' ability to understand and make meaning from a statistical argument, reduced anxiety, and increased the level of motivation of students. Students in the course reported that the whole course was entertaining for them and they found valuable outcomes of using real world examples in their statistics class.

## 2.5 The use of questions

Questions have always played a vital role in classrooms when delivering lessons (Farrell and Mom 2017). Brualdi investigated (1998) the use of questions in classrooms have many significant functions: (1) to promote active participation of students; (2) to allow students to share their thoughts about lesson materials among themselves; (3) to increase the opportunity for students to express their own ideas in class; and (4) to help teachers to check student improvement (As cited in Farrell and Mom, 2017). The benefits of the use of questions are not confined to classrooms, as they also have a positive impact on the quality of student learning in intercultural online projects. Yang (2017) found higher order thinking questions used during a synchronous intercultural online project between English learners in China and English-speaking Chinese learners in the United States promoted critical thinking and self-reflection in learners which thereby increased the quality and the productivity of online discussions. Gao, Wang, & Sun

(2009) proposed one of the directions for improving the quality of online discussions is raising questions; they discovered that posing questions helped students to construct knowledge by negotiating, reconsidering, refining, and revising their thinking among themselves.

## 2.6 The use of L1/making connections with students' native language

The "judicious, systematic, and strategic" (Chamberlin-Quinlisk and Senyshyn 2012: 31) use of ESL students' native language contributes to the successful acquisition of the target language. In ESL classes "L1 should not be used as a crutch", and the use of L1 should be kept to a minimum (Yough & Fang 2010: 31). L1 is considered an asset for the development of the target language when the choice is prudently made based on the proficiency level of both students and teachers, the motive, and the objective of the assigned task (McKay 2018). A number of benefits of the use of L1 in an ESL classroom have been researched. One advantage includes the use of students' native language to enhance vocabulary learning and better understanding of explanations (Yough & Fang 2010). Furthermore, Furthermore, Budash (2009) emphasized the need for making connections with students' previous knowledge, comprehension, as well as with students' L1 and its values in language classrooms (As cited in Chamberlin-Quinlisk and Senyshyn 2012). It is further stated by Ovando, Coller, and Combo (2005) that L1 is a valuable pedagogical tool to be used in classes where both language and content acquisition are intended learning outcomes. In other words, both cognitive and academic development are enhanced when the language the students are most proficient in is used (as cited in Huerta-Macias and Kephart, 2009). Auberach (1993) outlines another advantage of L1 use by highlighting the function of language as a tool of communicating ideas when prior experiences of students are connected with learning in class. Furthermore, a study carried out by Anton and Dicamillia (1999) on the socio-cognitive functions of collaborative interactions by using L1 reveals the advantages of the use of L1 in collaborative tasks.

# 3 The present study

Research that partners teacher candidates and language learners is growing (Dooly and Sadler 2013; Lenkaitis 2019a), and the aim of this article is to contribute to that knowledge base. Therefore, this study focuses on a virtual exchange that connected EFL learners majoring in International Business in a university in Colombia and TESOL (Teaching English to Speakers of Other Languages) candidates in a university in the US and addresses the following research question: What strategies do English teachers adapt to co-construct knowledge with ELLs when talking about what aspects make business pitches.

# 4 Method

## 4.1 Participants

The participants include 19 EFL learners in Colombia and 13 native/ near-native speakers of English in the US. The 19 EFL learners in Colombia were undergraduate students majoring in International Business. They all were enrolled in a Business English course at the university. Some of the participants in the US were pre-service English teachers pursuing a master's degree in TESOL. The other participants were undergraduate students majoring in linguistics. All these participants were enrolled in a course designed for graduate students focused on linguistics for teachers. This virtual exchange was part of the graded coursework for all participants.

## 4.2 Procedure

The participants in the US were partnered with one or two EFL learners from Colombia. They interacted in English with each other for at least 15 minutes each week for six weeks during the semester, via Zoom video conferencing (http://zoom.us) (Lenkaitis, Loranc-Paszylk and Hilliker 2019; Lenkaitis, in press). The participants were not assigned topics to discuss during their weekly meetings. However, most of the participants focused on a business pitch that the EFL learners were required to present in the Business English class. The goal was to compose a two-minute business pitch. All meetings were recorded and uploaded to a shared Google Drive folder. Before their first participants were asked to write and share a linguistic autobiography to introduce themselves to one another. This assignment required them to write about their own personal use of language and what role things such as family background, ethnicity, race, education, residence, place of living, occupation, class, hobbies, friends and the like have played in their language development and use. The meeting for week one revolved around a discussion and comparison of each other's' work. Weeks two through five were driven by topics that the EFL learners wanted to discuss as related to their coursework. The goal for the teacher candidates was to be a conversation partner and offer any suggestions to support their language learner. After the exchange was over for the week the teacher candidates went back to the recorded videos to analyze the language produced and focus on the topics of their course (pragmatics, semantics, syntax, phonology, and morphology). For the last week teacher candidates made an activity for their partner(s) that was implemented via Zoom to further their understanding of the pragmatics of a business pitch.

## 4.3 Data collection

The data for the research came from video recorded and transcribed zoom sessions of six-week interactions. Videos were uploaded and transcribed by YouTube. Then the researchers read through the transcriptions and watched the videos to make sure the two matched. The video recordings of participants who focused their discussions on the business pitch were selected.

## 4.4 Data analysis

The data were analyzed qualitatively using thematic analysis. After the selected video recordings were transcribed, the content was categorized by theme. The two researchers independently coded the transcripts with an interrater reliability of 88%. They then met and negotiated until 100% agreement was reached. In order to examine the strategies adopted by teachers in making students co-construct knowledge with them, the content of the video recordings was analyzed using three themes outlined in the review of literature: use of examples, use of questions, and drawing connections between students' L1 (Spanish) and L2 (English).

# 5 Results

Table 11.1 details the teams that used examples, questions and native language during the virtual exchange"lso demonstrates the number of instances each team used each strategy during the virtual exchange.

Below is a detailed description of how examples, questions, and ELLs' native language uplifted students' knowledge of creating business pitches. The narrative is embedded with examples taken directly from the conversations from different teams.

**Table 11.1:** The teams that used examples, questions, and native language to co-construct knowledge during the virtual exchange.

| Strategies used to co-construct the knowledge | Teams that used the strategy | The number of times each team used the strategy |
| --- | --- | --- |
| Appropriate language using examples | Team 1 | 11 |
| | Team 2 | 5 |
| | Team 3 | 2 |
| | Team 4 | 2 |
| | Team 5 | 1 |
| | Team 7 | 5 |
| Reflect on the funds of knowledge asking questions | Team 1 | 7 |
| | Team 4 | 1 |
| | Team 5 | 2 |
| | Team 7 | 2 |
| Giving a better understanding using students' native language | Team 1 | 1 |
| | Team 5 | 1 |
| | Team 6 | 2 |
| | Team 7 | 7 |

## 5.1 Use of examples

The first theme that emerged in teacher candidates is discussing the appropriate language that should be used in business pitch with their FL partners using examples. The participants were assigned to discuss the language choices they would like to make regarding their business pitch presentation. The register of language that complies with the audience or how language usage differs according to the targeted audience when making a business pitch presentation was a common topic discussed by several teams. However, native/ near native English speakers used different strategies in order to make the discussion more comprehensible for EFL learners. One such strategy is the use of examples. Olivia stated that in China "People talk with different people. If they [talk] with children and talk with adults or talk with elder people, they will have a different language usage". This example of how the use of language varies in register enhanced the understanding of Eva about language usage who began the conversation saying that she doesn't have any idea what the topic means. The example used by Olivia helped Eva apply that example to her own language use when she stated that she talks to her mother "in a different way than to [her] friends". It also helped to move the conversation forward with a deeper understanding in language learners of the importance of the selection of appropriate language when making the business pitch.

Since the EFL learners can be of lack of knowledge of how to use the language appropriately to sell their business ideas, native/ non-native speakers in many teams provided examples of language techniques to use in their pitch. In this example, Emily while praising Mia's idea of using numbers in her pitch, gave an example of how she can exaggerate her ideas to convince the audience to import recycling machines to the country. She said "fifty thousand tons of waste every single month is produced meanwhile we're only recycling 700 which is a minimal percentage of that waste. So, we just have so much left over that is not recycled that is just ruining . . . The teacher candidate suggested that she could exaggerate and say" . . . they are ruining the country, ruining the environment in the country and so like definitely keep the numbers in there because I really like that and it definitely it's so much better than saying we produce a lot of waste but we only recycle a little bit". Mia, who wasn't sure how to encourage people to think that it is important to improve recycling in Colombia in a few minutes, received a solid example from Emily on how to use the language appropriately to sell her idea in a few minutes.

The next example shows how teacher candidates explained how to be persuasive using examples. In week three of this virtual exchange native/ near native speakers in the United States were expected to watch the videotaped business pitch of their assigned virtual partner in Colombia and provide feedback on the pitch. Lucas's main feedback on Isabella's business pitch was on the incorrect pronunciation of long and complicated words that sometimes hinder the persuasiveness of her pitch. Lucas provides two options that help Isabella to overcome pronouncing unfamiliar words incorrectly. The first one was to "practice pronouncing a little better . . . to be able to be understood better by some people", however, as practicing takes more time, he gives her another alternative which is to "use a synonym or different word". He uses the word "accessibility" which he noticed Isabella struggling to pronounce in her pitch as an example to show her how using the phrases "ease of access or easier access" instead of using the word accessibility would make her pitch better understood by the audience. This use of example boosts Isabella's understanding of how to use alternative words instead of complicated words to enhance the persuasiveness of the business pitch. Examples helped students to understand what is explained to them by their partners.

Talking about presentation skills also played a significant role in most groups because students felt challenged to present their business idea in three minutes including all the required language elements. Hence, most of these students sought help from native/ near native speakers for some advice on how to present their ideas in a persuasive manner within the given short period of time. Mary provides a brief explanation including examples of how a presentation should be created aiming at an audience of people with different preferences to Mason who already has an idea of the topic he wanted to present. Mary said, "When you present to your teacher your classmates or whatever you definitely want to have like some sort of data, but not too much because then people will get bored. You want to have some sort of visual, but again not too much because people just their eyes will just glaze over and like you kind of just want to make it um like mediate everything so like you know have some statistics for the math people have some visuals for the visual people maybe even have like a video or something to like grab people's attention". Furthermore, Mason found presenting the business ideas difficult as he was not permitted to use technology, however, Mary provides flash cards as an example to show that there are ways to present their ideas visually without using technology. Hence, all these examples used by Mary give a preliminary idea about how to make a short presentation in an effective manner.

In this virtual exchange, discussing pronunciation was common in several teams as it has a strong impact on the comprehensibility of the pitch. Some native/ near native speakers in the United States also talked about how intonation, emphasis on important words, pausing can have a positive impact on the business pitch. Liam uses an example to give a better understanding to Sophia how emphasizing important words can better convey the important ideas. He used the example "I want to eat chicken" and emphasizes different words to show how emphasizing different words can change the message conveyed. This example makes Sophia recall that she has already learned it, and she concludes that "the main purpose is to like emphasize on those words [which] are going to catch people's attention". Hence, using examples to explain ideas better has a positive impact on recalling ELF learners' funds of knowledge which makes them apply these ideas to make their business pitch successful.

The next theme is talking about strategies to be persuasive in making a business pitch using examples. When talking about strategies that should be used in business pitch to persuade the audience, several teams talked about the use of intensifiers. When making the language choice regarding the business pitch these EFL learners, the use of intensifiers was a topic these EFL learners had already researched on. This virtual exchange partnered people of two fields: language and International Business and throughout the virtual exchange they co-constructed their knowledge. Native/ near native speakers in the United States could assist these EFL learners in terms of using English appropriately when making their business pitch. Hence, the use of questions was a significant strategy used by the native/ near native speakers of English in checking their knowledge and providing any assistance if they need. In this virtual exchange EFL learners showed their understanding on the use of intensifiers in business pitch. Thereby, native/ near native speakers of English in the United States asked these learners questions about intensifiers which made them reflect on the purpose of selecting powerful intensifiers. For example, Sophia's response to Liam's question whether the intention of using intensifiers to have a better impact on the audience was "Yeah because it's pitch so I'm selling my idea. I want that people you know pitch are many times made for investors and that kind of people. So, you want them to buy your idea to invest your project whatever you are selling."

## 5.2 Use of questions

In this virtual exchange partnership native/ non-native speakers of English not only gave advice and ideas to improve their business pitches, but they also tried to know the ideas of EFL learners when trying to help them improve their business pitch. Asking questions played a vital role in making students reflect on their funds of knowledge and making them realize how they can use these language ideas in their business pitch presentation. When discussing the appropriate language use in a business pitch presentation, Liam asked "How useful do you think it's to use the correct words in this presentation?". Sophia's responded that it's "extremely important" to select correct words which she explained giving examples "For example, [adding] one positive word to a list of negative words the impression that the person will get about the list will be different than if you have a list of just negative words. . . . Some people or companies that use this very often are airlines". This question made Sophia talk about the impact words can have on the audience by reflecting on a reading she did recently. Hence, the use of questions was a strategy used by participants in this virtual exchange project in co-constructing the knowledge with the English language learners.

When talking about the appropriate language to be used in business pitch not only native/ near native speakers of English in the United States, but also EFL learners asked questions to improve their business pitch. Susan, whose vocabulary is limited, sought help from her partner Jennifer in choosing different intensifiers other than almost, always, and very which she tends to use all the time. Jennifer helped Susan in two ways in using strong language to convince the audience of the importance of taking care of forests. First, Susan read out the sentence "This is a very important issue" which Jennifer replaced with "This issue tends to be very problematic". Secondly, Jennifer proposed some words and phrases Susan could use in her speech to convince the audience. The suggestions of Jennifer: extremely, crucial, tremendously, immensely, tremendously affects the environment, hugely affects the environment were accepted by Susan as perfect selections of language in her speech to make an impact on the audience within a very limited time assigned for them.

The next theme is talking about presentation skills using questions. Making a powerful presentation without using PowerPoint slides was challenging for these EFL learners. Hence, Susan asked Jennifer if she knows any strategies when presenting ideas to an audience. Jennifer's said that "I would try to find pictures of any kind of pollution, any kind of deforestation, any kind of things like that that are happening currently with our global problems I'm to present to them. I would have pictures to start off with my presentation and that I would present facts with how much." Susan poses another question to Jennifer to figure out how exactly she can use pictures and facts in an effective manner to make an impact on the audience. She asks "I make it more visual and not use like so much words to make them see the situation?" The response of Jennifer to this question was "I think facts are definitely important um make people aware how much garbage is in the landfills like in Colombia or in the United States or present a lot of back to back up how much garbage is pulled out of the ocean". Susan was really satisfied with Jennifer's answer as she was struggling to figure out a way to present her ideas without using technology. Susan is an inquisitive learner who wasn't hesitant to ask questions from her partner to make her business pitch successful.

## 5.3 Making connections with students' native language

In this virtual exchange, when talking about using language in accordance with the targeted audience, avoiding the use of slang in the business pitch was a common topic discussed by several groups. Most importantly, when talking about slang most native/ near native speakers in the United States referred to the Spanish language which is the native language of these students to give them a better understanding. When William and Emma were talking about how the use of language differs according to context, he further explained, "For example, if I'm speaking with my buddies, I speak colloquial English or Spanish it depends and sometimes it tends to be more of English can be slang or Spanish slang it depends on who I am with. I was speaking that way when I'm with my buddies with my friends". William makes a connection with the student's native language because she is more familiar with Spanish. Thus, talking about Spanish gives a better understanding to the students that using English in accordance with the audience is similar to how she uses Spanish in different contexts.

In this virtual exchange project participants in the American University made connections with ELF learners' native language and culture when discussing how to make their business pitch persuasive. Liam's question "how similar do you think Spanish language and English language in terms of selling ideas or conveying good ideas?" led to an insightful conversation with her virtual exchange partner. Sophia contrasted how Spanish speakers and English speakers differ in using the language as "Most Spanish speakers we have like similar culture. So, we are more relaxed and we speak a lot because then maybe we don't go straight to the point but we like to speak and tell many details" where as "the people that speak English that are in North Americans, Australians people from England . . . they go straight to the point they don't like to use many words like we do". Similarly as a person who is living in the United States Liam agreed with Sophia and provided an example to substantiate what she said as "In the United States . . . you go and introduce yourself like hello my name is . . . [but] in El Salvador you start talking hey you start talking. For example if you are in the bus sitting next to a person oh it's a wonderful day right and they start talking and they start talking and then when they are leaving or when you are getting up you say oh by the way my name is . . . ". Sophia concludes by connecting what they discussed to the topic of using language in business to suit the audience as "we have like more close relationships or some professional just professional relationships and it's also because they care about money. So every time they waste they are wasting money . . . .After a lot of while then then we decide if we want to buy or not". Making connections with the native language and culture led to a profound discussion among them by recalling their experience and knowledge. This insightful discussion between these two virtual exchange partners led to a better understanding of the things she should consider in the business pitch: how she can make her business pitch presentation more persuasive in a way that it suits the audience she is addressing.

For example, Jennifer asks Susan "what sounds specifically in English do you find difficult to pronounce? What letter combinations like which sound do you find difficult to pronounce?". Susan finds it difficult to pronounce words with double consonants which she explains using the word "committee". Jennifer who is learning Spanish could understand that her difficulty of pronouncing words with doubles consonants is due to L1 influence because "in Spanish like the Double L it's significant because you need to pronounce that differently than a single L [but in English] it doesn't change the double consonant sound" and could give a better explanation to Susan which helps her to overcome the difficulty of pronouncing words with double consonants.

# 6 Discussion

The results of this virtual synchronous partnership discussed how native/ near native speakers of English and EFL learners in Colombia co-constructed their knowledge using examples, questions, and making connections with students' native language. The virtual partners in this exchange represent two different areas of expertise: the EFL learners in Colombia are undergraduate students majoring in International Business with varying levels of English proficiency, whereas the partners in the United States are either TESOL teacher candidates or undergraduates majoring in linguistics who are proficient in English. Hence, these partners used questions, examples, and connections to students' native language in this collaboration, putting together two streams of knowledge in discussing what aspects make a good business pitch.

Using examples was a strategy used by native/ near native speakers in the United States in collaborating with the EFL learners in Colombia (Mvududu and Kanyongo 2011; Schewe 1980). Studying English in an EFL context and perhaps due to less exposure to the target language the Colombian L2 learners felt challenged accomplishing the task of creating a two-minute business pitch assigned to them using appropriate language. The examples used by their virtual exchange partners helped them in understanding strategies proposed by their partners to accomplish the task. Some examples used to explain the strategies suggested helped the students to identify how they can truly use them (Schewe 1980) in creating their business pitch. Furthermore, these students got further help in understanding the linguistic aspects addressed by their virtual exchange partners in the United States, for example, how language registers differ according to the audience and how to use the language in a persuasive manner. Hence, the teachers used examples to further explain and enhance an in-depth understanding by the students (Schewe 1980). And also, using examples when students do not understand what's being said was helpful in continuing their conversation. The use of examples was a strategy employed by the virtual exchange partners in co-constructing knowledge: students expressing their business ideas and talking about the difficulty they have in creating a pitch, and on the other hand, teachers boosting students' knowledge about how they can create a successful business pitch. The usefulness of examples was common throughout this exchange and for the first time in language learning just as the potential benefits of using examples have been found in a physics and statistics class (Mvududu and Kanyongo 2011). Therefore, more research should be conducted in ESL/ EFL classes, virtual exchange projects as well as other disciplinary learning to uncover the impact of the use of examples on students learning.

In this virtual partnership another strategy used by participants to co-construct knowledge is questions (Gao, Wang, and Sun 2009). Most importantly, questions were used by both students and native/ near native speakers in the United States. The questions posed by the participants in the United States served several functions: students shared their ideas (Farrel and Mom 2017) on how they were going to present their business ideas which increased their opportunity to practice the target language, helped them check students' knowledge (Farrel and Mom 2017) and determine what kind of help they need to improve their pitch. Questions also helped both groups of participants engage more actively (Farrel and Mom 2017) because they answered questions posed to one another. The EFL students posed questions to get help to improve their pitch and teacher candidates in the United States asked questions to check partners' understanding. In some instances, the questions posed by the participants in the United States made EFL learners reflect (Yang 2017) on their previous knowledge of readings, classroom lectures, and their experiences.

Lastly, in this virtual exchange partnership students were not supposed to use Spanish which is the native of the EFL learners. However, at some instances Spanish was used by the native/ near native speakers of English in the United States, most importantly, connections were made with the Spanish language when explaining certain ideas which were unable to be understood by the students clearly (Budash, 2009; Yough and Fang 2010). Making connections with students' prior experiences (Auberach 1993) associated with their native language led to meaningful and insightful conversations among the partners (Antón & DiCamilla, 1999) as students could better understand the concepts and could relate aspects to Spanish better than English as it is their lived experience. Hence, making connections with students' native language was helpful in collaborative tasks in co-constructing knowledge, sharing experience, and especially explaining ideas to partners with lower language proficiency in the target language.

All in all, using examples, questions, and ELLs' native language were strategies used in this virtual exchange to co-construct knowledge between teacher candidates and ELLs which there by enhanced the knowledge of ELLs of making business pitches.

A number of behaviors that have been shown to be positive for learning outside of virtual exchange contexts have also appeared in this exchange. However, we can't necessarily make a claim about the impact of these behaviors on either group in this study.In future, researchbetween the behaviors observed and learner products is an area for further research.

# 7 Limitations

The study was limited to six weeks. So, participants limited each topic for 15–30 minutes even though both ELLs and the TESOL teacher candidate participants would have benefited from more time for each session. ELLs could gain more language skills as they interact and receive feedback from native or native English speakers. In addition, teacher candidates could gain more pedagogical practice with more and longer exchanges.

## 8 Conclusion

This virtual exchange partnership that partnered EFL learners in a Colombian university with TESOL teacher candidates in the United States in this study outlines how productive such an endeavor can be for both groups of participants. Teacher candidates' use of examples, use of questions, and drawing connections between students' L1 (Spanish) and L2 (English) supported students in their language acquisition as they learned about and practiced business pitches. These students lack exposure to the target language as they are learning English in a foreign language context. This exchange created an opportunity to interact with native/ near native speakers of English (Akiyama and Saito 2016; Aristizábal and Welch 2017) which is important in improving the target language competence (Aristizábal and Welch 2017). Additionally, the feedback they received from the teacher candidates helped them to improve their language (Lenkaitis 2019a) and better accomplish the task of creating a business pitch. Furthermore, this exchange created a valuable and a rare opportunity to interact with language learners from another country (Tanghe and Park 2016) which was helpful in identifying areas language learners need support in improving their English proficiency. As there is a limited number of studies carried out partnering English language learners with teachers (Dooly and Sadler 2013), more studies should be carried out exploring the benefits of such exchanges for both learners and teacher candidates.

## References

Akiyama, Yuka. 2017. Learner beliefs and corrective feedback in telecollaboration: A longitudinal investigation. *System* 54 58–73. https://doi.org/10.1016/j.system.2016.12.007Get

Akiyama, Yuka & Kazuya Saito. 2016. Development of Comprehensibility and its Linguistic Correlates: A longitudinal study of video-mediated telecollaboration. *The Modern Language Journal.* 100 (3) 585–609. https://doi.org/10.1111/modl.12338

Antón, M. and DiCamilla, F.J., 1999. Socio-cognitive functions of L1 collaborative interaction in the L2 classroom. The modern language journal, 83(2), pp.233–247. https://doi.org/10.1111/0026-7902.00018

Antón, Marta. & Frederick J. DiCamilla. 1999. Socio-cognitive functions of L1 collaborative interaction in the L2 classroom. *The Modern Language Journal*. *83*(2), 233–247. https://doi.org/10.1111/0026-7902.00018

Aristizábal, Juanita. C. & Patrick M. Welch. 2017. Rio de Janeiro to Claremont: Promoting intercultural competence through student-driven online intercultural exchanges. *Hispania*. 100 (2) 225–238. https://www.jstor.org/stable/26387776

Auerbach, E.R., 1993. Reexamining English only in the ESL classroom. TESOL quarterly, 27(1), pp.9–32. https://ncela.ed.gov/files/rcd/BE019020/Reexamining_English_Only.pdf

Austin, Nick, Regine Hampel & Agnes Kukulska-Hulme. 2017. Video conferencing and multimodal expression of voice: Children's conversations using Skype for second language development in a telecollaborative setting. *System*. *64*, 87 103. https://doi.org/10.1016/j.system.2016.12.003

Chamberlin-Quinlisk, Carla & Roxanna M. Senyshyn. 2012. Language teaching and intercultural education: making critical connections. *Intercultural Education*. 23(1),15–23. https://doi.org/10.1080/14675986.2012.664750

Chun, D.M., 2011. Developing intercultural communicative competence through online exchanges. Calico Journal, 28(2), pp.392–419. https://www.jstor.org/stable/calicojournal.28.2.392

Chun, Dorothy M. 2015. Language and culture learning in higher education via telecollaboration. *Pedagogies: An International Journal*. 10 (1), 5–21. https://doi.org/10.1080/1554480X.2014.999775

C. J. Ovando, M. C. Combs and V. P. Collier, 2005 "Bilingual and ESL Classrooms: Teaching in Multicultural Contexts with Powerweb," McGraw-Hill, New York.

Dooly, Melinda & Randall Sadler. 2013. Filling in gaps: Linking theory and practice through telecollaboration in teacher education. *ReCALL*. *25*(1) 4–29. DOI: 10.1017/S0958344012000237

Farrell, Thomas S. & Vanbupa Mom. 2017. Exploring teacher questions through reflective practice. *Reflective Practice*, *16*(6). 849–866. https://doi.org/10.1080/14623943.2015.1095734

Gao, Fei. & Charles X. Wang. 2009. A new model of productive online discussion and its implications for research and instruction. *Journal of Educational Technology Development and Exchange*. *2*(1), 65–78.

Helm, F. and Guth, S., 2010. The multifarious goals of telecollaboration 2.0: Theoretical and practical implications. Telecollaboration, 2, pp.69–106. https://www.researchgate.net/profile/Francesca-Helm/publication/277357372_The_Multifarious_Goals_of_Telecollaboration_20_Theoretical_and_Practical_Implications/links/5569a5ba08aec22683035954/The-Multifarious-Goals-of-Telecollaboration-20-Theoretical-and-Practical-Implications.pdf

Hilliker, Shannon. 2020. Virtual exchange as a study abroad alternative to foster language and culture exchange in TESOL teacher education. *TESL-EJ*. 23(4),1–13. https://eric.ed.gov/?id=EJ1242714

Hilliker. S., Loranc-Paszylk, B., Lenkaitis, C. A. (2020). Transforming language teacher education: Utilizing virtual exchange as an alternative to study abroad. L. Baecher (Ed.), Study Abroad in Teacher Education: Transformative Learning at the Global Scale. Abingdon, UK: Routledge.

Hirotani, Maki, & Kiyomi Fujii. 2019. Learning proverbs through telecollaboration with Japanese native speakers: facilitating L2 learners' intercultural communicative competence. *Asia-Pacific Journal of Second and Foreign Language Education*. 1–22. https://link.springer.com/article/10.1186/s40862-019-0067-5

Huerta-Macias, Ana & Kerrie Kephart. 2009. Reflections on native language use in adult ESL classrooms. *Adult Basic Education and Literacy Journal*. *3*(2), 87–96. https://eric.ed.gov/?id=EJ845831

Jauregi, Krisite & Emerita Bañados. 2008. Virtual interaction through video-web communication: A step towards enriching and internationalizing language learning programs. *ReCALL*. 20 (2) 183–207. DOI:10.1017/S0958344008000529

Jauregi, Kristie, Rick De Graaff, Huub V. Bergh & Milan Kriz. 2012. Native/ non-native speaker interaction through video-web communication: A cue for enhancing motivation? *Computer Assisted Language Learning* 25 (1) 1–19. https://doi.org/10.1080/09588221.2011.582587

Kurek, Malgorzata & Andreas Müller-Hartmann. 2017. Task design for telecollaborative exchanges: In search of new criteria. *System*, 7–20. https://doi.org/10.1016/j.system.2016.12.0046

Lenkaitis, Chesla Ann. 2019a. Rethinking virtual exchange: EFL learner and TESOL teacher candidate partnership. *NYS TESOL Journal*. 6 (2) 3–14. https://www.researchgate.net/profile/Chesla-Lenkaitis/publication/340439060_RETHINKING_VIRTUAL_EXCHANGE_EFL_LEARNER_AND_TESOL_TEACHER_CANDIDATE_PARTNERSHIPS/links/5e890be292851c2f527f788b/RETHINKING-VIRTUAL-EXCHANGE-EFL-LEARNER-AND-TESOL-TEACHER-CANDIDATE-PARTNERSHIPS.pdf

Lenkaitis, Chesla Ann. 2019b. Technology as a mediating tool: Videoconferencing, L2 learning, and learner autonomy. *Computer Assisted Language Learning*. 33 (5–6) doi: 10.1080/09588221.2019.1572018

Lenkaitis, Chesla Ann. 2020. Teacher candidate reflection: Benefits of using asynchronous computer-mediated communication-based virtual exchange. *Teaching and Teacher Education*. 92 https://doi.org/10.1016/j.tate.2020.103041

Lenkaitis, Chesla Ann & Barbara Loranc-Paszylk. 2019. Facilitating global citizenship development in lingua franca virtual exchanges. *Language Teaching Research*. 1–18. https://doi.org/10.1177/1362168819877371

Lenkaitis, Chesla Ann, Barbara Loranc-Paszylk & Shannon M. Hilliker. 2019. Global awareness and global identity development among foreign language learners: The impact of virtual exchanges. *MEXTESOL Journal*, 1–11. http://www.mextesol.net/journal/index.php/index.php?page=journal&id_article=14468

Levak, Natasha & Jeong- Bae Son. 2017. Facilitating second language learners' listening comprehension with Second Life and Skype. *ReCALL*. 29 (2) 200–218. DOI:10.1017/S0958344016000215

Martí, Natalia. M. & Susana S. Fernández. 2016. Telecollaboration and sociopragmatic awareness in the foreign language classroom. *Innovation in Language Learning and Teaching*. 10 (1) 34–48. https://doi.org/10.1080/17501229.2016.1138577

McKay, Sandra L. 2018. English as an International Language: What it is and what it means for pedagogy. *RELC Journal 49*(1), 9–23. https://doi.org/10.1177/0033688217738817

Mvududu, Nyaradzo & Gibbs Y. Kanyongo. 2011. Using real life examples to teach abstract statistical concepts. *Teaching Statistics*. *33*(1), 12–16. https://doi.org/10.1111/j.1467-9639.2009.00404.x

O'Dowd, Robert. 2018. From telecollaboration to virtual exchange: State-of-the-art and the role of UNICollaboration in moving forward. *Journal of virtual exchange – UNICollaboration*. 1 1–23. https://eric.ed.gov/?id=ED592404

Rafieyan, Vahid. 2016. Effect of Telecollaboration on Translation of Culture-Bound Texts. *International Journal of Applied Linguistics & English Literature*. 5 (4) 127–134.

Schewe, Charles D. 1980. Using real world examples to teach undergraduates consumer behavior. *Journal of Marketing Education*. 2(2), 60–67. https://doi.org/10.1177/027347538000200210

Szedmina, Livia & Robert Pinter. 2010. Experiences from using Skype in language teaching. *Intelligent Systems and Informatics*. **DOI**: 10.1109/SISY.2010.5647340

Tanghe, Shannon & Gloria Park. 2016. "Build[ing] something which alone we could not have done": International collaboration teaching and learning in language teacher education. *System*. 57 1–13. https://doi.org/10.1016/j.system.2016.01.002

Terhune, N.M.. (2015). Language learning going global: linking teachers and learners via commercial Skype-based CMC. Computer Assisted Language Learning. 29. 1–21. 10.1080/09588221.2015.1061020. DOI:10.1080/09588221.2015.1061020

Thirunarayanan, M. O. & Jennifer Coccaro-Pons. 2016. A global information exchange (GIE) project in a graduate course. *TechTrends* 60(3), 289–298. Retrieved from https://link.springer.com/article/10.1007/s11528-016-0051-6

Uzum, Baburhan, Bedrettin Yazan, Netta Avineri & Sedat Akayoglu. 2019. Preservice Teachers' Discursive Constructions of Cultural Practices in a Multicultural Telecollaboration. *International Journal of Multicultural Education*. 21 (1) 82–104. https://eric.ed.gov/?id=EJ1208281

Wang, Jia, Ali Peyvandi & Betty S. Coffey. 2014. Does a study abroad class make a difference in a student's global awareness? An empirical study. *International Journal of Education Research*. 9 (1). doi:10.1155/2012/490647

Ware, Paige D. & Claire Kramsch. 2015. Toward an intercultural stance: Teaching German and English through telecollaboration. *The Modern Language Journal*. 89 (2) 190–205. https://doi.org/10.1111/j.1540-4781.2005.00274.x

Yang, Rong. 2017. The use of questions in a synchronous intercultural online exchange project. *ReCALL*. 30(1), 112–130. DOI:10.1017/S0958344017000210

Yough, Michael S. & Fang, Ming. 2010. Keeping native languages in ESL class: Accounting for the role beliefs play toward mastery. *Mid-Western Educational Researcher, 23*, 27–32. DOI:10.1017/S0958344017000210

Alexandra Laletina, Anna Zhiganova, Elena Gritsenko
# Chapter 12
# Developing linguistically responsive pedagogy among K-12 mainstream teacher candidates through virtual exchange

## 1 Introduction

There is a uniform consensus that mainstream, or content-area, teachers need special knowledge and skills to work successfully with multilingual students (Bunch 2013; Coady, Harper, & de Jong 2016; de Jong, Harper, & Coady 2013; Hansen-Thomas et al. 2016; Lucas 2010; Lucas, Villegas, & Freedson-Gonzalez 2008; Wernicke et al. 2021). This specialized knowledge stretches beyond general teacher knowledge and includes three large components: linguistics-related knowledge, knowledge of culture, and knowledge of pedagogy based on a nuanced understanding of language- and culture-related processes (see de Jong, Harper, and Coady 2013; Lucas, Villegas, & Freedson-Gonzalez 2008; Villegas et al. 2018). In this paper we define mainstream teachers as content area teachers, that is teachers whose content area is other than Teaching English to Speakers of Other Languages (TESOL) or teaching a foreign language.

Unlike language teacher education, mainstream teacher preparation rarely includes an in-depth coverage of linguistic and cultural phenomena. The effectiveness of telecollaboration to enhance initial language teacher education and develop intercultural, digital-pedagogic, and linguistic competencies has been well-documented in the field of language teacher education (Baroni et al. 2019; Dooly 2020; Jager, Kurek, & O'Rourke 2016; Turula, Kurek, & Lewis 2019). Yet, there is limited knowledge of how virtual exchange can be implemented in mainstream teacher preparation, particularly as it relates to developing linguistically responsive knowledge and skills of how to work with multilingual students.

The article provides an overview of a pilot virtual exchange project between US pre-service mainstream teachers and learners of English in Russia and highlights mainstream teacher candidates learning outcomes as stated in their post-

---

**Alexandra Laletina,** Binghamton University, USA, e-mail: alaleti1@binghamton.edu
**Anna Zhiganova,** Linguistics University of Nizhny Novgorod, Russia,
e-mail: ann-zhi1@yandex.ru
**Elena Gritsenko,** HSE University, Russia, e-mail: egritsenko@hse.ru

https://doi.org/10.1515/9783110727364-013

project reflections. The project was part of the fieldwork, or clinical, experience within a second language acquisition course and pursued a pedagogical objective to develop linguistically sensitive knowledge, skills, and pedagogy. The chapter extends the discussion on the use of telecollaboration in initial mainstream teacher education and suggests ways of how to integrate virtual exchange into mainstream teacher preparation alongside traditional fieldwork experiences and second language acquisition coursework.

## 2 Conceptual framework

### 2.1 Linguistically responsive pedagogy

Mainstream teachers generally feel underprepared to work with multilingual students (Hansen-Thomas et al. 2016; Newman, Samimy, & Romstedt 2010; Rubinstein-Avila & Lee 2014) and may hold misguided views on the process of second language acquisition (Penfield 1987; Pettit 2011a, 2011b). Specialized training on how to work with multilingual students is a more consistent predictor of teachers' beliefs about such students than the length of their teaching experience (Pettit 2011a). Moreover, teachers who have received longer and more varied training tend to make more accurate assumptions about multilingual student education and hold more positive views on this student population (Coady, Harper, & de Jong 2016; Pettit 2011a).

Linguistically responsive pedagogy (Lucas, Villegas, & Freedson-Gonzalez 2008) is one of the earliest frameworks of mainstream teacher education regarding multilingual students. This framework integrates theory and practice along the lines of understanding principles of second language acquisition in academic contexts and enacting this knowledge in pedagogical practice. The knowledge base includes the following principles: (1) distinction between conversational and academic language proficiencies, (2) importance of comprehensible input and opportunities for comprehensible output, (3) importance of social interaction for language development, (4) advantages of strong native language skills for second language development, (5) importance of safe, welcoming classroom environment, and (6) importance of explicit instruction in linguistic forms and functions. Linguistically responsive pedagogical practices involve (1) learning about students' linguistic and academic background, (2) identifying language demands in classroom tasks, (3) leveraging the use of native language, (4) modifying written language used in class, (5) engaging learners in purposeful interactive activities, and (6) minimizing the potential for anxiety. Although the model provides a detailed list of language- and linguistics-related aspects of mainstream teacher expertise, it does not explicitly include culture and cultural knowledge as components of mainstream teacher preparation related to working with multilingual students.

To incorporate cross-cultural knowledge and ability to deconstruct school-related phenomena and everyday school procedures from a cultural perspective, de Jong, Harper, and Coady (2013) proposed an enhanced elementary mainstream teachers' expertise of bilingual students. It is not only the cultural background and heritage of multilingual students that teachers need to be aware of and take into consideration but the cultural aspects of host education system and school culture that they should not consider default. Instead, teachers are expected to adapt mainstream practices to ensure a linguistically and culturally inclusive learning environment. The focus on sensitivity to cultural aspects of schooling is not incidental but stems from other studies indicating that mainstream teachers tend to overlook the importance of cultural scaffolding (Pawan 2008) and may indeed hold on to surface definitions of culture as far as multilingual students are concerned (Hilliker & Laletina 2018).

Taken together, studies on mainstream teacher expertise regarding multilingual learners highlight three interrelated aspects: (1) knowledge of second language acquisition and language-related nuances of multilingual students' learning processes, (2) sensitivity to students' cultural background and cultural components of local schooling system, and (3) pedagogical skills to enact curriculum in a linguistically and culturally inclusive way.

## 2.2 Telecollaboration as a field experience

Virtual exchange has already been recognized as an effective tool for developing linguistic and intercultural skills in foreign language education (O'Dowd 2007). As far as initial teacher preparation is concerned, the EVALUATE research project documented the potential of telecollaboration to contribute to the development of initial teachers' linguistic, intercultural, and digital competencies (Baroni et al. 2019). The majority of participating teacher candidates expressed a highly positive view on the telecollaboration and recommended including a virtual exchange component into other teacher-education courses (Baroni et al. 26). As a result of telecollaboration, they also exhibited better awareness of situational context and better ability to communicate in a multicultural environment than their peers who did not participate in a telecollaboration project (Baroni et al. 29). However, the study did not differentiate between language teachers, special education teachers, and mainstream teachers. The majority of participants were enrolled in English as a foreign language training, therefore it is unclear to what extent virtual exchange contributed to mainstream teachers' linguistic and intercultural competencies, especially when mainstream teachers have limited foreign language learning background or limited experience interacting with people from other cultures. Preservice history teacher candidates in Fernandez's (2016) study showed varied abilities to use communicative strategies for meaning transfer with some participants being skillful at it and others impatient with their multilingual partners. Her finding reaffirms the need for a linguistics-related component in mainstream teacher preparation to enable them to work effectively with multilingual learners.

In the US teacher preparation context, international telecollaboration has also been recognized in TESOL teacher preparation as an effective tool to develop teacher candidates' reflective practices and understanding of the connection between language and culture (Hilliker 2020). Teacher candidates in her study reassessed the value of multilingualism and the role false stereotypes played in their perception of English language learners. There is also evidence that teacher candidates' telecollaboration with peers in a different community across the US contributes to deeper understanding of social issues (Damrow & Sweeney 2019).

This paper explores the potential of a virtual exchange project to develop mainstream teacher candidates' sensitivity to language and culture related phenomena and linguistically and culturally responsive pedagogy.

# 3 Methodology

## 3.1 Participants

The participants of the study included two groups of students: 14 students at a US private liberal arts college and 25 students at a small state-funded university in Russia. American students were enrolled in an initial teacher training program in the following disciplines: physical education (4), art education (2), English education (1), math education (3), social studies education (3). One student was training to be a speech-language pathologist. Eight students identified as male, and seven as female. Most students (12) identified as white, one student identified as black, and one student identified as Latina. All students had either taken prior coursework in a foreign language (Spanish, French, Italian) or American Sign Language. One student claimed fluency in Italian, and one student reported receptive proficiency in Spanish.

Russian participants were 13 first-year and 12 second-year students, majoring in international relations. All students were learning English for professional purposes as part of their major requirements. The group comprised 16 females and 9 males. All students had studied English at school for various periods (from 5 to 10 years). Their linguistic and cultural background was very similar as they all spoke Russian as a first language and were learning English as a foreign language (second or third). One student grew up in Germany and moved to Russia one year before graduating from high school. Most students had some experience of traveling abroad, and two students were planning to take part in an academic exchange program with a German university within the following academic year.

In this study, author 1 (Alexandra) and author 2 (Anna) assumed the double role of instructors and researchers. We were instructors of record for pre-service teacher candidates and English language learners, respectively. We coordinated project implementation, assigned student pairs in consultation with each other, provided prompts, and resolved any arising issues. To reduce researcher bias, we invited author 3 (Elena) to analyze data during the retrospective stage. All authors have been involved in language teacher education either during the time of the project or previously in their careers. However, none of us had previously taken part in virtual exchange projects.

## 3.2 The project

The project was part of a second language acquisition course for American teacher candidates. Students were given extra credit for participation. Russian students were enrolled in English for professional purposes course and received also extra credit for participation. Before the start of the project, American students submitted a language learner's autobiography in which they explored their prior language learning experience and factors that contributed to their success or failure in language learning and connected their experience to the language learning theories they had learned about in the first few weeks of the course.

Each American student was paired with two Russian students with different levels of language proficiency and/ or academic standing. After initial introduction via email students would collaborate to set the time for a virtual conversation. They met weekly for a 30-to-40-minute session on a medium of their choice (Skype, Zoom, WhatsApp, etc.). The nature of the exchange was conversational. Each week American teacher candidates were offered a list of prompts to explore the language learning process with their partners that would align with the topic of the course they were discussing in the second language acquisition course (see Appendix A for sample prompts). Russian partners were encouraged to discuss culturally relevant topics related to their learning content such as family, daily routines, meals, traveling, culture contact, and education.

Midway through the project, both groups submitted a blog entry to reflect on the benefits and challenges of their virtual exchange experience. Finally, as a concluding assignment, the students compared the two cultures and shared their overall impressions of the project in an asynchronous Flipgrid discussion.

### 3.3 Data collection and analysis

Given the small sample size, our research project was qualitative in nature. We collected the following data: administrative communication regarding remote instruction requirements, communication with students about the telecollaboration project, students' reflections, instructional prompts for students, class discussion regarding telecollaboration procedures and progress, and instructors' journals.

During the project implementation, authors 1 (Alexandra) and 2 (Anna) collected data from both groups of participants in a continuous and iterative manner. After the project was completed, we conducted a retrospective analysis with the following objectives: 1) gain a detailed and holistic understanding of the virtual exchange; 2) draw instructional implications about the effectiveness of the project; and 3) develop modifications in achieving the pedagogical goals.

We analyzed the data using a descriptive coding system (Miles, Huberman, & Saldana 2014) independently before virtually meeting to compare the codes and themes. This coding method was open-ended using a constant comparison technique as we identified general thematic patterns in participants' interviews. We drew thematic comparisons between students in each of the groups and between groups. We met regularly to negotiate differences and resolve disagreements in coding.

To assess and increase legitimation of the study, we relied on a qualitative legitimation model (Onwuegbuzie & Leech 2006) and used the following legitimation tools: multiple data sources, audit trail through personal journaling, engagement in the project implementation throughout its entirety, and reducing researcher effect and bias.

## 4 Findings

We discuss our findings as they relate to the three areas that we were seeking to enhance in our instructional practice through virtual exchange: (1) students' sensitivity to language aspects in intercultural communication; (2) sensitivity to culture, and (3) perceptions of cross-cultural interaction.

## 4.1 Linguistic competence

Participants' linguistic competence has developed in the following interrelated but distinct aspects: beliefs about language learning and sensitivity to language forms.

Mainstream teacher candidates entered the virtual exchange with a set of beliefs and attitudes towards language learning which they had voiced in their language learning autobiographies. The virtual exchange project allowed teacher candidates to test the second language acquisition hypotheses, observe different language skills (speaking, listening, reading, and writing), and engage in cross-cultural interaction. Before the project, teacher candidates stated that their lower than desired proficiency in a foreign language was a result of a monolingual environment. They grew up in areas where English was the dominant language and since they had never travelled abroad, they never "had to use language". After the virtual exchange project, they reconsidered this popular myth that language is best learned through immersion as they observed their Russian partners exhibit high language proficiency in a non-English speaking country. One American student noted, "the first thing that V. and L. taught me was that it is very possible to learn and love a language that you do not often have the opportunity to speak."

Another common misconception among teacher candidates before the project was the definition of language learning stemming from their own language learning experiences. In their language learning autobiographies, they commented that foreign language classes they had taken involved a lot of grammar and vocabulary memorization. After the project, they seemed to develop a more holistic communicatively oriented definition that language involves both receptive and productive skills and communication may take place notwithstanding errors. One teacher candidate commented on how one person's language proficiency may vary across different language skills, "I now understand that language proficiency is not the same for speaking and reading."

As far as sensitivity to linguistic aspects is concerned, such as pronunciation, grammar, or lexical items, teacher candidates reported noticing how similar sounding words are different, "I had to explain gorges and gorgeous. After I explained, he said, 'It's like a canyon', and I said, 'Yes, but not the Grand Canyon. It was great to see him make that connection."

It is noteworthy that this sensitivity to language did not come smoothly and easily to mainstream teacher candidates, nor did they develop an immediate understanding of what could cause misunderstanding or connect it to the way language works. Vocabulary differences between varieties of English or lexical lacunae and lexical approximation in translation were beyond their knowledge of linguistics. Although they understood that something was going on in language, they could not always understand or explain the linguistic processes. Several American students were confused by their partners' interchangeable use of 'college' and 'university'. In another instance, a physical education teacher candidate recalled that his partner asked him whether "she could post him a letter" and he perceived it as her not knowing the word 'mail' which he happily taught her. Teacher candidates' reflections testify to their increased sensitivity to vocabulary and simultaneous inability to explain these semantic differences from a linguistic or cultural perspective.

## 4.2 Cultural knowledge

The project, being a form of cultural exchange, allowed students to learn about their partners' country and culture and discuss a variety of topics such as politics, history, education, food, films, and music. All participants talked about different aspects of cultural knowledge in their reflections. They discovered a lot of similarities, shared interests, and hobbies and identified cross-cultural differences. The interaction challenged students' stereotypes about their partners' countries and allowed them to reassess and re-evaluate their own cultures which they may have taken for granted and did not perceive as a culturally specific way of doing things. For instance, several American students talked about perceptions and definitions of distance and how it varied from their Russian partners' experience, "When they asked me about how far I am from NYC, I said about 4.5-hour drive depending on traffic. But they wanted to know how many miles." The virtual exchange challenged them to deconstruct the cultural norms they considered the default and exposed them to alternative ways of thinking. Another example of re-evaluating American cultural forms was a social studies teacher candidate awakening to the concept of personal space, "My partner said she was writing an essay about personal space and asked me if it was true that Americans like to maintain a certain amount of distance from people. I never really thought about it. I have been awoken to new cultural things. We have never thought about them before."

The major difference between American and Russian students as it relates to cultural experiences lies in prior knowledge and orientation to cultural learning. American teacher candidates entered the project with little prior knowledge of their partners' culture aside from stereotypical portrayals in the media. Russian participants on the contrary had spent years learning the English language and about English-speaking countries including the USA. Because of this cross-cultural background, American participants set the goal to learn about

Russia, whereas Russian students were seeking to validate their knowledge about American culture.

In their reflections, American students mostly talked about having discussed surface cultural features such as holidays, food, and popular culture. Several participants admitted not having heard of the Victory Day as a holiday to commemorate World War II veterans in Russia. To their surprise, they learned that American movies, popular music, and computer games would be widely known and loved outside the United States. As one student commented, "I don't watch foreign movies, so I didn't expect why they would do that". Another teacher candidate observed, "We have so much in common, we watch the same Marvel movies, play the same games, listen to Billie Eilish." One participant was surprised that his Russian partner "knew something about the US I did not know" when his partner asked him about a specific music festival in California. He perceived himself as an expert on American culture and lifestyle and it struck him that a person from another country could have a broad knowledge of the US.

Another learning outcome of the virtual exchange as it relates to knowledge and understanding of cultural phenomena was developing an understanding of the multitude of personal identities. Participants in both groups explained similarities in their life experiences by such aspects of their identities as being young college/ university students, "We are both teenagers going to college. So, it was easy to relate." A substantial topic for their discussion was the COVID-19 pandemic, quarantine, and remote learning. Both American and Russian students commented that talking about these things increased their understanding of the COVID phenomenon and reframed their perspective, "It gave me a more global perspective on things. Sometimes we have a narrow focus on what's happening in the US and you forget that people in the rest of the world could have similar experiences."

## 4.3 Perceptions of intercultural interaction

Participants in both groups reported being surprised by the overall comprehensibility of the interaction and positive communicative climate. For most participants, the project was their first experience using English as a lingua franca. The overall tone of students' reflections in both groups was highly positive. Russian students reflected, "I think that it is a great opportunity to build relationships and bring happiness into your life", "It was a little uncomfortable at first, but I soon learned that the more I shared about myself the more they wanted to share. It did not take long for our weekly meetings to seem like conversations amongst friends."

American participants similarly expressed appreciation of the experience and mentioned that it positively surpassed their expectations, "Working with the students in Russia allowed me to learn more about how to assist someone practicing English, myself as an educator, and especially how to connect and engage with someone from a vastly different environment", "I learned that I really appreciate forming a friendship with an online partner. I liked being able to talk about whatever we liked including TV shows, hobbies, boyfriends, etc. It made it a lot more fun than I expected it to be." Having low expectations and being skeptical of the project was not an uncommon theme in American students' reflections, "I feel like I was skeptical of this conversation partner experience at first and its applicability to the course", "overall, I felt like I learned more from my conversations with the Russian students than I was initially expecting."

Along with surpassed expectations, American students felt a boost of confidence in their teacher identity as several students thought they would consider working as online English tutors. Specifically, they were able to connect second language acquisition theories to what they noticed during their virtual exchange interactions such as the importance of a positive and welcoming environment, "One thing that I learned about second language learners from my Russian partners was that idea of how you need to use the language in a low-stress environment." Other students felt confident they would be able to help English language learners in their classrooms because they learned to identify when second language learners were not comprehending their message properly ("Though A. doesn't typically have a hard time understanding what I saw, I can tell that A. has a difficult time") and they were able to stop, explain and move on ("This experience helped me as a teacher because I got better at explaining concepts and words that may be more abstract", "I was actually able to help them practice conversation and even teach them a few new words in English").

American participants also reflected on their own speech and being able to monitor their partners' understanding and adjusting their rate of speech, stopping to explain or paraphrase, "One thing I feel I must get better at is being able to simplify things so that someone who is trying to learn English can understand it. When I was trying to explain what something meant in English, I often struggled with breaking things down to make it easier for them to fully understand." This finding is corroborated by their Russian partners' comments on how supportive the American peers were in the interaction, "I am so grateful to [my partner] for supporting me during a conversation." Russian participants unanimously commented on developing confidence interacting in English and being able to understand their interlocutor, which serves as an indirect confirmation that American teacher candidates were able to adapt their speech to maximize comprehensibility. American partners noticed the change as the project progressed, "I can tell that one of my Russian partners was very nervous in the beginning and you could tell that she did not want to mess up her English, but once she got comfortable with me, she really started to speak the language very well. I could understand her a lot better and we honestly were having great and fun conversations."

## 5 Discussion

The objective of the project was to explore the potential of virtual exchange to develop mainstream teacher candidates' linguistically and culturally responsive pedagogy. The five-week virtual exchange increased mainstream teacher candidates' sensitivity to language- and culture-related phenomena and provided an opportunity to apply the linguistically responsive pedagogical skills in practice.

Among the understandings and skills of the linguistically responsive pedagogy, mainstream teacher candidates successfully developed the following essential understandings: the importance of comprehensible input, the importance of a safe, welcoming environment, and the importance of explicit instruction in linguistic forms and functions (Lucas, Villegas, & Freedson-Gonzalez 2008). The conversational nature of virtual exchange enabled them to learn about their partners' linguistic and academic backgrounds, modify their speech to make it comprehensible, and minimize the potential for anxiety. They developed a sensitivity to language forms that may potentially be confusing to English language learners either in their linguistic form or pragmatics of use. They noticed that comprehensible input is critical to the flow of interaction. They were also able to observe in practice what different levels of language proficiency mean for interaction and observe how language proficiency may vary across different language skills.

Given the conversational nature of the exchange and one-on-one interactions, the project offered limited opportunities for mainstream teacher candidates to observe group interactions in academic settings or notice any characteristics of academic language in their respective content area.

Their partners were similarly proficient in their mother tongue, which also limited teacher candidates' observations as to the role of native language competence and its role in second language acquisition. Even when they noticed some gaps in mutual comprehensibility and understanding, they were unable to name and explain what linguistic phenomenon, such as lacunae, or calque, or homonymy was at play and how it could be successfully overcome other than slowing down and simplifying their speech.

Evaluating the project as part of the course on second language acquisition, we believe it played a supplemental role because it provided experiences that would be otherwise missing in a combination of coursework and observational fieldwork only. A follow-up study would confirm previous studies on importance of varied training in mainstream teacher preparedness to work with multilingual students (Coady, Harper, & de Jong 2016; Pettit 2011a). The observational fieldwork in the classroom includes observing a class with at least one multilingual student and potentially developing an understanding of academic language and classroom interaction. However, the privacy policy does not identify the multilingual students to teacher candidates who observe a classroom not being given a focal student. This may not yield any linguistically and culturally responsive pedagogical knowledge and skills if multilingual students are competent English speakers and live in a demographically homogeneous rural community. Unlike rural teachers with no specialized training (Hansen-Thomas et al. 2016), the participants of the virtual exchange project felt confident in their ability to establish rapport and interact with multilingual students should they have them in their future classrooms.

An unexpected finding was American students' lack of awareness about the power of globalization and how widespread American popular culture has been in other parts of the world. The domination of American media monopolizes their experiences, which leads to very limited exposure to other cultures. The virtual exchange project has definitely increased participants' understanding of the globalization phenomenon and how social issues are lived and perceived in other communities with a similar effect to Damrow and Sweeney's (2019) study. Acknowledging the limitations of their cultural experiences puts them at a disadvantage of having to start learning about another culture "from scratch" -from the most explicit, or surface, aspects of cultural experiences, such as food, holidays, language, and music. This finding aligns with prior studies that mainstream teachers define culture and cultural experiences of their bilingual students on a basic surface level (Hilliker & Laletina 2018). The virtual exchange stimulated their exploration of their own culture and deconstructing some practices they had taken for granted to explain how things worked to their partners and learning that everyday practices, such as living at home vs. campus, organization of classes and curriculum, could have significant cultural differences. This competence aligns with the enhanced mainstream teacher expertise of bilingual students (de Jong, Harper, & Coady 2013) which focuses on being able to deconstruct the culture of schooling and adapt mainstream practices to make them inclusive for all learners. Mainstream teachers increased sensitivity to cultural deconstruction after the project also testifies to their oversight of the importance of cultural aspects of scaffolding before the project and aligns with the pattern observed in earlier studies that cultural scaffolding is the lowest priority for mainstream teachers (Pawan 2008).

Despite the general success of the project, we have encountered several challenges during the implementation stage. Recruitment is one of the first challenges we faced at the initial stage of the project. American students were more skeptical and apprehensive of the idea at first. It was not until a thorough discussion of the project and potential benefits that American students accepted the invitation to participate. Although the project was part of the course, participation was incentivized but not mandatory and involved a lot more onboarding for American students than their Russian partners.

Another challenge was matching up and assigning partners. Given a smaller pool of American students, they were paired with two Russian students. We paired students based on our knowledge of students' personalities and English language proficiency (for Russian students). However, our knowledge of students was limited to classroom context only and as some students reflected on their experience, it was hard to connect on a personal level for some pairs. We would recommend a more thorough procedure of identifying students' interests, for example, a questionnaire or survey, before partner assignment.

Finally, as communication progressed, as the project developed, some pairs of students required more targeted guidance since they all worked at a different pace. They needed more suggestions and instructions concerning what they could bring to their conversations, while others worked more independently. The ongoing communication and collaboration between the participants and instructors helped overcome this challenge.

Looking back on the project, we believe more guidance for the students and structured experiences could have been used throughout it. More prompts for the interaction and self-reflection along with feedback from the instructor could have added to the project effectiveness. More focused reflections regarding language use could also help develop deeper linguistically responsive pedagogy. The length of the project could also be extended to allow American participants to develop a more nuanced understanding of culture and second language learning and to give Russian participants space and time to develop their linguistic competence and reflect on their own cultural identity.

# 6 Conclusion

Being able to interact with linguistically diverse learners is one of the components of mainstream teacher expertise in the 21st century. The virtual exchange project between American mainstream teacher candidates and Russian learners of English was designed to enhance a second language acquisition course in the teacher preparation program and provide a real-life hands-on opportunity for mainstream teacher candidates to foster their intercultural communication skills. One-on-one virtual exchange partnership dispelled some language learning myths among teacher candidates and increased their sensitivity to linguistic difficulties in interaction that go beyond correct grammar or knowledge of basic vocabulary. Additionally, teacher candidates were challenged to deconstruct some everyday practices from a cultural perspective and reflect on their cultural experiences.

The small sample size and short duration of the project restricted the use of quantitative measurements of intercultural communicative competence development. Further research on virtual exchange with mainstream teachers is needed to fully understand the implications of telecollaboration for mainstream teacher education. A greater focus on the linguistic aspects of the interaction could yield useful findings on the account of how linguistics knowledge could enhance mainstream teachers' understanding of communicative difficulties when using English as lingua franca.

The results of the project suggest that virtual exchange may be a viable option for fieldwork experience for mainstream teachers within their preparation to work with multilingual students or may supplement existing clinical experiences. Prior work on virtual exchange in language teacher preparation suggests multiple benefits for teachers' professional development.

# Appendix A Sample prompts for mainstream teacher candidates to learn about their partners' language learning processes

## Writing

Your partners are required to write a weekly blog post in English as part of their English language course. Here's a set of questions to ask about their writing processes:
    What do you write in you blog about?
    Do you make an outline or draft?
    What do you do when you don't know a word or how to say things in English?

How do you proofread?
Do you allow comments?
What's the most helpful advice you can give about writing a blog post?

## Reading

There are two mandatory activities your partners do in their English language courses. One is called Home reading when the entire class read a book (a chapter, a story) in English and do accompanying exercises at home and then discuss the book (chapter/story) in class. This happens on a very regular basis – once or twice a week. Another activity is called Independent reading when they select a book to their liking, read, and narrate the plot either at a reading conference before other students or one-on-one to the instructor. In addition, there are other shorter texts that they read in class or at home. Here's a set of questions to ask about their reading processes:

What kinds of books do you read as independent reading?
How do you select books: original, abridged, adapted?
Do you ever read books in the original after you've read them in translation?
How do get around if there are too many unknown words?
How do you learn words you encounter?
What vocabulary exercises do you find most helpful?
To what extent do you think narrating/ retelling a story helps your English language development?

## Listening

When it comes to listening, you may recall a discussion of input and interaction. Among language learners and language teachers there is a widely circulated advice that listening to songs and watching movies with subtitles help with both listening comprehension and vocabulary development. Prompt your partners about the value of comprehensible input:

To what extent, if any, does listening to songs or watching movies help you learn new words?
Which do you prefer: watch movies with or without subtitles? Can you explain why?
What do you do if you cannot understand the lyrics in a song?
Do you always remember what the word means when you hear a song a second/ third time?

## References

Baroni, Alice, Melinda Dooly, Pilar Garcés García, Sarah Guth, Mirjam Hauck, Francesca Helm, Tim Lewis, Andreas Mueller-Hartmann, Robert O'Dowd, Bart Rienties & Jekaterina Rogaten. 2019. *The key findings from the EVALUATE European policy experiment project on the impact of virtual exchange on initial teacher education.* https://doi.org/10.14705/rpnet.2019.30.9782490057344 (accessed 28 March 2021).

Bunch, George. 2013. Pedagogical language knowledge: Preparing mainstream teachers for English learners in the New Standards Era. *Review of Research in Education 37*. 298–341. https://doi.org/10.3102/0091732X12461772 (accessed 28 March 2021).

Coady, Maria, Candace Harper & Esther de Jong. 2016. Aiming for equity: Preparing mainstream teachers for inclusion or inclusive classrooms? *TESOL Quarterly 50*(2). 340–368. https://doi.org/10.1002/tesq.223 (accessed 28 March 2021).

Damrow, Amy & Jaqueline Sweeney. 2019. Beyond the bubble: Preparing preservice teachers through dialogue across distance and difference. *Teaching and Teacher Education 80*. 255–265. https://doi.org/10.1016/j.tate.2019.02.003 (accessed 28 March 2021).

de Jong, Esther, Candace Harper & Maria Coady. 2013. Enhanced knowledge and skills for elementary mainstream teachers of English language learners. *Theory into Practice 52*(2). 89–97. https://doi.org/10.1080/00405841.2013.770326 (accessed 28 March 2021).

Dooly, Melinda. 2020. *Virtual exchange in teacher education: Is there an impact on teacher practice?* In Hauck, Mirjam; Müller-Hartmann, Andreas (eds), *Virtual exchange and 21st century teacher education: short papers from the 2019 EVALUATE conference*, 101–113. Research-publishing.net. https://doi.org/10.14705/rpnet.2020.46.1136 (accessed 28 March 2021).

Fernández, Suzanna. 2016. Communication strategies in a telecollaboration project with a focus on Latin American history. In Sake Jager, Malgorzata Kurek & Breffni O'Rourke (eds.), *New directions in telecollaborative research and practice: selected papers from the second conference on telecollaboration in higher education*, 239–244. Research-publishing.net. https://doi.org/10.14705/rpnet.2016.telecollab2016.513 (accessed 28 March 2021).

Hansen-Thomas, Holly, Lilliana Grosso Richins, Kanika Kakkar & Christine Okeyo. 2016. 'I do not feel I am properly trained to help them!' Rural teachers' perceptions of challenges and needs with English language learners. *Professional Development in Education 42*(2). 308–324. https://doi.org/10.1080/19415257.2014.973528 (accessed 28 March 2021).

Hilliker, Shannon. 2020. Virtual exchange as a study abroad alternative to foster language and culture exchange in TESOL teacher education. *The Electronic Journal for English as a Second Language 23*(4). 1–13. https://www.tesl-ej.org/wordpress/issues/volume23/ej92/ej92a7/ (accessed 28 March 2021).

Hilliker, Shannon & Alexandra Laletina. 2018. What do mainstream teachers think, know, and think they know about English language learners? *NYS TESOL Journal* 5(1),30–50. http://journal.nystesol.org/january2018/4Hilliker.pdf (accessed 28 March 2021).

Jager, Sake, Malgorzata Kurek & Breffni O'Rourke. 2016. *New directions in telecollaborative research and practice: Selected papers from the second conference on telecollaboration in higher education.* Research-publishing.net. https://doi.org/10.14705/rpnet.2016.telecollab2016.9781908416414 (accessed 28 March 2021).

Lucas, Tamara (Ed.). 2010. *Teacher preparation for linguistically diverse classrooms: A resource for teacher educators*. New York: Routledge.

Lucas, Tamara, Ana María Villegas & Margaret Freedson-Gonzalez. 2008. Linguistically responsive teacher education: Preparing classroom teachers to teach English language learners. *Journal of Teacher Education 59*(4). 361–373. https://doi.org/10.1177/0022487108322110 (accessed 28 March 2021).

Miles, Matthew, Michael Huberman & Johnny Saldana. 2014. *Qualitative data analysis: A methods sourcebook*. Third edition. Thousand Oaks, CA: SAGE Publications.

Newman, Karen, Keiko Samimy & Kathleen Romstedt. 2010. Developing a training program for secondary teachers of English language learners in Ohio. Theory into Practice 49(2). 152–161. https://doi.org/10.1080/00405841003641535 (accessed 28 March 2021).

O'Dowd, Robert. 2007. Evaluating the outcomes of online intercultural exchange. *ELT Journal*, *61*(2). 144–152. https://doi.org/10.1093/elt/ccm007 (accessed 28 March 2021).

Onwuegbuzie, Anthony & Nancy Leech. 2006. Validity and qualitative research: An oxymoron? *Quality & Quantity 41*(2). 233–249. https://doi.org/10.1007/s11135-006-9000-3 (accessed 28 March 2021).

Pawan, Faridah. 2008. Content-area teachers and scaffolded instruction for English language learners. *Teaching and Teacher Education 24*(6). 1450–1462. https://doi.org/10.1016/j.tate.2008.02.003 (accessed 28 March 2021).

Penfield, Joyce. 1987. ESL: The regular classroom teacher's perspective. *TESOL Quarterly 21(1)*. 21–39. https://doi.org/10.2307/3586353 (accessed 28 March 2021).

Pettit, Stacie Kae. 2011a. Factors influencing middle school mathematics teachers' beliefs about ELLs in mainstream classrooms. *Issues in the Undergraduate Mathematics Preparation of School Teachers: The Journal* 5. 1–6. http://www.k-12prep.math.ttu.edu/journal/5.attributes/pettit01/article.pdf (accessed 28 March 2021).

Pettit, Stacie Kae. 2011b. Teachers' beliefs about English language learners in the mainstream classroom: A review of the literature. *International Multilingual Research Journal* 5(2). 123–147. https://doi.org/10.1080/19313152.2011.594357 (accessed 28 March 2021).

Rubinstein-Avila, Eliane & En Hye Lee. 2014. Secondary teachers and English language learners (ELLs): Attitudes, preparation and implications. *The Clearing House: A Journal of Educational Strategies, Issues and Ideas* 87(5). 187–191. https://doi.org/10.1080/00098655.2014.910162 (accessed 28 March 2021).

Turula, Anna, Malgorzata Kurek & Tim Lewis (eds). 2019. *Telecollaboration and virtual exchange across disciplines: in service of social inclusion and global citizenship*. Research-publishing.net. https://doi.org/10.14705/rpnet.2019.35.9782490057429 (accessed 28 March 2021).

Villegas, Ana Maria, Kit SaizdeLaMora, Adrian D. Martin & Tammy Mills. 2018. Preparing future mainstream teachers to teach English language learners: A review of the empirical literature. *The Educational Forum 82*(2). 138–155. https://doi.org/10.1080/00131725.2018.1420850 (accessed 28 March 2021).

Wernicke, Meike, Svenja Hammer, Antje Hansen, Tobias Schroedler (eds.). 2021. *Preparing teachers to work with multilingual learners*. Multilingual Matters.

Blanka Babická, Barbara Loranc-Paszylk, Josef Nevařil
# Chapter 13
# Virtual exchange to enhance English language teacher trainees' professional development – insights from a Czech-Polish project

## 1 Introduction

Although the most common ways for language teacher trainees to apply the knowledge and skills they are gaining in their teacher development programmes is to visit classrooms and teach their practicum classes, teacher trainees need more opportunities to bridge the theory and practice gap (Turunen & Tuovila 2012). With the rapid expansion of new technologies into education in recent years also the professional development of teacher trainees should be enriched with these tools. It has been agreed that virtual exchange can offer unique opportunities and prepare teachers to incorporate technology into their pedagogical practice and also be a beneficial addition to teacher training for a number of other reasons (Helm 2015; O'Dowd 2016). Virtual exchange has been recently defined as "an educational practice which involves the engagement of groups of learners in extended periods of online intercultural interaction and collaboration with international peers as an integrated part of their educational programmes and under the guidance of educators and/or facilitators" (The EVALUATE Group 2019: 4). Several research studies have demonstrated the ways in which the development of both intercultural and language competences among language teachers can be supported (Helm 2015; Lenkaitis 2019; The EVALUATE Group 2019). The main objective of the virtual exchange discussed in this study was to enhance language teacher trainees' teaching skills (specifically teacher trainees enrolled at universities in the Czech Republic and Poland), and to explore their ideas about using peer assessment for their professional development.

---

**Blanka Babická,** Palacký University Olomouc, e-mail: blanka.babicka@upol.cz
**Barbara Loranc-Paszylk,** University of Bielsko-Biała, e-mail: bloranc@ath.edu.pl
**Josef Nevařil,** Palacký University Olomouc, e-mail: josef.nevaril@upol.cz

https://doi.org/10.1515/9783110727364-014

## 2 Virtual exchange in language teacher development

Researchers have been exploring affordances of telecollaboration in the foreign language settings to demonstrate its potential in enhancing language teacher education. For example, Bueno-Alastuey & Kleban (2016) while discussing their telecollaborative project, emphasize benefits which such an experience brings to student teachers regarding development of their digital-pedagogical competences.

In a study by Dooly & Sadler (2013) language teacher trainees from the USA and Spain engaged in telecollaborative activities over a period of two years. In these activities the student teachers both prepared individual teaching sequences with the use of new technologies and offered peer assessment on the sequences created by members of their teams. The authors analysed participants' coursework, their final reports, transcripts of their chats and presentations of learning objectives. They found that the participation in the project helped teacher trainees to develop professionally and also made them recognize the importance of peer feedback.

Likewise, the telecollaborative experience of student teachers of English from universities in Poland and Spain who developed culture-oriented didactic materials and lesson plans and received feedback from peers from the partner culture was very much appreciated by the participants. Peer evaluation in the intercultural settings was utilised to maximize the virtual exchange experience by enhancing the participants' engagement and encouraging deeper reflection and collaboration in the tasks set (Loranc-Paszylk, 2018).

In a study by Wach (2015) language teachers from Romania and Poland recognized the benefits of the email exchanges with one another. The self-reported data collected from the questionnaires, related to their teaching context and programme of study, and their own experiences demonstrated that they valued the opportunity of having their hands-on experience with another teacher.

## 3 Community of practice

Important components of modern pedagogy, such as for example, experiential learning, social constructivism, and connectivism can all be related to the concept of communities of practice. Defined by Wenger (1998), communities of practice are groups of people who share a concern or a passion for something they do and learn how to do it better as they interact regularly. A community of practice differs from a community of interest or a geographical community in that it includes a common practice: ways of doing things that are shared to some degree by members. Wenger (1998) further argues that, while individuals learn by participating in a community of practice, the amount of the group's action is more important in terms of generating newer or deeper levels of experience. In conclusion, it is clear that in an increasingly uncertain and complex environment, virtual communities of practice are to become much more significant, especially given the openness of the internet, the social media tools now accessible, and the need for knowledge sharing on a global scale.

## 4 Peer assessment

Navigating between collaborative interaction and independent intellectual functioning, peer evaluation is an important element of modern pedagogy, recognized in both sociocultural and cognitive perspectives on learning. As defined by Falchikov (1995: 175), peer assessment refers to "the process whereby groups of individuals rate their peers. This exercise may or may not entail previous discussion or agreement over criteria". Peer assessment affords students the opportunity to not only notice and learn from each other how to construct, and to provide and receive feedback, but it also encourages them to reflect and interpret the experience in order to eventually develop greater learner autonomy (Fukai, Nazikian & Sato 2008). Furthermore, peer assessment means that the numerous cognitive operations needed for successful task completion are presumably internalized for potential independent problem-solving after being practiced in collaboration (De Guerrero & Villamil 2000). It is also thought to trigger motivation and encourage "deep rather than surface learning" (Cassidy 2006: 509).

From a language learning perspective, peer assessment, when properly introduced, gives students opportunities to develop and practise skills important in language acquisition (Hansen & Liu 2005). Studies in second language writing report that peer assessment is advantageous not only to the students whose work is being peer assessed, but also to the students who perform the assessment task. For example, Lundstrom & Baker (2009) found that the students who peer assessed other students' writing on a regular basis made more significant gains in their own writing skills than those who received peer feedback.

To conclude, several advantages of peer assessment have been found by researchers, for example: opportunities to collaborate with others, creation of space in which peers can support each other, and self-reflection on the learning experience (Fukai et al. 2008), stronger motivation to perform well (Cassidy 2006), and significant gains in content knowledge due to performing the role as assessor or rater (Lundstrom & Baker 2009). Peer assessment as an alternative to traditional teacher-based assessment seems therefore to be a suitable answer to the growing demand for lifelong learners and reflective practitioners.

# 5 Research questions

This study, while being the first study that explores the way Czech and Polish language teacher trainees collaborate in a virtual exchange, adds to the growing body of research examining the affordances of virtual exchange in language teacher training by exploring the self-reported data based on the participants' experiences in the virtual exchange project. Therefore, this study addressed the following research questions:

RQ1 What are language teacher trainees' perceptions of peer assessment in the intercultural settings?
RQ2 How do teacher trainees perceive virtual exchange as a way to help them develop their teaching expertise?

# 6 Methodology

## 6.1 Participants

Altogether 42 students (23 Czech and 19 Polish students) participated in the project. The Czech students were the first-year master's degree students who worked on the project during their first teaching practice. The Polish students were second-year master's students with some teaching experience already. It must be noted that the academic cultures in the Czech Republic and Poland differ, Palacky University students take two teaching practices during their master's studies (three weeks and four weeks), both organized by the university. In comparison, University of Bielsko-Biała students organize their teaching practice themselves.

## 6.2 The project design

The aim was for Czech-Polish teams of teacher trainees to communicate, cooperate and create a collaborative output, share it with others and peer assess each other's outputs. The main focus of the project was to enable students, trainee teachers of English, to cooperate with colleagues from a different university and country and share their knowledge and teaching practice experience. Students from universities in Olomouc, Czech Republic and Bielsko-Biała, Poland took part in this short-term project. The project was supervised by three teacher trainers – one Polish and two Czechs. The three co-authors worked as a team, setting the project in motion by instructing their students, helping them throughout the individual stages, monitoring and facilitating the students' work. The project was conducted in several stages; the procedure being as follows:

### 6.2.1 Stage 1

The teacher trainers divided the teacher trainees in nine groups to create teams of a relatively same size, each consisting of 2–3 Czech and 2–3 Polish students. The Czech students were asked to initiate the first contact between the members of their team. The students were offered the possibility to use Zoom for their virtual meetings, but, eventually, none of them took that opportunity as they used other means of communication instead (see research findings below). The teams communicated in English.

### 6.2.2 Stage 2

Each team was asked to choose four topics from four main English Language Teaching (ELT) areas (Teaching Language Systems and Language Skills, Using Resources, Class Management, Feedback and Recording Learners' Progress, see the details in the appendix, part 1). Each team was then supposed to meet in a virtual environment to create one collaborative output, integrating all the four chosen subtopics (a paper, a presentation, a poster or a short video). The final outputs needed to follow problem and solution as a pattern of organization. The students were asked to identify at least two problems within the selected topics and suggest at least one solution for each problem. When finished, each team uploaded their final output to the online drive managed by the teacher trainers.

### 6.2.3 Stage 3

The teacher trainers prepared a list of students who were to peer assess other teams' outputs. Each output needed to be assessed by at least two Polish and two Czech teacher trainees. The peer assessment was based on assessment criteria including the use of language, cohesion and coherence, topic coverage and originality (see the details in the appendix, part 2). Each output was awarded points by the assessors (up to 30 points). The assessors could also add their own comments on the outputs, providing information to their peers about the strong points of their outputs as well as suggesting areas for improvement. Among the strong points, students mentioned issues such as "easy to follow, well arranged," "the given examples of teaching vocabulary in context," "problems are clearly introduced, well logically structured and provided by many suggested solutions." As for the room for improvement, students often highlighted the need "to include more practical advice and suggestions," sometimes they missed "more specific examples." Quite often, though, they negatively commented on the layout of the output, in the words of one of the assessors "graphics should be less sophisticated." The assessments were then again uploaded to the shared drive by the teacher trainers. Due to the time span of the project, the students were not asked to improve upon their outputs after receiving the assessment. The assessment was provided and taken as suggestions for the students' future work.

The students were given deadlines for completing each stage of the project, which was monitored by the teacher trainers. Certain adjustments to the original schedule were necessary to allow the students enough time to cooperate and complete their outputs and assessments. Finally, the whole procedure took approximately three months.

At the end of the project the students were asked to complete a questionnaire evaluating their experience and giving feedback on the project. The final questionnaire consisted of six close-ended questions in which the students were asked to provide feedback on their experience doing the tasks, collaborating with their teammates, using different channels of communication, what helped them do the tasks and how much they would say they learned from the experience of working on their products, assessing their peers' products and receiving peer-assessment. The students were also asked to provide a comment to each question.

# 7 Results and discussion

The first and second question asked the students to indicate how much time they spent on individual work, communication and collaborations with their peers when working on the tasks and to specify the frequency of using different means of communication when working on the assignments with their teammates.

Based on the students' feedback, 17 of them (40%) spent 2–4 hours on individual work and 2–4 hours on collaboration with their peers and approximately

25% of them spent between 4 and 8 hours on these (10 and 11 respondents respectively). Slightly fewer students spent less than two hours on these two types of activities and there were only a few students who claimed to have spent more time on individual work and collaboration. Quite a lot of students commented that the project had not been time-consuming in the end, but several students stated it had been difficult to find enough time for the project due to their other duties.

However, the majority of the students – 28 (67%) and 27 (64%) respectively – spent up to two hours only having informal talks with their peers and communicating with others/seeking advice. According to their comments, the students mostly had initial meetings online, distributed work and then worked on their tasks individually as they considered it less time-consuming. As for the channels of communication, 36 (86%) of the students frequently used written chat or messenger and about a half of them occasionally used email. 37 and 40 students respectively (88–95%) never used voice or video calls to communicate during the project. Messenger seemed to be the most practical way of communication for most of the students, according to their comments, as it was demanding to coordinate their different work and study schedules. As far as can be judged, the cooperation styles within the teams did not seem to vary significantly and did not depend on the particular cultures in question.

## 7.1 Language teacher trainees' perceptions of peer assessment in the intercultural settings

First, teacher trainees were supposed to evaluate how useful the experience of assessing the other teams' work as well as having their own work assessed by other teams was for them (see Table 13.1).

In both cases, teacher trainees mostly agree the experience was useful (27 in case of assessment of their peers' work and 23 in case of receiving peer-assessment). A single sample t-test was calculated at the 0.05 significance level for each of the experiences. It was ascertained that both the results are statistically significant at the 0.05 significance level and therefore it can be concluded that the respondents find the experience useful.

Additionally, the chi-square test for independence was calculated and the following null ($H_0$) and alternative ($H_A$) hypotheses formulated:

$H_0$: The extent to which teacher trainees find the listed aspects useful is independent.

$H_A$: The extent to which teacher trainees find the listed aspects useful is <u>not</u> independent.

**Table 13.1:** The usefulness of the experience of assessing the peers' outputs and having own outputs assessed by peers.

| value | 1 | 2 | 3 | mean | | t value |
|---|---|---|---|---|---|---|
| | not useful | hard to say | useful | calculated | hypothetical | |
| assessing the outputs prepared by my peers | 7 | 8 | 27 | | | |
| frequency x value | 7 | 16 | 81 | 2.48 | 2.00 | 3.994 |
| receiving the feedback on my output from my peers | 8 | 11 | 23 | | | |
| frequency x value | 8 | 22 | 69 | 2.36 | 2.00 | 2.926 |

In this case, the null hypothesis cannot be rejected at the 0.05 significance level. It is therefore impossible to say which experience is more useful for students – giving or receiving peer-assessment.

In their comments the respondents expressed some drawbacks of assessing and being assessed. Several teacher trainees felt that their colleagues had misunderstood the assessment scale (confusing 1 and 5 as the best). This must have been a random mistake since the scale was clearly specified in the instructions at the beginning of the project (1 = unacceptable, 5 = excellent). Some teacher trainees thought the assessments were not honest or reliable enough. However, positive comments were in the majority. The respondents often commented on the usefulness of such an activity for their future teaching profession, the benefit of learning the strong points of their outputs and areas for improvement. Specifically, participant CZ 15 wrote that, "Peer assessment is always a good thing. You can learn and find space for improvement at the same time." Participant CZ 25 maintains that, "It is good to assess others as we all are supposed to become teachers; we should practise assessing others." On a similar note, participant PL 7 is of the opinion that "while assessing the outputs prepared by my peers, I could find out some new interesting information concerning the teaching process. The feedback received helped me to discover the room for improvement."

Participant PL 4 evaluated the experience at some length balancing the pros and cons: "It is a difficult issue to assess. To be honest, I prefer working individually because in the case of collaborating with a few people, there might sometimes appear some difficulties. Everyone can have a different vision of our cooperation and its details. There is no wrong vision. Every vision is individual because every person is unique. One thing can be unacceptable for me, and another one may be considered totally differently by another group member. Although sometimes it is difficult to find one solution accepted by every member, it is good to develop cooperation skills and to meet other peoples' views on different topics."

Next, the participants were asked to decide whether the experience of assessing or being assessed by their colleagues was a positive or negative one for them (see Table 13.2).

**Table 13.2:** Overall experience of assessing the peers' outputs and having own outputs assessed by peers.

| value | 1 | 2 | 3 | mean | | t value |
|---|---|---|---|---|---|---|
| | negative | neutral | positive | calculated | hypothetical | |
| assessing your peers' outputs | 1 | 14 | 27 | | | |
| frequency x value | 1 | 28 | 81 | 2.62 | 2.00 | 7.445 |
| having your outputs assessed by your peers | 2 | 16 | 24 | | | |
| frequency x value | 2 | 32 | 72 | 2.52 | 2.00 | 5.712 |

As can be seen in Table 13.2 above, most of the respondents see the experience of giving and receiving peer assessment as positive (27 and 24 respectively) or neutral (14 and 16 respectively). Very few teacher trainees saw the experience as negative.

The single sample t-test at the 0.05 significance level shows that the participants tend strongly towards the positive evaluation. However, the chi-square test for independence does not show any preference, it has to be deduced that assessing or being assessed is perceived similarly.

The teacher trainees' comments show what particularly they value about the experience. Participant PL 26, for example, wrote, "It was a great experience to find so many useful tips and so much information in my peers' projects. I could not have assessed them badly. However, I am truly glad for their honest assessment of the presentation of ours." Participant CZ 34 supports this opinion stating, "It was positive because it made us think what the others think of our project. It was in a written form, so very useful."

Even teacher trainees who did not find the experience entirely positive were able to see its benefits, e.g. PL 32: "Overall, it was neutral for me. But I am really glad that I could see the work of my peers. I saw there some things I could change and improve in my own work." As well as CZ 40, who wrote, "Overall the experience was positive. Sometimes it was difficult to decide the optimal degree of criticism when assessing my peers' work. I did not want to be too harsh, but sometimes I felt that I expected a better outcome of my peers' work."

## 7.2 Language teacher trainees' evaluation of the telecollaboration experience

In the other part of the questionnaire, the teacher trainees were asked to decide how useful the given aspects of their teacher-training preparation or collaboration with other teacher trainees were in helping them complete the assigned tasks (see Table 13.3).

**Table 13.3:** The extent of usefulness of: i/ teaching practice, ii/ methodology classes at university, iii/ collaboration with foreign teacher trainees, iv/ collaboration with peers from own university – in providing ideas to complete the final output.

| value | 1 | 2 | 3 | mean | | t value |
|---|---|---|---|---|---|---|
| | not useful | hard to say | useful | calculated | hypothetical | |
| teaching practice | 4 | 4 | 34 | | | |
| frequency x value | 4 | 8 | 102 | 2.71 | 2.00 | 7.281 |
| courses in EFL methodology at the university | 4 | 9 | 29 | | | |
| frequency x value | 4 | 18 | 87 | 2.60 | 2.00 | 5.802 |
| collaboration with foreign teacher trainees | 16 | 10 | 16 | | | |
| frequency x value | 16 | 20 | 48 | 2.00 | 2.00 | 0 |
| collaboration with peers from your university | 6 | 11 | 25 | | | |
| frequency x value | 6 | 22 | 75 | 2.45 | 2.00 | 3.966 |

Table 13.3 seems to show that a substantial proportion of participants find all four listed aspects quite useful. In case of teaching practice, ELT methodology courses and collaboration with their university peers, this is true for the majority of them (34, 29 and 25 out of 42 respectively). The calculation of the t-test at the 0.05 significance level shows that the participants tend strongly towards the option "useful" in these three aspects. When it comes to collaboration with foreign teacher trainees, the respondents appear to be undecided. Of the 42 participants, 16 find the foreign cooperation useful, the same figure (16) stands for not useful and the rest (10) cannot decide. In this case, the t value for this aspect equals 0, as the calculated mean equals the hypothetical mean 2.00.

The chi-square test for independence was used as well to determine whether the extent to which teacher trainees find the listed aspects useful is or is not independent.

Once again, the alternative hypothesis can be accepted at the 0.05 significance level. The participants see some of the aspects as more useful than others. Their teaching practice experience seems to be the most useful aspect of their preparation, followed by the EFL methodology courses. Collaboration with the foreign trainees, on the other hand, is seen as the least useful part of the whole experience. This might have been caused by the possible communication difficulties due to differences in study schedules. In addition, the students might have felt that the collaboration with peers from their university was helpful enough and more straightforward as it did not require them to communicate in English.

According to the respondents' additional comments, 15 trainees consider the teaching practice and/or the ELT courses at university particularly useful. Five trainees emphasized that all the mentioned aspects were beneficial to completing the tasks. Although the results above indicate that the participants did not see the collaboration with the foreign teacher trainees as particularly useful, there were five who specifically stressed the importance of such collaboration and sharing ideas. A few trainees mentioned the internet, recommended literature and their diploma or bachelor's theses as useful sources of information when working on the tasks.

In particular, participant PL 9 believes "that such a project should be included into teaching practice more often. The activity of collaborating with other students (future teachers) is needed to exchange experiences as well as the knowledge of methodology." It would be beneficial to incorporate a similar exchange of ideas into the students' teaching practice on a regular basis. However, this might prove difficult due to the different organization of teaching practices. It would seem more practical to organize more long-term projects spanning over the whole academic year to give the participants more space and time to find an effective way to communicate and share ideas. Another participant (CZ 34) highlights the following: "Teaching practice and methodology classes were essential for the final output of the project as I used my own teaching practice experience. Then, collaboration with the Polish students was useful, but it would be better if we could see each other face to face. Moreover, collaboration with peers from our university turned out to be the most effective and helpful, because we have all experienced teaching practice, so we exchanged our experiences." Participant CZ 22 comments positively even on the Czech – Polish collaboration: "Our methodology classes are always very inspiring and beneficial for me; and the teaching practice was amazing, which inspired me a lot, too. It was interesting to find out how it is like in Poland."

Lastly, the respondents were asked to indicate whether or not they were satisfied with the whole telecollaboration experience (see Table 13.4).

**Table 13.4:** The level of satisfaction with the teamwork, the learning outcomes, and the students' findings.

| value | 1 | 2 | 3 | mean | | t value |
|---|---|---|---|---|---|---|
| | dissatisfied | hard to say | satisfied | calculated | hypothetical | |
| teamwork | 8 | 9 | 25 | | | |
| frequency x value | 8 | 18 | 75 | 2.40 | 2.00 | 3.287 |
| findings included in the paper, presentation, etc. | 4 | 4 | 34 | | | |
| frequency x value | 4 | 8 | 102 | 2.71 | 2.00 | 7.281 |
| overall learning outcomes | 5 | 5 | 32 | | | |
| frequency x value | 5 | 10 | 96 | 2.64 | 2.00 | 6.019 |

Once again, the data seem to show a relatively straightforward tendency towards the "satisfied" option. A single sample t-test was calculated for each of the listed aspects with the result that in all three cases it is statistically significant at the 0.05 significance level and therefore it was determined that the respondents are satisfied with the experience.

Additionally, the chi-square test for independence was used to determine whether the extent to which teacher trainees are satisfied with the listed aspects is or is not independent. In this case, the alternative hypothesis cannot be accepted at the 0.05 significance level. The participants are, overall, satisfied with the aspects of the experience listed in Table 13.4 equally, without any significant difference between them.

Apart from a few negative comments such as the one from participant CZ 41: "I am not happy about the whole project because as I have mentioned above the co-operation wasn't very enriching for me," most comments were on a positive note. For example, participant PL 35 simply stated that "it was a pleasure to work with such motivated and determined students," while participant CZ 34 highlights the collaboration: "I am satisfied with our teamwork because we worked effectively. All of us worked effectively and equally. It was a real collaboration between Czech and Polish students."

# 8 Conclusions

Generally speaking, the project's significant advantage lies in developing the students' ability to cooperate with others, which is a crucial part of the teaching profession, be it cooperation with other teachers, schools, or parents and the public. The language teacher trainees could engage in collaborative activities and become more prepared to form communities of practice in their professional careers (Wenger 1998).

The overall results of this study are in line with the findings shown by Loranc-Paszylk (2018) and suggest that incorporating the peer assessment task in virtual exchange between language teacher trainees can be considered beneficial. As students see the benefits in both, giving as well as receiving feedback (see 6.1 above), it seems teacher trainees benefit in much the same way as language learners do according to Lundstrom & Baker's findings (2009) and in this setting both their pedagogical and linguistic needs can be addressed (Bueno-Alastuey & Kleban 2016). It can be seen from the data collected that peer assessment activates involvement and enhances collaborative learning on the part of students.

It is evident that the language teacher trainees broadly valued peer assessment as it gives them feedback on their strengths as well as areas for improvement. As a result, engagement and collaboration in peer assessing enhanced their professional expertise, since assessing is seen as an important teacher's skill by the trainees.

Furthermore, it could be stated that the teacher trainees mostly view the virtual exchange as a positive and professionally enriching experience as they learned useful teaching ideas from their international peers' inputs. Having to cooperate and share ideas in English with colleagues from another culture contributed both to the trainees' language proficiency and intercultural competence. Furthermore, virtual exchange that included peer assessment gave the students opportunities to practise their assessment skills in a novel, intercultural environment. They could also develop a sense of shared professional experience and thus become more prepared for future functioning in professional communities of practice in which they could exchange ideas about teaching English. This type of telecollaborative experience could therefore constitute a valuable means of preparing future language teachers to navigate successfully in the globalized world and for future work with linguistically and culturally diverse students.

## The appendix, part 1

Each team (consisting of 2–3 students from PL, 2–3 students from CZ) was to choose one subtopic from each of the four main areas and had to prepare **ONE** final "product", a presentation that would integrate the four subtopics.
1. **Teaching Language Systems and Language Skills**
a. teaching vocabulary
b. teaching pronunciation
c. teaching grammar
d. teaching spelling
e. providing for a balance of the 4 skills
f. teaching speaking
g. teaching listening
h. teaching reading
i. teaching writing

2. **Using Resources**
a. producing appropriate materials
b. using visual aids
c. using the black / white board effectively
d. using the Interactive board / data projector effectively
e. use of a textbook or resource packs in correspondence with targets set by the curriculum
f. use of computers to assist learning

3. **Class Management**
a. use of classroom English
b. use of L1 and L2 by teacher / learners
c. giving clear instructions
d. organising pair / group work
e. generating interest and enthusiasm
f. giving appropriate and genuine praise
g. providing equal opportunities for learners of all abilities
h. helping learners with specific learning difficulties
i. handling large and mixed ability classes
j. controlling the class
k. dealing with discipline problems
l. getting on with learners
m. pacing lessons
n. timing the stages of a lesson

4. **Feedback and Recording Learners' Progress**
a. marking learners' work
b. identifying individual learning difficulties
c. monitoring learners' progress
d. creating and using proper assessment tools (tests, portfolios, etc.)
e. setting and checking homework
f. handling errors, accuracy and fluency

# The appendix, part 2

Peer assessment sheet and criteria

## Assessment sheet

|  | 1 | 2 | 3 | 4 | 5 |
|---|---|---|---|---|---|
| Organisation _/5 | | | | | |
| Language _/5 | | | | | |
| Relevance _/10 | | | | | |
| Insights _/10 | | | | | |
| Total /30 | | | | | |
| Comment on one strong point of this work | | | | | |
| Indicate any room for improvement | | | | | |

## Assessment criteria

|  |  | Unacceptable | Poor | Acceptable | Good | Excellent |
|---|---|---|---|---|---|---|
|  |  | 1 | 2 | 3 | 4 | 5 |
| Clear, logical order, easy to follow, cohesive and coherent | Organisation /5 points | | | | | |
| Appropriate grammar & vocabulary; appropriate register | Language /5 points | | | | | |
| On topic, focuses well and provides clear (reader friendly) examples and details | Relevance /10 points | | | | | |
| Original ideas, insights, fresh perspectives, critical comments | Insights /10 points | | | | | |
|  | Total /30 | | | | | |

# References

Bueno-Alastuey, Maria Camino & Marcin Kleban. 2016. Matching linguistic and pedagogical objectives in a telecollaboration project: A case study. *Computer Assisted Language Learning* 29, (1), 148–166.

Cassidy, Simon. 2006. Developing employability skills: Peer assessment in higher education. *Education + Training*, 48(7),508–517.

De Guerrero, Maria C. & Olga S. Villamil. 2000. Activating the ZPD: Mutual scaffolding in L2 peer revision. *The Modern Language Journal*, 84(1), 51–68.

Dooly, Melinda & Randall Sadler. 2013. Filling in the gaps: Linking theory and practice through telecollaboration in teacher education. *ReCALL*, 25(1),4–29.

EVALUATE Group. 2019. *Executive summary – The key findings from the EVALUATE European policy experiment project on the impact of virtual exchange on initial teacher education*.

Falchikov, Nancy. 1995. Peer feedback marking – developing peer assessment. *Innovations in Education and Training International*, 32, 175–187.

Fukai, Miyuki, Nazikian, Fumiko & Shinji Sato. 2008. Incorporating sociocultural approaches into assessment: Web-based peer learning and portfolio projects. *Japanese Language and Literature*, 42(2),389–411.

Hansen, Jette & Jun Liu. 2005. Guiding principles for effective peer response. *ELT Journal*, 59, 31–38.

Helm, Francesca. 2015. The practices and challenges of telecollaboration in higher education in Europe. *Language Learning and Technology*, 19(2),197–217. https://doi.org/10.10125/44424

Lenkaitis, Chesla Ann. 2019. Rethinking virtual exchange: Partnering EFL learners with TESOL teacher candidates. *NYS TESOL Journal*, 6(2),3–15.

Loranc-Paszylk, Barbara. 2018. Marking the difference – use of peer assessment in a cross-cultural telecollaborative project involving EFL teacher trainees. In Pitura, Joanna & Shannon Sauro (Eds.) *CALL for Mobility*, 13–28. Bern, Switzerland: Peter Lang.

Lundstrom, Kristi & Wendy Baker. 2009. To give is better than to receive: The benefits of peer review to the reviewer's own writing. *Journal of Second Language Writing*, 18, 30–43.

O'Dowd, Robert. 2016. Emerging trends and new directions in telecollaborative learning. *CALICO Journal*, 33(3),291–310.

Turunen, Tuija A. & Seija Tuovila. 2012. Mind the gap: Combining theory and practice in a field experience. *Teaching Education*, 23(2),115–130.

Wach, Aleksandra. 2015. Promoting pre-service teachers' reflections through a cross-cultural keypal project. *Language Learning and Technology*, 19(1),34–45.

Wenger, Etienne. 1998. *Communities of practice: Learning, meaning, and identity*. Cambridge: Cambridge University Press.

# Conclusion

This edited volume provided practical ideas and continued evidence of the value of virtual exchange in the language and language teacher education classroom. The chapters contained in this volume gave a plethora of accounts with practical ideas and research findings and discussion that support virtual exchange. Collectively, the authors in this book contributed their accounts of virtual exchange so we can continue to expand important conversations between learners and educators and impact education around the globe. The three sections of this book 1) Language and Virtual Exchange; 2) Culture and Virtual Exchange; and 3) Teacher Education and Virtual Exchange demonstrated how effective virtual exchanges can be implemented.

## Language and virtual exchange

During a virtual exchange it is often the case that at least one of the participants is participating in the discussion and activities in a foreign language. Purposeful exchanges allowed participants to have access to native speakers or near native speakers of a target language or participants at similar language acquisition levels communicate in a lingua franca. In virtual exchange this was supported by course instructors with goals and objectives for the interaction as well as time for participants to ask questions and debrief with faculty. The activities devised by the instructors of the courses provided language practice within the context of course. In the chapters of this book the authors presented findings that point to the positive impacts on their language learners' skills through interaction with their partners. The consistent theme that ran through this section of the book was that purposeful activities were important to language skill development among the participants. It is evidenced that activities need to be scaffolded and supported by the instructors for maximum benefit of the learners. For example, feedback was given, tasks with detailed instructions or guiding questions to support discussions were necessary, and learning objectives that created a space where fruitful interactions occurred were all imperative to constructive exchanges.

## Culture and virtual exchange

Language and culture are inseparable as displayed in this section of the book. The important feature of virtual exchange for cultural exchange was that students have a common language at a level of proficiency that they can talk about topics as related to their own experiences. In the chapters in this book the shared content of participants was influential to successful exchanges. The projects outlined showed evidence of developed cultural awareness though participants sharing different perspectives on topics that also lead to deeper course understanding. Internationalization of the curriculum with virtual exchange led to improved attitudes and understanding of one another's cultures. It also raised awareness for topics and pushed participants to act as global citizens on issues that are outside their immediate contexts. In addition, they realized that some of their local issues discussed are more global or participants learned of matters that they had not encountered previously.

## Teacher education and virtual exchange

Exchanges pairing teacher candidates together as well as those that paired teacher candidates with second language learners were both configurations that were valuable for participants. This last section of the book provided studies that display how virtual exchange can help teacher candidates develop their craft through interaction on cultural and linguistic based exchanges. Cultural topics allowed teacher candidates to continue to learn about the classroom and benefitted teacher candidates on both sides of the exchange as they gained different perspectives on issue related to education. Teacher candidates paired with language learners received practical experience as they supported language learners' target language acquisition. They also benefitted from studying more about their course content as they had the opportunity to practice course concepts with actual students. Virtual exchange can be a way that teacher education programs offer teacher candidates more practical experience beyond local opportunities for observations and field work. Teacher candidates were afforded additional opportunity to practice what they were learning in their courses coupled with feedback from a faculty member. These exchanges continued to lay the groundwork for the realities of working with language learners through clinically rich exchanges.

In conclusion, this book offers exemplar instructor led virtual exchanges for language learner and teacher education programs. Virtual exchange is a ripe venue for supporting global understanding and 21$^{st}$ Century skills. Also, during

Covid-19 online learning became essential to the continuation of education in a global pandemic. Virtual exchange, due to its online nature, can be leveraged this day in age to support educational goals. Some of these studies in this book were carried out and they were able to continue without interruption as faculty and students interacted during the time of uncertainty with the effects of Covid-19. Both synchronous and asynchronous exchanges can be valuable while flexibility remains key when implementing a virtual exchange as cultures, times differences, and general technology issues can be obstacles that are worth overcoming.

# Index

chat 11, 57, 60, 201, 264, 269
collaboration VII, 1, 4, 9, 11, 13, 17–18, 20, 36, 52, 67, 97, 118, 121–122, 147–148, 192, 197, 202, 210, 239, 257, 263–265, 268–269, 272–275
communicative competence 2
Covid VIII, 3, 11, 97, 101, 150, 157, 163, 170, 189, 191, 195, 201, 211, 253, 281

discussion VII, 2, 14, 37, 39–40, 56, 61, 63, 68–69, 78, 83, 97–98, 101, 108, 110, 122, 127, 130–131, 136, 161–162, 168, 175, 181, 184, 190, 192, 195, 197, 214, 219, 226, 228–233, 238, 246, 250, 253, 257, 265, 279

e-tandem VII, 3, 13, 98, 161–162, 165, 167–168, 170, 174, 179–181, 184, 186

feedback 13–14, 15, 18–23, 25, 27–29, 74, 77–84, 98, 100, 102–103, 106–107, 109–110, 147, 150, 227–228, 234, 241, 257, 264–265, 267–268, 270, 275, 279–280

global VII, IX3–17, 37, 46117, 121, 127, 139, 145, 147, 161–166, 183, 185–186, 189, 191, 211–212, 221, 228, 237, 253, 265, 280–281

I feedback 27
intercultural communicative competence 10, 36, 38, 98, 117–118, 122–123, 128, 132, 136, 140, 258
intercultural exchange 2, 9, 37, 68, 157, 226–227
interview 22, 25–28, 49, 75, 102, 106–107, 130, 132, 134, 136, 250
interviews 2

journals 14, 250

language acquisition VIII, 17, 226, 241, 265, 279–280
language learner 36, 100, 109, 232, 249, 280
likert scale 56, 130, 133, 152, 167–168
listening VIII, 43, 227, 251, 259, 276

mixed method 49, 53, 56

native speaker VIII, 2, 4, 27, 54, 97–101, 106–108, 110, 225–227, 231, 234–241, 279

online learning VII, VIII, 107

pedagogical VIII, 2–3, 9, 14, 37, 68, 73–75, 82, 84, 97, 99–100, 110, 118, 120–121, 162–164, 166, 184, 189–192, 204, 209–210, 212, 219, 221, 230, 241, 245–248, 250, 255–257, 263–265, 275
pragmatic IX, 13, 99, 149, 232, 255

qualitative 22, 49, 52, 56, 131–132, 134, 136, 139, 167, 190, 210, 232, 250
quantitative 49, 56, 132, 137, 167–168, 210, 258
questionanaire 264
questionnaire 44–45, 55–56, 60, 130, 132–133, 135, 137, 257, 268, 272
questionnaires 2–3

reading VIII, 43, 54, 62, 73, 76, 80, 85–86, 88, 92, 104, 166, 170, 236, 251, 259, 276
reflection IX, 2, 14, 22, 26, 37, 41, 43, 45, 68, 99, 102–104, 106–107, 109–110, 127, 130–132, 134, 136, 140, 190–191, 195, 199–201, 210–211, 219, 229, 246, 250, 252–254, 257, 264–265
reflections 22
rubric 13, 20, 78, 80–81

**286** — Index

second language 9–10, 12, 16, 29, 36–37, 51, 56, 98, 101, 118–119, 209–210, 226, 246–247, 249, 251, 254–255, 257, 265, 280
second language acquisition 1
speaking VIII, 14, 26, 27–28, 51, 54, 106, 108–109, 122, 137, 162, 193, 229, 237, 251–252, 275–276
survey 35, 44–45, 49, 110, 130, 146, 151–152, 156–157, 166–173, 175, 178–179, 181–184, 203–204, 211, 257
surveys 3

teacher candidate 211–212, 234, 240, 252–253
teacher candidates 3–4, 209–213, 219–221, 225, 228, 230, 232–234, 239–241, 245, 247–249, 251–252, 254–258, 280
teacher education 1, 4, 119, 226, 228, 245–246, 249, 258, 264, 279–280
telecollaboration VII, 2–3, 4, 9, 49–54, 60–61, 66–69, 73–75, 78, 84, 98, 118–121, 149, 156–157, 189, 210, 245–248, 250, 258, 264, 274

video IX, 2–3, 11, 17–18, 21–22, 25–28, 40, 62, 74, 98, 102–106, 108, 121, 137, 147, 150, 157, 162, 167–168, 171, 176, 182–185, 195, 203, 211, 213, 226, 231–232, 235, 267, 269
virtual exchange VII, IX1–2, 3, 4, 9, 11, 14, 17, 22, 29, 36–39, 46, 49, 51, 67–68, 73–75, 82–84, 97–102, 107–110, 118–122, 125, 128–130, 134–137, 139–140, 166, 181, 184–185, 189–193, 196–197, 199–202, 204, 209, 225–232, 234–241, 245–258, 263–264, 266, 275–276, 279–281
virtual exchanges VIII, 108, 119, 162, 227–228, 279–280
vocabulary 13–14, 19, 22, 25, 80, 103–106, 108, 110, 138, 230, 236, 251–252, 258, 268

writing VIII

www.ingramcontent.com/pod-product-compliance
Lightning Source LLC
Chambersburg PA
CBHW020223170426
43201CB00007B/295